Palm OS™ Programming For Dummies®

Events

More events are available than you can shake a stick at, but these are the ones you'll need to deal with most often:

- ✔ `frmLoadEvent`: Sent when a form is loaded via the `FrmGotoForm()` Palm OS function. The form ID of the loaded form is in the event member variable `data.frmLoad.formID`.
- ✔ `frmOpenEvent`: Sent when a form is opened. This is where you draw the form and initialize its interface elements.
- ✔ `menuEvent`: Sent when the user makes a selection from a menu. The menu item ID of the selected item is in the event member variable `data.menu.itemID`.
- ✔ `ctlSelectEvent`: Sent when the user taps a control. The control ID of the tapped control is in the event member variable `data.ctlSelect.controlID`.
- ✔ Variations of `ctlSelectEvent` named `lstSelectEvent`, `popSelectEvent`, `frmTitleSelectEvent`, and `tblSelectEvent` are sent when the user makes a selection in a list, popup, form title, or table.
- ✔ `appStopEvent`: Sent when your application needs to exit. Your application needs to finish up and return from the `PilotMain()` function when it receives this event.

Launch Codes

Launch codes are one important way the Palm OS communicates with your application. A good place to handle these launch codes is in the `PilotMain()` function. Of the 17 launch codes, these 4 are the most commonly used in applications:

- ✔ `sysAppLaunchCmdNormalLaunch` is the normal launch code sent when the user selects your application for running.
- ✔ `sysAppLaunchCmdSaveData` is the launch code your application receives when it is running and the user performs a Find.
- ✔ `sysAppLaunchCmdFind` is the launch code your application receives to locate matches in response to the user doing a Find.
- ✔ `sysAppLaunchCmdGoTo` is the launch code your application receives when the user selects some matching item you returned from a `sysAppLaunchCmdFind` launch code.

...For Dummies®: Bestselling Book Series for Beginners

Palm OS™ Programming For Dummies®

Cheat Sheet

Memory

Always remember that memory is very limited on a Palm device:

- Stack space is between 2KB and 4KB. That's all you have for local variables.
- Dynamic Heap space is between 12KB and 60KB. That's all you have for dynamic handles and pointers, as well as all your global variables.
- Even database storage space is limited, especially on older Palm devices. Don't use fixed-sized char arrays to store strings in a record.

Following are the key Palm OS functions used for memory allocation:

- `VoidHand MemHandleNew(ULong size)`

  `MemHandleNew()` allocates a new handle big enough to hold `size` bytes of data and returns the handle. You cannot use the memory until you lock the handle by calling `MemHandleLock()`. If not enough memory is available, the returned handle is 0.

- `Err MemHandleResize(VoidHandle h, ULong newSize)`

  `MemHandleResize()` makes a chunk of memory allocated via `MemHandleNew()` larger or smaller. The handle should not be locked when you resize it.

- `VoidPtr MemHandleLock(VoidHand h)`

  `MemHandleLock()` takes a handle and returns a pointer to memory. You can then use the pointer as you normally would in C to modify the allocated memory. After you're done, you should unlock the handle by calling `MemHandleUnlock()`.

- `Err MemHandleUnock(VoidHand h)`

  `MemHandleUnock()` takes a handle, and unlocks it. You cannot use pointers that reference the handle after you unlock it.

- `Err MemHandleFree(VoidHand h)`

  `MemHandleFree()` releases the allocated memory you allocated via `MemHandleNew()`.

  If you want to avoid locking and unlocking handles, use these functions:

  `VoidPtr MemPtrNew(ULong size)`

  `Err MemPtrFree(VoidPtr p)`

  `MemPtrNew()` allocates a handle and locks it for you, while `MemPtrFree()` unlocks the handle and then frees it.

...For Dummies®: Bestselling Book Series for Beginners

PALM OS™ PROGRAMMING FOR DUMMIES®

PALM OS™ PROGRAMMING FOR DUMMIES®

by Liz O'Hara and John Schettino

IDG Books Worldwide, Inc.
An International Data Group Company

Foster City, CA ◆ Chicago, IL ◆ Indianapolis, IN ◆ New York, NY

Palm OS™ Programming For Dummies®

Published by
IDG Books Worldwide, Inc.
An International Data Group Company
919 E. Hillsdale Blvd.
Suite 400
Foster City, CA 94404
www.idgbooks.com (IDG Books Worldwide Web site)
www.dummies.com (Dummies Press Web site)

Library of Congress Catalog Card No.: 99-63443

ISBN: 0-7645-0563-7

Printed in the United States of America

10 9 8 7 6 5 4 3 2 1

1O/SQ/QX/ZZ/IN

Distributed in the United States by IDG Books Worldwide, Inc.

Distributed by CDG Books Canada Inc. for Canada; by Transworld Publishers Limited in the United Kingdom; by IDG Norge Books for Norway; by IDG Sweden Books for Sweden; by IDG Books Australia Publishing Corporation Pty. Ltd. for Australia and New Zealand; by TransQuest Publishers Pte Ltd. for Singapore, Malaysia, Thailand, Indonesia, and Hong Kong; by Gotop Information Inc. for Taiwan; by ICG Muse, Inc. for Japan; by Norma Comunicaciones S.A. for Colombia; by Intersoft for South Africa; by Eyrolles for France; by International Thomson Publishing for Germany, Austria and Switzerland; by Distribuidora Cuspide for Argentina; by Livraria Cultura for Brazil; by Ediciones ZETA S.C.R. Ltda. for Peru; by WS Computer Publishing Corporation, Inc., for the Philippines; by Contemporanea de Ediciones for Venezuela; by Express Computer Distributors for the Caribbean and West Indies; by Micronesia Media Distributor, Inc. for Micronesia; by Grupo Editorial Norma S.A. for Guatemala; by Chips Computadoras S.A. de C.V. for Mexico; by Editorial Norma de Panama S.A. for Panama; by American Bookshops for Finland. Authorized Sales Agent: Anthony Rudkin Associates for the Middle East and North Africa.

For general information on IDG Books Worldwide's books in the U.S., please call our Consumer Customer Service department at 800-762-2974. For reseller information, including discounts and premium sales, please call our Reseller Customer Service department at 800-434-3422.

For information on where to purchase IDG Books Worldwide's books outside the U.S., please contact our International Sales department at 317-596-5530 or fax 317-596-5692.

For consumer information on foreign language translations, please contact our Customer Service department at 1-800-434-3422, fax 317-596-5692, or e-mail rights@idgbooks.com.

For information on licensing foreign or domestic rights, please phone +1-650-655-3109.

For sales inquiries and special prices for bulk quantities, please contact our Sales department at 650-655-3200 or write to the address above.

For information on using IDG Books Worldwide's books in the classroom or for ordering examination copies, please contact our Educational Sales department at 800-434-2086 or fax 317-596-5499.

For press review copies, author interviews, or other publicity information, please contact our Public Relations department at 650-655-3000 or fax 650-655-3299.

For authorization to photocopy items for corporate, personal, or educational use, please contact Copyright Clearance Center, 222 Rosewood Drive, Danvers, MA 01923, or fax 978-750-4470.

About the Authors

Liz O'Hara: Liz is also known as Elizabeth Anne O'Hara-Schettino, but no one can ever pronounce that, so things had to be shortened. Liz has a Ph.D. in Information Technology. In spite of spending a great deal of her life acquiring this degree, she's also done quite a bit of hands-on work in the "real world." Liz has done it all in the computer field. She's worked on commercial software, done research (really cool stuff with NASA satellites), and taught at several universities. Liz's specialty is teaching people difficult concepts without putting them to sleep. These days, she spends her non-writing hours as a mom to her 3-year-old daughter Kiera, and as a family activities coordinator, laundress, house cleaner, paperwork organizer, financial manager, decorator, scrapbooker, cook, . . . you know . . . as a wife.

John C. Schettino, Jr.: John's first name is pretty easy to pronounce, so he didn't have to change it for the book. However, his last name is a doozy. John has been involved with computers for the past 20 years or so. He started out as a consultant, even before finishing high school. Today, John's non-writing job is as the Manager of Software Development, in the Mobile Computing department at Sharp Laboratories of America, Inc. This is where he gets to learn about the latest advances in Computer Science and Mobile Computing. Prior to this, John was a Principal Member of the Technical Staff at GTE Laboratories, Inc. Of course, he carries the usual barrage of degrees associated with Computer Scientists. John and his co-author Liz have written a several other computer books, including CORBA For Dummies with IDG Books Worldwide, Inc. Their other two books were written for another publisher. That's probably why you haven't heard about them.

ABOUT IDG BOOKS WORLDWIDE

Welcome to the world of IDG Books Worldwide.

IDG Books Worldwide, Inc., is a subsidiary of International Data Group, the world's largest publisher of computer-related information and the leading global provider of information services on information technology. IDG was founded more than 30 years ago by Patrick J. McGovern and now employs more than 9,000 people worldwide. IDG publishes more than 290 computer publications in over 75 countries. More than 90 million people read one or more IDG publications each month.

Launched in 1990, IDG Books Worldwide is today the #1 publisher of best-selling computer books in the United States. We are proud to have received eight awards from the Computer Press Association in recognition of editorial excellence and three from Computer Currents' First Annual Readers' Choice Awards. Our best-selling *...For Dummies®* series has more than 50 million copies in print with translations in 31 languages. IDG Books Worldwide, through a joint venture with IDG's Hi-Tech Beijing, became the first U.S. publisher to publish a computer book in the People's Republic of China. In record time, IDG Books Worldwide has become the first choice for millions of readers around the world who want to learn how to better manage their businesses.

Our mission is simple: Every one of our books is designed to bring extra value and skill-building instructions to the reader. Our books are written by experts who understand and care about our readers. The knowledge base of our editorial staff comes from years of experience in publishing, education, and journalism — experience we use to produce books to carry us into the new millennium. In short, we care about books, so we attract the best people. We devote special attention to details such as audience, interior design, use of icons, and illustrations. And because we use an efficient process of authoring, editing, and desktop publishing our books electronically, we can spend more time ensuring superior content and less time on the technicalities of making books.

You can count on our commitment to deliver high-quality books at competitive prices on topics you want to read about. At IDG Books Worldwide, we continue in the IDG tradition of delivering quality for more than 30 years. You'll find no better book on a subject than one from IDG Books Worldwide.

John Kilcullen
Chairman and CEO
IDG Books Worldwide, Inc.

Steven Berkowitz
President and Publisher
IDG Books Worldwide, Inc.

**Eighth Annual
Computer Press
Awards ≥1992**

**Ninth Annual
Computer Press
Awards ≥1993**

**Tenth Annual
Computer Press
Awards ≥1994**

**Eleventh Annual
Computer Press
Awards ≥1995**

Dedication

To the memory of John C. Schettino, Sr., who will never be forgotten. We miss you Dad.

Authors' Acknowledgments

Thanks go to several people at IDG books. First, to Joyce Pepple, our acquisitions editor. That's the technical term for being the person who gave us the opportunity to write this book. Next, to Colleen Totz, our project editor. Colleen also had the ill fortune to have to copy edit every single word you're about to read. Finally, there are a lot of other people at IDG without whom this book would have never reached your hands. You know who you are, and we do appreciate the effort.

We sincerely thank 3Com, who graciously supplied Palm devices and lots of software, as well as lots of technical support. We couldn't have done it without your support!

Thanks also goes to Metrowerks, Inc. who supplied CodeWarrior Lite for the CD-ROM. Without CodeWarrior Lite, we wouldn't have much hands-on work, and that's no fun at all.

Finally, thanks and lots of hugs go to our wonderful daughter Kiera, who gave mommy and daddy the time to write this book when we could have been playing with her. What a special kid! Kiera, we hope that the world of words will excite and enlighten you as it has for us.

Publisher's Acknowledgments

We're proud of this book; please register your comments through our IDG Books Worldwide Online Registration Form located at http://my2cents.dummies.com.

Some of the people who helped bring this book to market include the following:

Acquisitions, Editorial, and Media Development

Project Editor: Colleen Totz

Acquisitions Editors: Joyce Pepple and Greg Croy

Technical Editor: JB Parrett

Media Development Editor: Joell Smith

Media Development Coordinator: Megan Roney

Associate Permissions Editor: Carmen Krikorian

Editorial Manager: Mary C. Corder

Media Development Manager: Heather Heath Dismore

Production

Project Coordinator: Tom Missler

Layout and Graphics: Tom Emrick, Angela F. Hunckler, David McKelvey, Barry Offringa, Brent Savage, Michael A. Sullivan, Brian Torwelle, Dan Whetstine

Proofreaders: Christine Berman, Arielle Carole Mennelle, Marianne Santy, Rebecca Senninger,

Indexer: Ann Norcross

Special Help
Suzanne Thomas

General and Administrative

IDG Books Worldwide, Inc.: John Kilcullen, CEO; Steven Berkowitz, President and Publisher

IDG Books Technology Publishing Group: Richard Swadley, Senior Vice President and Publisher; Walter Bruce III, Vice President and Associate Publisher; Steven Sayre, Associate Publisher; Joseph Wikert, Associate Publisher; Mary Bednarek, Branded Product Development Director; Mary Corder, Editorial Director

IDG Books Consumer Publishing Group: Roland Elgey, Senior Vice President and Publisher; Kathleen A. Welton, Vice President and Publisher; Kevin Thornton, Acquisitions Manager; Kristin A. Cocks, Editorial Director

IDG Books Internet Publishing Group: Brenda McLaughlin, Senior Vice President and Publisher; Diane Graves Steele, Vice President and Associate Publisher; Sofia Marchant, Online Marketing Manager

IDG Books Production for Dummies Press: Michael R. Britton, Vice President of Production; Debbie Stailey, Associate Director of Production; Cindy L. Phipps, Manager of Project Coordination, Production Proofreading, and Indexing; Shelley Lea, Supervisor of Graphics and Design; Debbie J. Gates, Production Systems Specialist; Robert Springer, Supervisor of Proofreading; Laura Carpenter, Production Control Manager; Tony Augsburger, Supervisor of Reprints and Bluelines

Dummies Packaging and Book Design: Patty Page, Manager, Promotions Marketing

◆

The publisher would like to give special thanks to Patrick J. McGovern, without whom this book would not have been possible.

◆

Contents at a Glance

Cartoons at a Glance

By Rich Tennant

page 7

page 105

page 295

page 329

page 219

Fax: 978-546-7747 • E-mail: the5wave@tiac.net

Table of Contents

Introduction

*P*alm OS Programming For Dummies is a complete Palm OS programmer's reference. If you are a beginner or intermediate programmer, a shareware programmer, or a professional software developer who is working on commercial Palm OS software applications, you can use this book to quickly gain proficiency developing such applications. In fact, because the Metrowerks Codewarrior IDE includes a Palm device emulator that runs under Windows and MacOS, anyone interested in learning about PDA programming can use this book — even if they don't have a Palm device!

Like any good operating system, the Palm OS provides a standard interface, or API, to the services and hardware of the Palm device. This API is in the form of functions, callable from a C or C++ program. Each function performs one well-defined action. Also, because Palm applications are graphical in nature (that is, they present a graphical user interface, or GUI), and because you use a pen to navigate the interface, Palm programs are event-based. This approach to application development leads naturally to a form-based approach to program development. A programmer defines one or more forms (or screens) containing the interface elements (buttons, text boxes, tables, lists, and so on) and then writes a program in C that processes the user interaction with the forms. Because a PDA is intended to hold information, the Palm OS includes a rich and powerful database. Many applications need to store information, and they use the database API to accomplish this. Finally, no PDA is an island, and the Palm OS addresses this with a rich set of communications APIs for serial, network, and infrared communications. Palm OS programming even has a desktop component, called *Conduits,* that lets the developer synchronize information between his or her Palm program and a Windows or Macintosh desktop computer. All in all, the Palm OS is a simple, powerful computer operating system.

This book has been created to help you graduate from being a person who can *use* a Palm device to being a person who can *program* a Palm device. Although that may sound daunting to some of you, it really isn't that bad. That's why it takes only one book to do it and not a stack of books, an audio cassette series, and 2 or 3 months of intensive training at a Top Gun Programmers Workshop. Of course, when we say *program,* that means that you're going to need to know how to write a program. We use the C language for the Palm OS application examples, and we keep it as simple as possible. We also use Java for the Conduit example. If you've done any programming at all in C, you'll be fine.

For those of you who already know a bit about Palm OS programming, this book gets you even further into the Palm OS world. We foresee that you'll spend a great deal of your free time and energy creating applications that you could easily and cheaply buy right off the shelf. We think that you'll find Palm OS programming so much fun that you'll want to create all your applications yourself! (Just kidding, of course.) Although we can't vouch for everyone out there, we think that most of you hard working application developers will simply gain a great deal of good information from reading this book and will use that knowledge to reduce the time and effort you spend creating Palm OS applications.

About This Book

Palm OS Programming For Dummies is a reference book. It consists of self-contained chapters that each cover a single topic. This way, you can choose chapters that cover the topics that are of immediate importance and get the information you need quickly and easily. Palm OS Programming For Dummies is arranged so that it can be read from beginning to end in order to get all the information you need about Palm programming.

Conventions Used in This Book

This book is a reference. You can move freely from chapter to chapter, dig in, get what you need, and get out. We use C — and a little Java — in a standard style. Program source code listings appear this way:

```
void Example() {
    int myInt;
    myInt = 1;
}
```

When we describe source code listings and refer to variables, such as myInt, they will be in a special font, like this: myInt. When we refer to a function, we include the parentheses, as in the Example() function. If the function is a Palm OS function, we tell you — such as the MemHandleLock() Palm OS function.

What You're Not to Read

Palm OS programming is generally straightforward, but there are occasional topics that pop up that we can talk about in two ways. The short way is to gloss over the messy details and just tell you what you need to get something done. The long way is to tell you exactly what we glossed over. We call these detailed discussions technical stuff, and they're flagged with a special icon. (See the section "Icons Used in This Book.") You can safely skip over the technical stuff and come back to it later.

Foolish Assumptions

Before you read this book, you must know certain things and have certain stuff. We have made certain assumptions about what you already know as well as assumptions about the tools you have for programming Palm OS applications.

Target languages and their tools

When you create Palm OS applications, you're going to use a target language such as C, Java, C++, or BASIC. In this book, we provide examples in C, so you need to know the C language well enough to follow along. We also assume that you have access to, and know how to use, a development environment for your target language. You need to be able to create files to compile, link, and run. In this book, we use both the CodeWarrior for Palm OS IDE (Integrated Development Environment) by Metrowerks and the GNU distribution by the Free Software Foundation. You must know at least one of them. See Chapter 2 for information about CodeWarrior and Chapter 6 for information about GNU.

Hardware

Pencil and paper just won't cut it. You're going to have to access either a machine with Windows 95/NT or later, or a machine with Macintosh OS (PowerPC processor, or MC68020, MC68030, or MC68040 machine.) Plus, it is helpful to have access to a Palm device.

Since an emulator, called POSE, is available for the Palm device, you don't need access to a Palm device in order to create and use all the examples presented in this book. POSE has its limitation, however, so you should always test your applications on an actual Palm device before shipping it.

We provide more specific hardware and software requirements in Chapter 3.

How This Book Is Organized

If you're anything like us, you'll have numerous scraps of paper and sticky notes inserted all over the pages of your book. Somewhere amidst the sticky notes, you should also find the following five parts.

Part I: Tools of the Trade

To create a Palm OS application, you need to know how to use the tools. This part gets you off to a very quick start by showing you CodeWarrior and its related tools in action. We use a step-by-step approach to build a simple application. This way, you get the instant gratification of building a working Palm OS application in your first sitting. You also gain experience with the development tools.

Part II: Building Blocks

When you create Palm OS programs, you get to build on top of a wealth of building blocks supplied by the Palm OS. This part shows you how to structure your program correctly and then take advantage of all those wonderful building blocks to create powerful applications.

Part III: Targeted Applications

You'll find a few applications that are just a pretty interface. This part shows you how to do things within an application — important things like saving and retrieving information and synchronizing information with the desktop.

Part IV: Flying on Instruments

When you're ready to get fancy, come to this part. You see how to go beyond the static interfaces of resource-based applications and add dynamic behavior to your applications. In this part, you debug your program on the emulator and directly on a Palm device.

Part V: The Part of Tens

What's a ...For Dummies book without a Part of Tens? The first three "tens" chapters help reinforce key concepts presented throughout the book, and the last points you to Web-based information on Palm OS programming.

About the CD

A CD-ROM accompanies this book. You can use the CD-ROM to get:

- ✔ All the example programs
- ✔ Code snippets useful for your own purposes
- ✔ CodeWarrior Lite, a demo version of CodeWarrior by Metrowerks and 3Com that runs on Windows 95/NT and Windows 98 PCs
- ✔ Pilot-GCC Win32, a GNU C development environment
- ✔ Documentation about CodeWarrior Lite, Constructor, and the GNU distribution
- ✔ The Java 2 SDK
- ✔ Internet Explorer 5.0, in case you don't already have it
- ✔ Adobe Acrobat Reader 3.02, which is handy for reading documentation!
- ✔ Lots of interesting Shareware and Freeware, from very generous folks, including ErrorFinder, The Pilot Icon Editor, Flash!, Pandora for Windows, SetUp MAX, the TUser Data Class for Delphi, Pilrc, AstroInfo, Chess Timer, and Doodle (with source code)
- ✔ A demo version of CASL for the Pilot, version 2.6

Basically, we included everything that we could to help you become a Palm OS programmer.

Icons Used in This Book

An icon is just a little picture that captures your attention to a particular part of a page. This graphics technique often comes in handy when we want you to notice something and we aren't there to point over your shoulder and show you.

A step-by-step description of what you should do when performing a task gets a Blow By Blow icon.

A paragraph alongside a Definition icon provides the meaning of one or more terms.

An On the CD icon means that you can find the item described on the CD-ROM. We got real creative here, huh?

An idea or concept that we want you to pay attention to but isn't as critical as a Warning and not as trendy as a Tip gets a Remember icon.

A Technical Stuff icon paragraph provides a more in-depth look at a subject. You can skip this information.

Tip icons indicate actions you can take to make things easier, better, and tastier, too!

Be extremely cautious when taking an action described in a paragraph attached to a Warning icon, or simply don't do it.

Where to Go from Here

Palm OS programming isn't the easiest thing you'll ever do, but it isn't the hardest either. However, as with all new endeavors, there are times when you'll need a bit of a self-esteem booster and spirit recharger. In those cases, repeat this six P tongue twister:

Persistent Palm OS Programming Produces Prodigious Payouts

We aren't talking only about your future financial rewards from creating new software applications; we're also talking about all the new skills you'll gain and all the new ideas that you'll produce when you really get into creating Palm OS applications. So loosen up your tongue with the twister and roll up your sleeves to begin your journey into mobile application development.

Part I
Tools of the Trade

The 5th Wave   By Rich Tennant

"So much for the Graffiti handwriting system."

In this part . . .

Part I is where you discover how to enjoy Palm OS programming. It's just not that hard. If it were, Palm devices wouldn't be as popular as they are. That makes sense doesn't it? Another thing that makes sense is getting you off to a quick start by having you create a simple but informative program. You do this by using the CodeWarrior Lite development environment. We show you how to use it, including its various editors and an associated emulator. We also introduce you to the GNU free development environment. This is just another set of tools that you can use to create Palm OS programs.

After you read this part, you'll know what a Palm OS program looks like, how it is created, and how you can test it by using the emulator.

Chapter 1

In the Palm of Your Hand

In This Chapter

▶ Examining Palm device characteristics and their implications for applications

▶ Developing applications

*W*e are guessing that right now you have access to this book and to a Palm device. (We're clairvoyant, you know.) What do you do next? What kinds of applications are best suited to the Palm device? After you figure this out, what kinds of applications are you going to develop, and how are you going to go about creating them? This chapter addresses these issues and provides some insights into the unique characteristics of Palm devices and how they can be used to your advantage when you create applications.

Of course, not all Palm device characteristics are to your advantage; some of them can be a bit annoying. We'll talk about these characteristics, as well, and help you come to terms with some necessary limitations in your Palm applications.

Determining the Kinds of Applications You Develop

When we first held the Palm device, we couldn't get over how small it was and how concise its functions were. The folks at 3Com have struck on a winning theme and have stuck to it throughout all the successive Palm device incarnations. These themes have blossomed into Palm device characteristics (with some features and limitations thrown in for good measure). In the sections that follow, we briefly look at each of these themes and their implications for the kinds of applications that are best suited for the devices.

In Chapter 7, we talk more about designing Palm applications.

Small is okay

Palm designers have stuck with the idea that for a handheld device to be successful, it must fit easily into a shirt pocket, rest comfortably in a hand (thus the "Palm" part of the deal), and weigh a modest amount.

This has worked well for all the Palm devices. We don't know about you, but we have regular-sized shirt pockets, and our hands aren't the size of Big Foot's, so we need something that won't tear our shirts and won't require two hands to hold steady. Remember, these things are supposed to be mobile computing devices, not luggable computing devices.

Unfortunately, this has lead to a 160 x 160 pixel screen. Yowzaa! Now that's a tight squeeze for any application developer.

The overriding implications of such a small screen size is that you must be absolutely ruthless when cutting things out of an interface so that only the most important information and controls remain. This is no time to be a wimp. Ask yourself if data or controls can be viewed/handled in ways other than constant display. Attempt to put as much as you can in menus, popup lists, and other interface techniques that remove things from a user's view until they are required.

You can create applications that work well with this screen space limitation by keeping the following tips in mind:

✔ If you have many functions to perform, you don't use separate buttons for each of them. Instead, you need to provide menus and popup lists.

✔ Keep your application's interface as simple as possible by creating screens that do one thing really well, like display an overview of data, without a great deal of excess features.

✔ Make your forms the same size as the Palm device screen: 160 x 160 pixels.

✔ Don't use toolbars or status lines. They aren't supported directly in Constructor, and although you can create interfaces that look like they have these elements, they take up too much screen space to be useful.

✔ Hide user elements that aren't valid at a given moment. Don't "gray them out."

A little memory is better than none at all

We are going out on a limb here, but we must say that the Palm devices aren't the motherships of memory. Depending on the operating system, a Palm device can have as little as 32K of usable program memory and as much as

128K. This memory is broken up into memory that is used exclusively by the operating system, for the application stack, and for free space. We talk more about memory and its allocation in Chapter 13.

Although this amount of memory sounds like a minuscule amount compared to the monoliths of memory we have today, it is very usable and is one of the key factors in keeping Palm applications sleek and not bloated with unnecessary features. Unfortunately, as the saying goes, "There is no such thing as a free lunch." Sleek is nice, but it does constrain the kinds of applications that work well on Palm devices.

The short list of things that you should know about this memory limitation and application design is as follows:

✔ Data-intensive applications that display images in GIFs and JPEG format are not good candidates for Palm applications. They take up too much memory.

✔ Spreadsheets are another category of applications that wouldn't be our first candidates when selecting applications to develop. They need a great deal of of memory and screen space to be truly useful.

✔ Pay attention to how much memory is being allocated and where it's allocated.

✔ Pack the data in records as tightly as possible. Don't use fixed widths for strings stored in records.

✔ Edit the information in a record in place. Don't copy the contents of a record into local or dynamic memory.

Faster than a tortoise, slower than a hare

Palm applications must be fast. That's a fact. Mobile users are generally looking for data in a hurry and don't have time to wade through multiple levels of menus and button taps in order to get to the information they want. We aren't talking about desktop users that hit a key and then go get a cup of coffee to wait for their information. Mobile users are just that — mobile. They need information on the go.

On this note, we suggest:

✔ An application should require no more than a single button tap to get to overview information.

✔ Check all user tasks for their speed under loaded conditions. This means having a full database and then performing tasks — not testing tasks with just two records present in the database.

✔ No task should take longer than one minute to complete.

✔ Palms are not meant to be computation-intensive machines. Computations slow down processes, thereby slowing down users. Leave computations for the desktop part of your application. Of course, this means two things. First, you must have a desktop component to your application. Second, you must create a conduit by which information can be transferred back and forth between a Palm device and the desktop computer. Conduits are the way you can extend the Palm supplied HotSync desktop synchronization application so it knows all about the data in your application and how to keep it in sync with a desktop application.

Data display overrides data input

As far as we are concerned, this is the Golden Rule of designing Palm applications. All applications must focus on displaying data and allowing for some minimal data input instead of focusing on data input as the primary modus operandi of the device.

The Palm device provides a Graffiti shorthand and a tap-able keyboard along with user interface elements such as popup lists and check boxes to enter data into an application. These input mechanisms aren't exactly designed for high speed entry of voluminous data. Instead, the designers of Palm devices correctly decided that Palm devices should be used primarily for viewing information and provided these input mechanisms for those times when data entry is necessary.

The short list of things that you should know about this design characteristic is as follows:

✔ Follow the design of the built-in applications. Create applications that focus on data display and not data input.

✔ Provide overview and detail views of data. Be sure to put all necessary information in the overview view so that users aren't forced into retrieving the detailed view. Also, be sure that the detailed view requires only one screen.

✔ Palms are not meant to be data-entry–intensive machines. Leave most of the data entry for the desktop computer. Of course, this means you must create a conduit by which information can be transferred back and forth between a Palm device and the desktop computer.

A very small powerhouse

If we wrote a children's book about the Palm device, we would call it The Two AA Batteries That Could. We're sure you've heard horror stories about Palm devices eating batteries by the dozens. Well, they're not true . . . not really true . . . well some of them are true, but it's not as bad as it seems . . . okay, it can be bad, but you can take precautions when you create your applications to ensure longer battery life.

The things you should know about this characteristic of Palm devices are:

- ✔ Computationally-intensive applications like spreadsheets and chess games are voracious battery eaters. You'll have to create these for some other device.

- ✔ Very frequent database sorting and resorting is computationally-intensive and therefore has the same effect as spreadsheets do. This means that you need to create at least one index for your database and keep that database in sorted order.

A single thread of execution

Applications are given a single thread for execution. There is no such thing as a multi-threaded Palm application. Does this means that all your seams are going to come apart? Probably. It also means that your applications cannot have any background processes. So such applications as spreadsheets aren't realistic choices for Palm applications.

The Connected Organizer

The Palm device is often called The Connected Organizer. That's because it supports IR (infrared) beaming, serial and network connections, HotSync, and custom conduits. The Palm device is a reasonably decent device for accessing data via a modem. This means that applications using e-mail, newsgroups, terminal emulation, and Web-page data extraction are good application candidates because they take advantage of the Palm device's strength.

IR beaming is the fast and easy way to send information between two Palm devices, without wires. You just point them at each other and choose the Beam menu item.

Not too pricey

Cost is a major consideration when people buy mobile computing devices, unless of course they're Bill Gates. 3Com has kept the price below the $500 mark for most incarnations of the Palm device. This price is quite competitive.

The overriding idea is that such fast and sleek devices must also have fast and sleek capabilities at affordable prices. It makes sense then that the applications must not be expensive. This means that you must price your applications to be competitive with other Palm applications. No one in their right mind would pay more for an application than they paid for the device to run it on. How do you keep the price down? Using the age old business creed: Volume. If you build it, they will come. If you price it right, a lot of them will buy it, too.

Last but not least

Ultimately the two things that you must keep in mind when creating applications are:

- ✔ Be selective in what you display, capture, and store in your application.
- ✔ Organize the data in such a way that it is easy for users to retrieve and potentially manipulate without too many steps, too much use of memory, and too much use of the batteries.

Developing Applications

Now that you have some idea of the kinds of applications that you'll be writing, you need to know the steps involved in creating these applications. Chapter 2 gives you the opportunity to work step-by-step through the building of a small application. In that chapter, you use CodeWarrior to create the application.

In this chapter, we take a much broader view. We discuss the same steps, but we look at application development as a general process. Accordingly, the steps involved in creating applications are:

1. Lay out the graphical user interface (GUI).

2. Show the interface to others for feedback.

3. Add form handling and form navigation.

4. Test what you have built thus far and make appropriate changes.

5. Implement fully the behavior of each menu.

6. Test what you have built thus far and make appropriate changes.

7. Add launch code handlers.

8. Test what you have built thus far and make appropriate changes.

9. Create a conduit for to support desktop HotSync of the application data.

10. Test what you have built thus far and make appropriate changes.

When you get to Chapter 2, you should notice that the steps in both lists do not contradict each other. Instead, they complement each other by making a more complete picture of what you need to do when you create Palm applications.

The following sections examine each step. Because testing is involved at almost every step, we consider testing as a single step that is repeated throughout the process, and we discuss it only once.

Laying out the GUI

All applications are collections of resources. The most noticeable resources are the forms, menus, and user interface elements that users see and interact with. Unlike functional programming or procedural programming that begins from the code level and works its way up to the interface, Palm OS programming begins at the interface and works from there. This distinction is important because it affects not only the way you produce code, but it also affects the structure and function of the code itself.

Steps 1 and 2 of creating Palm OS applications relate to laying out the interface. To do this you:

1. Make selections from the standard set of user interface elements.

2. Adjust the properties of these elements to meet the specific needs of the application.

3. Get feedback from others about form and menu appearance and style.

The user interface elements don't come out of space. They come from Constructor, the part of CodeWarrior that deals with the interface. If you are using GNU, you can find out about how to create interface elements in Chapter 6. Begin by creating forms and add the necessary interface elements to them. Then move on to menus and their menu items. We discuss forms, menus, menu items, and other resources in Chapters 2, 3, and 4.

CodeWarrior is the integrated development environment that is most commonly used to create Palm OS applications. It is the favorite of the folks at Palm. GNU is a free software development environment that can also be used to create Palm OS applications. For the majority of this book, we use CodeWarrior in our examples. Chapter 6 discusses GNU.

Once you have selected the interface elements, you can use the various Constructor editors to modify each element's properties to more closely match the needs of your application. We describe the resources and their editors in Chapters 3 and 4.

Before you move to the next step, it is very important to get some feedback from other people. The best candidates to get information from are the potential users of your application. We strongly recommend finding some and employing them as testers. If no one is available, then at the very least talk to other programmers to see how they might do things differently.

Naming object identifiers

An *object identifier* is the name that programs use to refer to objects and resources in your applications. You create object identifiers when you are adjusting the properties of the forms, menus, user interface elements, and all other resources for an application in Constructor. These names are so important that we are suggesting that you use the convention that we follow throughout this book.

When creating an object identifier, end the identifier with an underscore (for example, Overview_). This may sound a bit strange, but there is a very important reason for doing it. When you refer to a resource in your program, you have two choices. You can either use the resource ID (a number) or a name that Constructor makes up for you and places in the resource header file. Constructor doesn't just make up names willy-nilly. Instead, it appends the object identifiers you provide in the preferences by using a simple rule. If a resource item is defined within another resource item (such as

an element in a form) the object identifiers you provide are concatenated together. When header files are generated, #define statements are created that associate the names generated in this way with the corresponding resource IDs. Using resource IDs in your programs can be very confusing, because it's hard to tell if you're using the right number. They can also change if you edit the resources by using Constructor at a later time, so it is also very unreliable. Instead, you want to use the object identifiers from the header file.

If you append the underscore to the resource's name, the #define statements become much easier to read because you can clearly see the names of objects and resources. Consider the following #define statement: #define OverviewPinList becomes #define Overview_Pin_List. (Note that the word *List* refers to the resource type and is automatically attached by Constructor.)

Adding form handling and navigation

In Steps 3 and 4 of creating Palm OS applications, you add the behavior of the forms and their associated user interface elements. This involves the following steps:

1. Write code to handle user interaction in each form individually.

2. Write code to take care of how users move from one form to another.

3. Create necessary database(s).

4. Test what you have built thus far and make appropriate changes.

User interface elements come with some very rudimentary behavior, such as highlighting when selected, but that's about it. To get more sophisticated activity, you must write the code yourself and include it in one or more source files.

Throughout the majority of the book, we provide detailed examples of source code. We include all source files on the CD-ROM.

After you complete each form, you must determine how users are going to move from one form to another. Will they tap a button? Will they make a selection from a list, table, or menu? Will they tap a selector trigger? Will they just wish really, really hard?

When you make these decisions, keep in mind that users want fast access to information and therefore do not want to wade through several layers of choices before seeing what they want. Also, keep navigation between forms fast, don't add time-consuming activities such as computations in order to go from one form to another.

Forms are not complete unless you create the databases that store the information that forms display. Now's the time to decide what your database(s) contain and what data is shown and not shown on each form. We talk about databases in detail in Chapter 13.

As always, after you complete a significant step such as adding behavior to a form or user interface element, you need to test, test, and test. It has been our experience that the creators of applications make lousy testers of their own work. Find someone else. Anyone else.

Implementing menu behavior

In Step 1 of creating Palm OS applications, we briefly talked about creating menus and menu items. Now's the time to add the behavior to these resources. Implementing menu behavior involves the following steps:

1. Add shortcuts to menu items.

2. Handle events that are generated when users make selections from menus.

3. Dynamically swap menus for a form.

4. Test and make changes.

When you created the menus, you probably added the keyboard shortcuts to them. If you haven't already done so, it's time to do that now. The next item of business is to add menu behavior. This involves the Steps 2 through 4 in the preceding list. The first thing you need to do is handle events that are generated when users make selections from menus.

Events are the way that the Palm OS lets your application know something important has happened. Important things include the user making a menu selection. Your event handlers are where your program performs much the behavior of the application.

When a user makes a menu selection, an event is generated. Code must be written that handles this event. We talk about events in detail in Chapter 8.

Step 3 isn't as obvious as Step 2. Palm OS applications don't provide support for "graying out" or removing menus or menu items that are not appropriate under certain circumstances. Therefore, it is up to you to create several menus (and often menu bars) that you can, at the necessary time, dynamically and programmatically swap out so that users see only menus and menu items that are valid at any given time. An example may help to explain this.

Older Palm devices that lack infrared hardware don't support beaming of information. Suppose that you have an application that does support beaming. In this case, you would check to see what device your application is running on and then provide only those menus and menu bars that are appropriate for the device. It seems silly to provide a menu item for Beaming, have the user select it, and then display a dialog that states that that choice is unacceptable! Instead, it is much wiser, and a much cleaner design, to never provide the option in the first place. To do this, you must create two menus — one with the option and one without. We provide this example exactly on the CD, in Bonus Chapter 2.

It should go without saying now that the last step for any major achievement is testing, testing, testing, so this is the last time we'll say it. (Aren't you happy about that?)

Adding launch code handlers

A launch code is the way that the Palm OS specifies to an application the reason for launching it and what the application is to do. Launch codes allow direct communication between an application and the Palm OS, and between two applications.

Step 7 in creating a Palm OS application involves the following steps:

1. Write code for the launch code.

2. Add code for other application feature support.

3. Test and make appropriate changes.

Step 1 of handling launch codes involves writing code. The Palm OS uses launch codes to request information from an application or to request that an application do something. An application's `PilotMain()` function receives the launch code and its parameters. You must write code to provide the behavior that occurs when this function receives a launch code.

Step 2 also involves writing code for certain scenarios when launch codes are sent. We are talking about the handling of launch codes for the following types of things:

✔ Doing a Find

✔ Notifying each application after data is synchronized by using HotSync

✔ Resetting the Palm device

✔ Powering up

✔ Changing the country or the system date and time

✔ Beaming data

✔ Saving data

We talk about launch codes in detail in Chapter 12.

Supporting conduit for desktop HotSync

As we stated earlier in the chapter, the Palm device is known as "The Connected Organizer." It gets this name because it provides its own means of data transmission to and from Palm devices and desktop computers. This is called HotSync.

A conduit is essentially an application or plug-in that interacts with HotSync to allow data to be moved from a Palm device to the desktop and vice versa.

To perform a two-way synchronization of data, your application must support HotSync. We talk about conduits and HotSync in Chapter 17.

Chapter 2

Discovering the CodeWarrior Within

In This Chapter

▶ Installing CodeWarrior

▶ Creating a new project

▶ Creating and editing resources and code

▶ Making and running the application

*A*pplications don't magically appear; you have to create them. What a shame. So in order to create applications, it seems logical that there must be tools to use to build and test them. Lucky for us two widely used approaches are available that you can take for Palm programming. You can use:

✔ CodeWarrior for Palm OS by Metrowerks to create C and C++ programs on Windows 95/NT and Macintosh systems

✔ GNU C Compiler by the Free Software Foundation to compile C/C++ under Windows and many UNIX variants

Other tools are available, such as assemblers and form builders, but the two described in the preceding list are the primary ones. We could discuss each and then give you our opinions, but in the end all would still be the same. You would have to investigate each option yourself in order to identify which development environment best fit your needs. Instead of doing this, we take the fast way out and use CodeWarrior by Metrowerks for the majority of the book. We spend Chapter 6 discussing GNU. We chose CodeWarrior because it is a great development environment and because the folks at Metrowerks have made it the official development environment for the Palm OS. Because some of you will end up using the GNU tools, we made sure that all the examples would work with GNU as well. Aren't we nice?

You can find CodeWarrior Lite for Windows 95/NT and Windows 98 and the GCC Win32 port for Palm devices (also known as the GNU distribution) on the CD-ROM in their respective folders, CodeWarrior and GNU.

Like any good development environment, CodeWarrior has many features to help you create your applications. A development environment is a set of tools that assist in creating, editing, browsing, linking, compiling, running, and testing programs. This chapter gets you up and running by showing you step by step how to create a simple application. You see:

- How to build an entire application in C
- Most of the tools you'll be using to build applications using CodeWarrior
- POSE, an emulator of the Palm OS that runs on your desktop so that you can try out your fantastic creation
- Little gray men from outer space because they love to use Palm devices and they hang out wherever one can be found

What you won't see is a great deal of detailed descriptions or explanations. If something doesn't make a whole lot of sense right now, just skip over it. We get to everything in good time.

The example code for this chapter is on the CD-ROM in the Examples\Chap02 folder.

If you're going to try the examples in this book, you need to do a little leg-work. You need to:

- Install a development environment on your desktop computer.
- Use the POSE emulator to test your applications. We talk about the emulator at the end of this chapter and in more detail in Chapter 5.

Installing the Warrior

This section shows you how to install CodeWarrior, but you can choose GNU or another less widely used environment to develop your applications. Just be sure that your selection builds applications for the Palm OS. If you choose something other than CodeWarrior, skip this section and use the time you save to install your choice. We need to say that this section is not intended to be the final end-all and be-all for information about CodeWarrior and how to install and use it. Instead, we want to provide a quick and dirty explanation to get you going so that we can trot out our first stellar sample application.

You can find much more information about CodeWarrior on the CD-ROM in the CodeWarrior folder. To read some of this information, you need Adobe Acrobat and Internet Explorer. You can find these applications in the Tools folder. Use Adobe Acrobat to read the .pdf documents and Internet Explorer to read .html documents.

The Web is also a great place to get information about CodeWarrior. See www.palm.com and www.metrowerks.com.

Windows installation

Before you begin installation, you must be sure that your Windows system has the following minimal hardware and software:

- ✔ Intel Pentium-class processor or 80486-class processor
- ✔ 24MB of RAM
- ✔ CD-ROM drive
- ✔ Windows 95/NT 4.0 or later
- ✔ 70MB free hard disk space
- ✔ An espresso machine to keep you awake for those late night programming stints

To install CodeWarrior on a Windows computer, follow these steps:

1. Insert the CD-ROM that comes with this book into your CD-ROM drive.

2. In the CodeWarrior folder, double-click the file named Setup.exe to launch the program.

   The Welcome Screen appears. This screen recommends that you quit all programs before you run the setup program.

3. Click Next to continue.

   The software license appears.

4. To install CodeWarrior, you must accept this agreement. To do so, click the Yes button.

   A Destination Location screen appears. The setup program creates a destination folder on your hard drive for CodeWarrior. The path of the destination folder is given at the bottom of the Destination Location screen.

5. If you do not want to use the destination folder suggested by the setup program, click Browse and select another destination. When you are satisfied with the destination location, click Next.

   The Component Selection screen appears.

6. Select an installation type.

   You can choose from three kinds of installation. The CodeWarrior Heaven option provides "The Full Monty" — all the CodeWarrior development tools, languages, linkers, and documentation. The second option is the Minimal CodeWarrior. As you would expect, this is the bare bones version, but it's enough to develop and test applications. Finally, there is the Custom option that allows you to pick and choose what you want installed. Unless you are very limited in space, select the CodeWarrior Heaven option.

7. After you select a type, click the Next button at the bottom of the screen.

   The Program Folder screen appears.

8. The setup program adds a CodeWarrior icon to the program folder. The setup program assigns a default name of Metrowerks CodeWarrior. This name is as good as any name, so we suggest that you accept it by clicking the Next button.

   When you click Next, the installation occurs. You can have fun by watching the gauge move up, or you can take a break and get a snack. We always prefer to snack while we watch the installation.

What about the Mac?

Metroworks does not currently provide a "lite" version of CodeWarrior for the Macintosh, so you need to visit www.metroworks.com and download the full program if you are working on a Macintosh. The minimal hardware and software requirements to run CodeWarrior on a Macintosh are:

- ✔ PowerPC processor, or MC68020, MC68030, MC68040
- ✔ 24MB of RAM
- ✔ CD-ROM drive
- ✔ Mac OS System 7.5.3 or later
- ✔ 80MB free hard disk space

Remember to quit all other applications before you begin the installation. Also, disable any system extensions.

Creating an Application

In this section, we show you how to create a simple application. It won't take all day to do it, either. When you're done with this example, Palm programming will seem more real and easier than it might have before.

This chapter is not intended to give you a detailed description of what makes up a CodeWarrior application or how you, the application developer, go about deciding what goes into an application and how it is designed. These topics are covered in detail throughout the book. In this chapter, we want you to become familiar with the CodeWarrior environment. It doesn't do you any good to have a great application in mind if you can't execute any tasks to create it or save it.

We don't cover everything you need to know about the environment. That's what the CodeWarrior documentation is for, and it does a great job. Instead, think of this chapter as a cheat sheet that gets you going quickly.

The general steps involved in creating any application are:

1. Launch CodeWarrior.

2. Create a new project.

3. Edit the project's resources.

4. Create the project's code.

5. Make the application.

6. Load the application into the POSE emulator. POSE (rhymes with nose). If you want something different, call it "Paw-see" (rhymes with saucy). Run the application to see what happens.

7. Load the application on the Palm device. Run the application there.

8. Do the boogie woogie across your desk because your application is destined to make millions of dollars for you.

Launching CodeWarrior

In order to create your application, you must launch CodeWarrior. Lucky for us it doesn't require a trip to NASA or a degree in rocket science. Instead, all you need to do is follow the steps outlined in the following sections.

Launching CodeWarrior from Windows

To launch CodeWarrior from Windows, follow these steps:

1. Click the Start button in the taskbar.

2. Select Programs.

3. Select Metrowerks CodeWarrior.

4. Select CodeWarrior IDE.

   Following Steps 1 through 4 launches CodeWarrior without an existing project. When CodeWarrior launches, its menu bar appears at the top of the screen.

IDE stands for Integrated Development Environment. An IDE is just a fancy way of saying that the tools all work together smoothly. Generally speaking, this means that the tools for program creation (such as editors) are under the same roof as the tools required to link, compile, and run the program. It's kind of like having a matched set of luggage.

If you have an existing project, you can launch CodeWarrior and open the project simultaneously by locating the project's .mcp file and double-clicking it. Another way is to select Open from the File menu. Of course, the Macintosh doesn't rely on file extensions like .mcp, so you just locate the project file and double-click its icon.

Launching CodeWarrior from a Macintosh

After you install CodeWarrior on a Macinstosh, you can launch it by following these steps:

1. Go to the CodeWarrior For Palm OS folder and open the Metrowerks CodeWarrior folder.

IDE Preferences

Certain settings for the environment can be set for all projects. You can find these settings in the IDE Preferences dialog box. For example, you can view and change Editor Settings by selecting its preference panel from the IDE dialog box. To open this dialog box, select Preferences from the Edit menu. The Preferences dialog box appears with two parts. The left side of the dialog box lists the available preference panels. The right side shows the details of the chosen preference panel. Changes made to the right side of the dialog box are reflected in all projects created afterward.

Use the Preferences dialog box if you want to change the default settings and behavior of the IDE. For our purposes, we just leave things as they were given to us. We come back and change things when we are using POSE or installing our application on the Palm device, but we talk about that at the end of this chapter.

You can use three buttons to select settings:

✔ **Factory Settings:** Click this button to return the panel's contents to the settings that were provided when CodeWarrior was originally installed.

✔ **Revert Panel:** Click this button to return the panel's contents to the settings that it had prior to this session's changes.

✔ **Save:** Click this button to save the changes in the current panel.

When you are finished, close the window by clicking the Close box or by selecting Close from the File menu.

2. Open the Metrowerks CodeWarrior folder.

3. Double-click the CodeWarrior IDE icon.

   CodeWarrior launches and its menu bar is displayed at the top of the screen.

Creating a new project

Throughout this book we repeatedly say stuff like "create a file" and "enter this." If you don't want to go to all that trouble, you can simply copy the file from the CD-ROM. The example in this chapter can be found in Examples\Chap02.

Step 2 in the development of an application is to create a new project. We are going to create a simple project called SimpleCalc. This application:

✔ Allows a user to enter an integer into a field and obtain the square root of that number

✔ Allows a user to enter an integer into a field and obtain the square of that number

✔ Performs data entry and the displays results on one form

✔ Has three menus — Options, Edit, and Trig. The Options menu provides an About SimpleCalc menu item. The Edit menu provides Copy and Paste menu items. The Trig menu provides alternative ways to obtain the square root and square of the entered integer.

A project is the container for all the pieces that comprise an application. After all, CodeWarrior has to put them somewhere. CodeWarrior doesn't actually store everything in one file, but it does keep track of the names of the files in the project, and your project setting, using the project file.

Follow these steps to create a project:

1. Create the project in one of the following ways:
   - Select New Project from the File menu.
   - Click the New Project icon.
   - Execute the Ctrl+Shift+N key sequence.

   A new project window appears.

2. Click the plus sign to the left of the Palm OS item to see its options (see Figure 2-1).

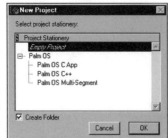

Figure 2-1:
New project
window.

3. Select Palm OS C App.

Palm OS C App is a stationary that acts as a template. A stationary gives you a head start on the project by providing program source code for common functions, one form and one Menu resource. It's a bare bones project. Alternatively, you can select Empty Project to start without help from Metrowerks. Selecting a stationary or Empty Project causes a Naming Screen to appear.

4. Save the project.

To follow the example, enter SimpleCalc as the name of the project file and then click the Save button. The project window appears, as shown in Figure 2-2. The filename has an .mcp extension.

To access all the files associated with a project, you need to start somewhere. CodeWarrior has a "home screen," so to speak. It is the project's .mcp file. Open this file to gain access to the project's files.

Figure 2-2:
The project
window.

The project window consists of:

- ✔ View tabs: The View tabs present three different views of information about a project. The Files tab enables you to view file information. The Segments tab enables you to specify the order in which files are compiled. The Targets tab enables you to configure the targets a project builds and the order in which they are built.

✔ Toolbar: The Toolbar displays icons that correspond to the CodeWarrior commands and functions. These include Target Settings, Synchronize Modification Dates, Make, Run/Debug, and Project Inspector. You'll see Starter in the left part of the Toolbar. Starter is the default target for this project.

✔ Project Window Columns: The first column in the window is the Touch column. It indicates whether a file needs to be compiled. The second column is the File column, and it provides the names of files and groups in the project. The third column is the Code column, and it shows the size of the compiled executable code. The fourth column is the Data column, and it shows the size of non-executable data. The fifth and last column is the Debug column. It shows whether debugging information will be generated for an item.

A target is the executable that will be built when this project is made. Because "target" isn't a very descriptive name, you need to change it. We change this name in the next step in the step-by-step process for creating the SimpleCalc application, which happens in the next section.

Editing the project's resources

Step 3 is to edit the project's resources, such as forms and menus. This step also includes editing the project's settings.

You create and edit all resources by using Constructor. Constructor is a gateway to the numerous editors that you'll use to create your application. It is CodeWarrior's resource editor. You'll spend a great deal of time here doing project stuff. Constructor is the place to get things done when you are creating and modifying your project and its resources. It has its own menu separate from CodeWarrior. It is easy to get confused when you are flipping back and forth between Constructor and CodeWarrior. Just pay attention to the active window and its menu.

To access all the resource editors you need to start somewhere. Constructor has a jumping-off point to the various editors: the project's .rsrc file. Open this file to gain access to the resources and their editors.

A resource is a data structure that describes the characteristics of a project. For example, the user interface of an application consists of interface elements such as forms and menus. An application would therefore have a Form resource for each form in the interface and a Menu resource for each menu. You get the picture.

Many types of resources are available. We discuss them in more detail in Chapter 3. For now, here's a short list to give you a general idea of what you're getting into when you create an application:

✔ Application resources: These include the version of the application and its icon name that is displayed on the Palm device.

✔ Form resources: Each screen in an application has one Form resource. Each resource describes the appearance of the screen including the title of the screen, and the number, type, and position of every control (textbox, button, and so on) in it.

✔ Menu resources: Every menu bar in an application has one resource. Every menu in an application also has one resource. Each Menu Bar resource lists the Menu resources that it contains. Each Menu resource lists the menu title and all menu items and their command sequences.

✔ String resources: These resources provide a place to store string literals in the resource file rather than in your program code. Also, the Form and Alert resources may refer to String resources.

✔ Alert resources: These resources are a lot like Form resources except that the number and type of controls they contain are not user-editable. You get what you get and that's all you get. Got it?

✔ Icons and bit maps: These resources hold pretty pictures. These include the icon that appears in the applications list of the Palm device.

Editing the project's settings

Now that you know what a resource is, we can get into the details of how to edit them. To edit the project's resources:

1. In the project window (the .mcp file shown in Figure 2-2), click the plus sign adjacent to the AppResources folder to display its contents.

2. Double-click the Starter.rsrc file.

   This is a resource file. Opening the .rsrc file causes Constructor's project window to appear, as shown in Figure 2-3.

   Constructor's project window lists each type of resource and the individual resources available for each type. The gray bars are the resource types. The white ones are the current project's resources. At the bottom of the window are the project's settings.

To close the display of current project resources for a particular type (that is, to make the white lines disappear), click the little triangle to the left of the resource type's name. If you don't see a triangle, the project does not currently have resources of that type. To reopen the list of resources, simply click the triangle again. This is a Macintosh kind of thing, so if you are using a Macintosh, this seems a reasonable thing to do. However, most of us are expecting a tree view like the one in the project window (refer to Figure 2-2). As they say, "Get used to disappointment."

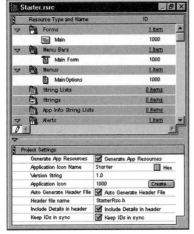

Figure 2-3:
Constructor's
project
window.

To continue with the example, we're going to change the Project Settings shown at the bottom of the window. Editing these settings changes the application resources and also controls the output of Constructor.

3. In this step, we change the name of the application icon. Click the word Starter in the second column second row of the settings. This is the application icon name. Change this name to something more descriptive of the project. In our case, we change it to SimpleCalc.

4. The project needs an icon that appears on the desktop of the Palm device so that the user can tap it to start the application. This is called the application icon. Change its number to 1000 if it isn't already set to that number.

5. Click the Create button in the Application Icon row.

   An Icon Editor appears.

6. Draw the project's icon in this editor. The Icon Editor is a simple pixel by pixel editor similar to any kind of paint program that you probably have used before.

   We are going to create a very simple icon, as shown in Figure 2-4. You're on your own here. It would be too tedious to describe each step, so we wish you the best of luck. It's okay. The editor is really simple.

7. The only other setting to change is the Header File Name. Change this setting from StarterRsc.h to SimpleCalcRsc.h. By default, Constructor names the header file after the project filename and adds res.h. We just want a different name, so we change it.

Now it's time to create the Forms, Menus, and other resources that our project will have. Each type of resource has its own resource editor. This means that there is a Form Editor, a Menu Bar Editor, a String Editor, and so on.

Figure 2-4:
SimpleCalc's
application
icon in the
Icon Editor.

Creating and editing the project's forms

Projects usually have more than one form. To keep things simple, our project has only one form. To see how to create more than one form, see the sidebar, "Having more than one form in a project."

Before you create the single form, you need to change the name of the default Forms resource. Then you can edit this resource to hold the interface elements that SimpleCalc needs.

1. Be sure that you are in Constructor's project window (.rsrc file), shown in Figure 2-3. Select the Main resource (in the white bar underneath the forms' gray bar.)

2. Change the name to Main_.

   Now it's time to create the form.

Having more than one form in a project

Since our project only has one form, we walked you through only the steps required to change the name of the default Forms resource and the steps necessary to edit it so that it can hold the interface elements that SimpleCalc needs. Unfortunately, this doesn't tell you much about adding an additional form. To add an additional form, do the following:

1. **Be sure that you are in Constructor's project window (.rsrc file), shown in Figure 2-3. Select New Form Resource (Ctrl+K) from Constructor's Edit menu.**

An untitled Form resource appears in the Forms resource list just under the Main Form resource.

2. **Change the name of the form to something more descriptive for your project.**

3. **Double-click the name to cause the Form Editor to appear. Now you can add interface elements to it as we describe in the text.**

3. Double-click the Main_Form resource.

    A Form Layout window appears with Layout Properties on the left and the Layout Appearance on the right, as shown in Figure 2-5.

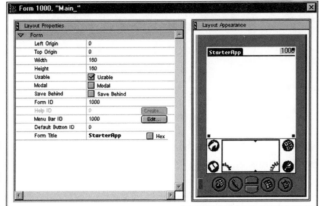

Figure 2-5:
Form Layout
window.

4. Change the Form Title setting from StarterApp to SimpleCalc.

    When you click the mouse or press Enter, the title change is made in the Layout Appearance portion of the editor. The next step is to add the interface elements that we'll need to:

    • Enter the integer

    • Display the results of its square root computation

    • Display the results of its square computation

    • Command that the computations be made

    The way you add interface elements is to use something called the Catalog.

5. Open the Catalog window by selecting Catalog from the Window menu in Constructor.

    The Catalog is shown in Figure 2-6.

    The Catalog is a repository of interface elements that you use to create applications. The Catalog consists of resources such as buttons, check-boxes, and fields. We talk about these interface elements in greater detail in Chapter 3. For now what you need to know is that you drag an interface element from the Catalog and drop it onto a form in order to add it to the project.

Figure 2-6:
The Catalog
window.

Because this example is a simple one, we are not going to follow strict user interface design principles, such as labeling what users see and where they enter information. Also, we are going to have data entry and data display use the same field. This is not a great way to design an application, but it does keep our example simple and easy. After all, that's what we want in this chapter. We talk about design issues throughout the book.

6. We need a field to enter the integer and to display the results of the computations. Select the Field interface element from the Catalog window and drag and drop it onto the SimpleCalc form.

   The Field interface element should be centered somewhere in the upper third portion of the screen. The Field's Layout Properties Window should be displayed on the left. If it isn't, double-click the field.

7. Change the layout properties as follows:

   • Object Identifier from Unnamed 1001 to Display

   • Left Origin to 40

   • Top Origin to 48

   • Width to 80

   • Height to 21

   • Single Line to being checked

   • Font to Large

   • Numeric to being checked

You can change some of the properties by editing their settings in the right column of the Properties Layout, or you can move the interface element around and change their appearance on the form itself.

You can use different numbers if you don't like the placement of
the Field.

8. The next thing you need to do is to add the button to tap to initiate the
square root computation. As before, we use the Catalog to pick a user
interface element and then drag and drop it onto the form. Select the
`Button` interface element and drag and drop it just below and to the
left of the `Field` you just added. The button's Layout Properties
window should be displayed on the left. If it isn't, click the button.

9. Change the layout properties as follows:

    • Object Identifier to `SqrRoot`

    • Left Origin to 25

    • Top Origin to 98

    • Width to 62

    • Height to 14

    • Label to `Square Root`

10. Next, you need to add the button to tap to initiate the square computation. Use the Catalog. Select the Button interface element and drag
and drop to the right of the button you just added.

    The button's Layout Properties window should appear on the left. If it
doesn't, click the button.

11. Change the layout properties as follows:

    • Object Identifier to `Square`

    • Left Origin to 104

    • Top Origin to 97

    • Width to 44

    • Height to 14

    • Label to `Square`

    The layout appearance should look like Figure 2-7.

Congratulations, you've just created a form in Constructor. To continue editing the resources for this project, you need to create the menus.

Creating and editing the project's menus

This project has three menus: Options, Edit, and Trig. The Options menu provides an About SimpleCalc menu item. The Edit menu provides Copy and
Paste menu items. The Trig menu provides ways other than using the buttons
to obtain the square root and square of the entered integer.

Figure 2-7:
SimpleCalc's
layout
appearance.

Six tasks are involved in creating and editing menus:

1. Change the name of the default menu bar and default menu.

2. Edit the default menu.

3. Add menus.

4. Add menu items to a menu.

5. Link menus together into a single menu bar.

6. Create additional menu bars.

Changing the name of the default menu bar and default menu

To change the default name for the menu bar, do the following:

1. Go to Constructor's project window (SimpleCalc's .rsrc file), shown in Figure 2-3.

2. Change the name of Main Form to Main_. The Menu Bar form is the white line underneath the gray line called Menu Bars. That was pretty easy.

   Now we need to change the default menu inside that menu bar. You can do this in two places. You can edit the default menu here or you can select the default menu resource and open it to edit it. Since we are already here, we've decided to stay.

3. Change the name of the menu from MainOptions to Options_.

4. Double-click Options_ to open the Menu Editor in Constructor.

   You'll see a bare bones menu with a single menu item named About Starter App.

5. Click this menu item and change its name to About SimpleCalc.

6. Close the window.

Adding menus

We are now going to add Edit and Trig menus. To add a new menu, follow these steps:

1. Be sure that you are at Constructor's project window (SimpleCalc's .rsrc file) shown in Figure 2-3.

2. Be sure that the Menus resource type (in the gray bar just above the Options_ Menu.) is highlighted. Select New Menu Resource (Ctrl+K) from the Edit menu in Constuctor's menu bar. This causes a new Menu resource to appear with the name untitled.

   Instead of choosing this menu item you can select New Menu Resource... from the Edit menu. (The difference in the two menu options is the ellipse after one and not the other.) A Naming Screen appears. Change its name and then close the window to go to the Menu Editor.

3. Change the menu name from Untitled to Edit_.

4. Repeat Steps 2 and 3. This time, change the menu name from untitled to Trig_.

If you open a newly created menu, you'll see the default menu name of Untitled. Change this name to be something more descriptive for your application. For this project, you change the names to Options, Edit, and Trig.

Adding menu items to a menu

It's now time to enter menu items into the two new menus that we just created. To add new menu items to a menu:

1. Be sure that you are at Constructor's project window (SimpleCalc's .rsrc file), shown in Figure 2-3.

2. Open the Edit_ menu and select New Menu Item.

   An untitled item appears in the emerging menu.

3. Change the name to Copy. Double-click Copy. A Property Inspector Window appears that lists the properties and their values for this menu item. Create a shortcut for this item by entering C for the Shortcut Key.

4. Repeat Steps 1 and 2 except this time the new menu item's name should be Paste with a shortcut of P.

5. We are now going to add two menu items to the Trig_ menu. As you may have guessed, it's just the same as the steps above except the two menu items are Square Root (with a shortcut key of R) and Square (with a shortcut key of S). When you are finished, close the Trig_ window.

Linking menus together into a single menu bar

The next step is to link menus together so that they all appear at the top of SimpleCalc when it is running. To link all menus together:

1. Be sure you are at Constructor's project window (SimpleCalc's .rsrc file), shown in Figure 2-3.

2. Open Main_ from the Menu Bars resource. The Menu Bar window appears with only the default Options menu in it.

3. Re-select the .rsrc window to make it active. Then drag and drop the Edit_ Menu resource onto the Menu Bar window. Be sure to drop the Menu resource to the right of the Options menu. A new menu appears in the menu bar with the name untitled. Change the name to Edit.

4. Repeat Step 2 except add the Trig_ Menu resource.

Congratulations, you have successfully created and edited menus for this project. Now's a great time to take a break and have some fun with those little gray men that we talked about at the beginning of the chapter.

Creating and editing the project's alerts

The project comes with an alert called Rom Incompatible. We need to add another Alert resource to the project.

1. Open Constructor's project window (SimpleCalc's .rsrc file), shown in Figure 2-3. To see this resource, scroll the bar located to the left of the Resource Type and Name column.

2. Select Alerts, and then select New Alert Resource (Ctrl+K) from Constructor's Edit menu.

   A new alert is added to the resource list. Change the name from untitled to About_.

3. Double-click About_ to see the Alert Editor.

   This editor looks similar to the Forms Editor in that it has properties on the left and a layout appearance on the right.

4. Change its layout properties as follows:

   • Alert Type to Information

   • Help ID to 1000

   • Title to SimpleCalc

   • Message to A very simple trig calculator

5. Click the Edit button next to the Help ID property. A window appears. Enter the text that you want displayed when the user taps the Info icon. For this example, enter Example program for Chapter 2 of Palm OS Programming For Dummies. Close the window.

Creating additional menu bars

The project in this chapter doesn't have multiple menu bars, but many projects do. If you have a project that requires more than one menu bar, you need to know how to create one. Creating an additional menu bar is very similar to creating new menus and menu items. To create an additional menu bar:

1. **Be sure that you are at Constructor's project window (SimpleCalc's .rsrc file), as shown in Figure 2-3.**

2. **Be sure that the Menu Bars resource type is highlighted. Select New Menu Bar Resource (Ctrl+K) from the Edit menu in Constructor's menu bar.**

This causes a new Menu Bar resource to appear with the name *Untitled*.

3. **Change the name of the menu bar to be more descriptive for your project.**

Instead of choosing this menu item, you can select New Menu Bar Resource... from the Edit menu. (The difference in the two menu options is the ellipse after one and not the other.) A Naming Screen appears. Change its name and then close the window to go to the Menu Editor.

Instead of choosing the New Alert Resource menu item, you can create the resource by selecting New Alert Resource... from Constructor's Edit menu. (The difference in the two menu options is the ellipsis after one and not the other.) A naming screen appears. Enter the name of the alert and click the Create button. The alert appears in the Alert Editor.

Writing the C Code for the Project

At the beginning of this chapter, we stated that the following general steps are involved in creating any application:

1. Launch CodeWarrior.
2. Create a new project.
3. Edit the project's resources.
4. Create the project's code.
5. Make the application.
6. Load the application into the POSE emulator and run it.
7. Load the application on the Palm device and run it.

So far in this chapter, we've covered the first three steps. This means that we have an interface and some settings, but nothing actually works. In this section, we cover the next step — writing the C code for the SimpleCalc project. We create the implementation (.c) file. CodeWarrior creates the header (.h) file automatically. These two files are pretty much what you'd expect to see when coding in C.

Are you excited? You should be — it's a lot easier than. . . . (Please select one of the following.)

- ✔ You might think.
- ✔ Teaching an old dog a new trick.
- ✔ Teaching a young dog any trick involving bodily functions and your new carpet.

Because this chapter doesn't focus on writing C applications, we don't discuss the how to's and details. Instead, we are going to have you copy the source code from the CD-ROM and paste it into your project's .c file.

Using the template without the silly Starter names

Somebody thought it would be a good idea to use Starter as the filename for every project you create by using CodeWarrior templates. We're not fond of Starter as a descriptive filename, so we figured out how to change the names. Here's the scoop:

1. **Open the project file (.mcp) in CodeWarrior.**

2. **Select Project, Remove Object Code, and then click OK in the dialog box that appears.**

3. **In the project window, delete** `Starter.c` **and** `Starter.rsrc`. **Don't worry, this doesn't delete the actual files. Remove them by selecting each and then choosing Project, Remove Selected Items.**

4. **In Windows or the MacOS, navigate to the folder where your project's .mpc file is stored.**

5. **Open the folder named Src.**

6. **Rename the files in this folder. Change Starter to whatever you want, but be sure to leave the file extensions unchanged if you're using Windows.**

7. **Again only for Windows, open the Resource.frk folder in the Src folder, and rename the file named Starter.rsrc as desired.**

8. **Back in CodeWarrior, use the Project, Add Files menu choice to add the renamed files to your project. Navigate to the project directory, and select the .c and .rsrc files in the Src directory.**

Follow these steps to copy the pre-written C code for the SimpleCalc example into your project:

1. Open the SimpleCalc folder on your desktop. (Note that you are not in CodeWarrior or Constructor at this time.)

2. Open the Src folder. You are now ready to copy the contents of the files from the CD-ROM. Open the Examples\Chap02\copyfiles folder.

3. Open the SimpleCalc.c file. Select all text (Ctrl+A) and copy it (Ctrl+C).

4. Open the project window (the .mcp file shown in Figure 2-2). You are now in CodeWarrior. Click the AppSource folder. A file named Starter.c appears. Double-click its icon to open it. You are now in the Program Editor. What you see is a template for a generic program that Metrowerks provides for you.

5. Select all text (Ctrl+A). Paste the code into the file by using Ctrl+V or by selecting Paste from the Edit menu. Be sure to save the file and close it.

Making the Application

So we've come quite a ways from stumbling around with installing CodeWarrior to having a nearly completed application. Now it's time to put the fruits of our labor to the test and see if they actually work. This involves making an application.

Make is the process of applying the necessary compilation and linking tools to the pieces of a project to generate a Palm application that you can run. An application is the compiled resources and code for a single project in a form that can be run on the Palm.

Before we do the actual make, however, we need to edit some settings. To edit the settings, follow these steps:

1. Be sure that you are in CodeWarrior. Select Settings from the Edit menu. A Settings window appears. Scroll the left side of the window until the Linker group shows.

2. Select PalmRez Post Linker. The PalmRez Post Linker settings appear in the right panel of the window.

3. Change the Output File to be SimpleCalc.prc. Change Creator to PFDe. Be sure to save these changes.

The Creator is the application's Creator ID. It is a four-character code that is unique for each Palm application. You can use any four characters while you're learning how to program the Palm. However when it's time to put your creation out into the world, you must visit the Palm developer Web site at `www.palm.com/devzone/crid/cridsub.html` to register a unique Creator ID with Palm. We've registered PFDe as a Creator ID for our example programs.

To make an application:

1. Be sure you are in CodeWarrior.

2. Select Make from the Project menu. The application is made.

   If the make didn't work, the project has errors. An Errors and Warnings window appears that lists the errors on the top and the corresponding code on the bottom. Fix all errors if you want to. We assume that you've followed our directions perfectly, so you should have no errors. If you are experiencing errors, we suggest that you just use the example from the CD-ROM and move on.

Loading and Running with POSE

POSE is the emulator for the Palm device. It runs on your desktop computer. Use POSE as a substitute for an actual Palm device to try out and debug your applications while you develop them. But don't use it as a complete replacement. Eventually, connect your Palm device to your desktop so that you can download your application. Test your application on the handheld. As the pop song goes "There ain't nothing like the real thing, baby." So always be sure to test your final application on the device. We aren't going to show you how to debug here. Instead, we talk about debugging in Chapter 16. What we are going to show is how to get your application into POSE in a way that it can be debugged. We also show you how to exit POSE when you are done, which can come in handy.

Note: We talk about installing POSE onto your desktop computer in Chapter 5. If you haven't already installed POSE, do it now. We'll go get a cup of coffee.

To load the application into POSE in such a way that it can be debugged, do the following:

1. Set some IDE Preferences.

2. Launch POSE.

3. Start the Debugger (which loads the application into POSE).

4. Run the application.

Now it's time to load your application. Follow these steps:

1. Open the project window (the .mcp file shown in Figure 2-2). You are in CodeWarrior, not Constructor.

2. Select the Preferences option from CodeWarrior's Edit menu.

   The IDE Preferences Window appears. To find out more about these preferences, read the sidebar, "IDE Preferences," near the beginning of this chapter.

3. Select Palm Connection Settings, which is located under the Debugger group.

4. Set the Target setting to Palm OS Emulator. Also, be sure that Always Download Application to Device and Show Palm OS menu are checked. Click the Save button and close the window.

5. Select Launch Palm OS Emulator from the Palm OS menu.

   Ta-da, the emulator appears.

6. Select Debug from the Project menu.

   Choosing this command causes the application to download into POSE. Also, the Debugger Window appears.

7. Click the Run button in the upper left corner. It looks like a right-pointing arrow. Or you can select Run from the Project menu.

   The application now appears in POSE. Use it to your heart's content (or until your fingers get tired).

8. When you are finished, click the X button in the debugger to quit the application. Or you can select Kill from the Debug menu.

9. To quit POSE, right-click anywhere on it and select Exit from the popup menu.

To load and run an application with POSE without going through the Debugger, select Launch Palm OS Emulator from CodeWarrior's Palm OS menu. When POSE appears, place the mouse pointer anywhere over the POSE image and right-click the mouse. Next, select Load app from the popup menu. Click Other... and then navigate to the project you want and select its .prc file. Select it. Click the Applications button. Tap the SimpleCalc Application Icon.

The screens that show the applications in POSE can't be visible when loading an application or crazy things happen. Be sure that another application like Prefs is showing and then load your application.

Loading and Running on a Palm Device

Okay, you've spent enough time testing your application, and now it's time to try it out on the real McCoy. The steps are a lot like the ones to use POSE, so it's a snap.

To load the application, follow these steps:

1. Open the project window (refer to Figure 2-2).

   This is the project's .mcp file. You are in CodeWarrior.

2. Select the Preferences option from CodeWarrior's Edit menu.

3. Select Palm Connection Settings, located under the Debugger group.

4. Set the Target setting to Palm OS Device. Select the Connection to correspond to the serial port that the Palm's cradle is connected to. In our case it's COM1. Also, be sure that Always Download Application to Device and Show Palm OS menu are checked. Click the Save button and close the window.

5. Select Debug from the Project menu. A dialog box appears asking you to put your Palm device into Console mode. You have to do this on the Palm.

6. Turn on your Palm device and put it into the cradle. Tap Find. In the left side of the Graffiti window, enter the shortcut stroke (like a lowercase cursive L). Then, on the right side, enter two periods followed by the number two. You can see the shortcut and two periods in the Find window, which is handy. Tap Cancel in the Find window. Now, go back to the desktop and click OK in the dialog box. Hey, we don't make this stuff up!

7. Click the Run button in the upper-left corner. It looks like a right-pointing arrow. Or you can select Run from the Project menu. The application now executes on the Palm device. Have a good time testing the application.

8. When you are finished, click the X button in the Debugger to quit the application. Or you can select Kill from the Debug menu.

   When you quit an application, your Palm device resets.

You've made it! You can now say you've built a Palm application. Even if you just followed along as we built it, you can say that. We won't tell.

Chapter 3

Natural Resources

In This Chapter

▶ Understanding resources

▶ Using Constructor

▶ Editing forms, menus, strings, alerts, and bitmaps

*R*esources are the heart and soul of a Palm application. Without them, you just have an empty project skeleton — and everyone knows that's a pretty scary sight. In the last chapter, we showed you how to create a simple application with some very simple resources. In doing so, we explained a bit about resources, what they are and how to edit them. We didn't get into everything you need to know about them because that would have clouded the example. So this chapter is our chance to dig into resources and mine this topic for all its valuable nuggets. This chapter provides:

✔ An explanation of what a resource is and how it fits into a Palm OS application

✔ A description of Constructor, the graphical interface that enables you to create and view your application's GUI

✔ A walk-through of each of the resource editors in Constructor

We get started by defining a Palm resource and describing the kinds of resources you'll be dealing with.

Understanding Resources

DEFINITION

A *resource* is a data structure that describes the characteristics of a user interface element such as a form, a menu, or a piece of text. You add resources to your application to present something to the user. Without resources, your application wouldn't exist. An example of a resource is a button that a user taps in order to perform an action, such as saving data.

Many types of Palm resources are available. In the following list, we provide the name, four-character code, and brief definition of each kind. The four-character code is used in program code to retrieve resources of specific types. Resource types are necessary because resource IDs are unique only to each resource type. This means that you can have a form with an ID of 1010 and also a button with an ID 1010. The resource type distinguishes between the two resources.

- ✔ Application resources (APPL and tAIN): These resources include the ID of the application and its icon name that is displayed on the Palm device.

- ✔ Forms and User Interface Elements (tFRM): Application Version is tver, Application Icon Name is tAIN. There is one Form resource for each screen in an application. Each resource describes the appearance of the screen, including the title of the screen, and the number, type, and position of every user interface element (such as a field) and control (textbox, button, and so on) in it.

- ✔ Menu Bars (MBAR) and Menus (MENU): There is one resource for every menu bar in an application. There is one resource for every menu in an application. Each Menu Bar resource lists the Menu resources available to the user at a specific time in the application. You can have more than one menu bar in an application. Menu resources list the menu options available to the user grouped by category. For example, an Edit menu would likely include Copy and Paste menu items.

- ✔ Character Strings (tSTR), String Lists (tSTL), and Category Names (tAIS): These resources provide a place to store string literals in the resource file rather than in your program code. A Character String resource holds a character string. A String List resource holds a group of Character String resources. Category Names resources hold a group of category names for a database. A Category Name resource is also called an App Info String List resource.

- ✔ Alerts (Talt): Alert resources are a lot like Form resources except that they contain controls that are not user-editable. Alert resources are modal dialog boxes that display information that the user must address immediately. An Alert resource contains an Icon, Text, and up to three Button controls.

- ✔ Icons and Bitmaps (Black and White Icons are ICON; multibit, 4-level grayscale Icons are cicn; Black and White and 4-level grayscale Bitmaps are PICT.) Icon and Bitmap resources hold pretty pictures. An Icon resource includes the icon that appears in the applications list of the Palm device. A Bitmap is a picture composed of individual pixels that you can modify at the pixel level. Icons and Bitmaps can be black and white or multibit, 4-level grayscale.

Using Constructor

You manage the resources described in the preceding section by using a CodeWarrior tool known as Constructor. Constructor is a graphical interface that enables you to create and view your application's GUI. You use Constructor as part of the development process to specify how your application appears. To specify how your application operates, you create source code in the Source Code Editor, which we describe in Chapter 4.

Starting Constructor

You can start Constructor in three ways:

- ✔ Without selecting a project first. For Windows machines, you select Start➪Programs➪Metrowerks➪Constuctor for the Palm OS. For the Mac OS, you double-click the Constructor icon.

- ✔ By selecting an existing project to open simultaneously. For both Windows and the Mac OS, you open the project's .rsrc file (also known as Constructor's project window for the project).

- ✔ By double-clicking the resource file name in the CodeWarrior project window. For both Windows and the Mac OS, you open the project in CodeWarrior. Then double-click the .rsrc file in the project window of CodeWarrior.

When you start Constructor by using the first method, only Constructor's menu bar appears with the following menus: File, Edit, Window, and Help. You will need to create a new project before you can access the editors. When you start Constructor the second or third way, you must follow the directions in each editor's section covered in this chapter to open the appropriate editor and its associated resource. Each kind of resource has a different editor.

Constructor's project window

Figure 3-1 shows the Constructor's project window (also known as the project's .rsrc file).

Constructor's project window lists each type of resource and the current project's resources. The gray bars are the resource types. The white ones are the current project's resources. At the bottom of the window are the project's settings.

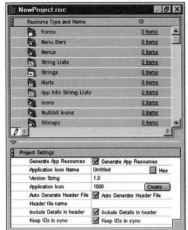

Figure 3-1:
Constructor's
project
window.

The three parts to Constructor's project window are the Resource Type and Name List, the File Control Status, and the Project Settings.

Resource Type and Name list

The Resource Type and Name list provides the list of resource types and the individual resources available for each type. You use this part of the window to gain access to the editors.

You need to know two things about this part of the window. The first is that when a resource has been changed and not yet saved, a dot appears to the left of that resource. The second is that you can copy resources from one project to another by having more than one project's resource file (.rsrc) open.

To close the display of the project's resources for a particular type (that is, make the white lines disappear), click the little triangle to the left of the resource type's name. If the resource type doesn't have a triangle next to it, then that project currently has no resources of that type. To reopen the list of resources, simply click the triangle again.

File Control Status

The File Control Status shows the read/write privileges for the project's .rsrc file. The File Control Status is used in conjunction with a revision control system. The Windows version of CodeWarrior on the CD-ROM included with this book does not include a revision control system, so you can ignore the File Control Status.

Revision control systems are used by programmers to help keep track of all the changes they make to a program over time. They're darn handy if you happen to be working with several other programmers on the same application, or if you need to maintain very tight control over all the changes you make to an application.

Project settings

Project settings are the options that you can set that will apply to the entire project. The settings are:

- ✔ Generate App Resources: When checked, a Version resource (tver) and an Application Icon Name (tAIN) are included in the project's resources. We suggest that you check this setting because the application won't run on a Palm device if it's not checked.

- ✔ Application Icon Name: Name that appears on the Palm's Launch window for the user to tap to start the application. This name appears under the Application Icon. The name is limited to 31 characters and is placed in the project's Application Icon resource (tAIN). Check the Hex box to edit the Icon Name in hexadecimal, allowing you to enter characters that aren't easily typed. For example, to enter a copyright symbol, enter the Hex code A9. If no name appears, the project's file name is used instead. This setting is not available if Generate App Resources is not checked.

- ✔ Version String: This is the text that is placed in the Version resource (tver) and is limited to 15 characters. Its format is MAJORVersion.MINORVersion. This setting is not available if Generate App Resources is not checked.

- ✔ Application Icon: The ID of the Application Icon and a button to Create/Edit the icon. Clicking the button causes the Icon Editor to appear. Enter an ID of zero to indicate that the application doesn't have an Application Icon. If you do want an Application Icon, it must have an ID of 1000.

- ✔ Auto Generate Header File: When checked, this setting causes a header file (.h) to be automatically generated. We suggest that you check this setting; otherwise, you must remember to choose the Generate Source menu item from the File menu to update the header file whenever you edit any of the resources.

- ✔ Header File Name: The name of the header file to be automatically generated. The default header file's name when using the Windows version of Constructor is the name of the project file with _res.h added to it. We suggest that you change this setting so that the file has an .h extension. You can change it to whatever you want, as long as it ends in .h.

- ✔ Include Details in Header: When checked, this setting causes Constructor to add comments for the items listed in the header file (.h). This setting is not available if Auto Generate Header File is not checked.

- ✔ Keep IDs in Sync: When checked, this setting tells Constructor to keep resource IDs consistent between Form resource IDs and Internal Form resource IDs. It also will renumber object IDs in a form when the form's ID changes.

Common Constructor tasks

Every well-designed tool has familiar and consistent interface elements to help you perform commonly performed tasks, such as editing and saving information. Constructor is no exception. This section describes how to perform editing tasks regardless of the resource type.

Throughout the chapter we refer you to this section to get these instructions instead of repeating these tasks and their steps over and over again and again because that would be redundant redundant redundant.

Opening and editing a resource

To open and edit a resource, follow these steps:

1. Open Constructor's project window (refer to Figure 3-1) for the project (.rsrc file).

   You can do this by double-clicking the .rsrc filename in the project's Src folder or in the project's .mcp file.

2. Use one of the following techniques to open the appropriate editor:

   • Double-click the resource in Constructor's project window.

   • Select the resource in Constructor's project window and press the Return or Enter key.

   • Select the resource from Constructor's project window and choose Edit Item from the Edit menu.

   Doing any of the preceding causes an editor to open. Each type of resource has a different editor.

Creating a new resource

To create a new resource, follow these steps:

1. If Constructor's project window (refer to Figure 3-1) for the project (.rsrc file) is not already displayed, open it.

2. Select the resource type you want from the Resource Type and Name List.

3. Select New Resource from the Edit menu.

   This causes a new resource to appear in the Constructor's project window underneath the previously selected resource type. The resource type is in a gray bar and the new resource instance is in a white bar.

4. Use the techniques described in the Opening/Editing a resource section to open the new resource and gain access to its editor.

Saving a resource

To save a resource, be sure the resource is active or selected. Choose Save or Save As from Constructor's File menu or press `Ctrl+S`.

To save all resources in Constructor, choose Save All from Constructor's File menu if you are working under Windows. To save all resources in Constructor when working under the Mac OS, press the Option key while choosing Save All from Constructor's File menu.

Deleting a resource

To delete a resource, select it and then use one of the following techniques:

- ✔ Press the Delete or Backspace key.
- ✔ Choose Clear from Constructor's Edit menu.
- ✔ Choose Cut from Constructor's Edit menu. Choosing this command places the item in the Clipboard.

Mac OS users can also drag and drop the offending items into the Trash.

The Property Inspector window

The Property Inspector window provides another way to view and edit the attributes of a selected item such as a resource in Constructor's project window, a pane in a Layout or Hierarchy window, or a menu or menu item in the Menu Bar Editor. Figure 3-2 shows the Property Inspector window for a form.

Figure 3-2:
Constructor's
Property
Inspector
window for
a form.

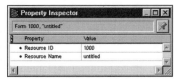

You should know the following about the Property Inspector window:

- ✔ To open the Property Inspector window, you first select a resource, pane, menu, or menu item and then choose Property Inspector window from the Window menu.

✔ The top line of the window identifies the item whose properties are displayed. The left side of the window shows the Property Name. The right side shows its value.

✔ To change a property's value, simply select its current value and type over it. Select another property or use the Tab key to finish.

✔ The Property Inspector window stays consistent with whatever other view is open. This means that modifying data in one view causes the same changes to be made in the other view.

✔ You can stop the consistency management by "pinning down" the contents of the Property Inspector window. To do this, click the icon of a thumb tack in the upper-right corner of the window.

Using the Form Editor

The Form Editor is what you use to work with Form resources. This section talks about the Catalog window, the Form Layout window, the Hierarchy window, and editing tasks.

Catalog window

The Catalog window (shown in Figure 3-3) contains the user interface elements that you add to forms to create the UI for your application. From this window you select an element like a button and drag and drop it onto the Layout Appearance part of the Form Layout window.

Table 3-1 lists the user interface elements in alphabetical order, their resource type, and a brief definition.

Figure 3-3:
The Catalog
window.

Table 3-1	User Interface Elements	
Interface Element	**Resource Type**	**What It Does**
Button	tBIN	Triggers an event after the user has tapped it
Checkbox	tCBX	Toggles on/off when the user taps it
Field	tFLD	Holds text entered by the user
Form Bitmap	tFBM	A placeholder for a Bitmap resource
Gadget	tGDT	A placeholder for a user interface element defined by an application
Graffiti Shift Indicator	tGSI	Displays the Shift Indicator for punctuation, uppercase shift and lock, and symbol
Label	tLBL	Non-editable text
List	tLST	A box containing a list of choices that is presented to the user
Popup Trigger	tPUT	Shows a Popup List's selection and lets user display another Popup to change the selection.
Push Button	tPBN	Permits user to make a single selection from a group of Push Buttons
Repeating Button	tREP	Triggers a continuous action while the Button is being pressed
Scrollbar	tSCL	Permits control of the display of a list or table by a user
Selector Trigger	tSLT	Displays a setting that can be changed through an associated dialog box
Table	tTBL	A two dimensional array of information

Form Layout window

You use the Form Layout window (shown in Figure 3-4) to create and edit forms and add user interface elements to them.

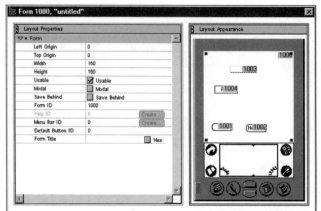

Figure 3-4:
The Form
Layout
window.

To open a Form Layout window for viewing/editing, see Opening/Editing a resource under the "Common Constructor tasks" section in this chapter.

Following those instructions causes the Form Editor to launch along with a display of the selected Form resource's Form Layout window. The window has Layout Properties on the left and the Layout Appearance on the right. The Layout Properties are the characteristics of the form such as whether or not it is modal. The Layout Appearance part of the window displays a What You See Is What You Get (WYSIWYG) view.

Hierarchy window

The Hierarchy window (shown in Figure 3-5) provides a hierarchical listing of the contents of a form. This window just provides another view of the form. This view lets you select interface elements that are underneath other elements, or are otherwise difficult to select in the Form Editor. To open a Hierarchy window, be sure that the form's Layout window is active and select Show Object Hierarchy from the Layout menu. To select an interface element in the Form Editor using the Hierarchy window, just double-click it. The Form Editor appears with the element selected.

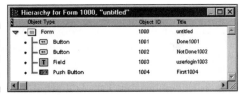

Figure 3-5:
A Hierarchy
window.

The Hierarchy window shows, in a tree structure, the form and its user interface elements, their Object IDs, and their titles. When you change information
in other views (such as the Form Layout view), the information in this
window changes to maintain consistency.

Form editing tasks

To work with forms, you need to know how to create and edit them and their
parts. This section shows you how to go from a project with no forms to one
that has forms with user interface elements on them and menus associated
with them.

Creating a form

To create a form, follow the instructions in the "Creating a new resource" section in this chapter.

Setting form properties

Every form has properties. Properties are characteristics of the form that
affect its layout and behavior. You can set a form's properties in two ways: by
using the Property Inspector window or by using the Form Layout window.
See the "Property Inspector window" section in this chapter to find out more
about the Property Inspector window. To set properties by using the Form
Layout window, open the Form's Layout window and then edit its property
values in the Layout Properties part of the window.

A dialog box is a kind of form that displays information that the user must
respond to immediately. Dialog boxes are modal — they appear on top of all
other windows and force the user to respond before anything else can be
done. To create a dialog box, follow the instructions for creating a form and
check the Modal checkbox in the form's Layout properties.

We suggest you look at Metrowerks documentation (found on the CD-ROM
that accompanies this book) to learn more about each form property, the user
interface elements' properties, and the particular values for these properties.

Help I need somebody, help!

Modal forms may have Help icons in their upper-right corners. When a user taps this icon, another modal form appears that contains information that is helpful to the task at hand. To add a Help icon to a form:

1. Open the form to which you want to add a Help icon. Recall that you can open the form by selecting the form's resource from Constructor's project window (Figure 3-1) for the project (.rsrc file). Make sure that the Modal checkbox setting is checked.

2. Enter a resource ID for the Help ID setting. If you have already created a character string to be used as Help, enter the resource ID for that character string; otherwise enter a new ID. See the section titled "Strings and Things" later in this chapter for more information on string resources.

3. Click the button that appears next to the Help ID setting in order to create or edit the Help text. Save the form.

Adding user interface elements

Forms are nice, but they aren't terribly interesting or useful unless they contain user interface elements. A user interface element is a vis-able, tap-able, select-able, or data-entry-able item on a form that a user interacts with in order to communicate with your application. Examples are checkboxes and buttons.

You can add up to 99 interface elements to a form. You will probably never come even close to reaching this limit seeing as though the Palm device's screen is 160 x 160 pixels.

You can add user interface elements to a form in two ways. You can copy and paste from another form, or you can drag and drop from the Catalog window (refer to Figure 3-3).

To prevent runtime problems, be sure that the Keep IDs in Sync project setting (found in Constructor's project window) is selected. This ensures that resource and form IDs are consistent. Inconsistent IDs cause major headaches, not to mention late-night error-finding sessions.

Deleting items in a form

To delete items in a form, you use the techniques described in the "Deleting a resource" section.

Adding a menu bar to a form

To add a menu bar to a form, follow these steps:

1. Open the form to which you want to add a menu bar.

2. Enter a resource ID in the Menu Bar ID property.

   This causes a Create button to appear next to the ID if the resource ID you entered is new and unique. If you entered the resource ID of an already existing menu bar, the word Edit appears. In either case, clicking the Create/Edit button causes the Menu Bar Editor window to appear.

3. Edit the menu bar. When you are finished, close the window and save the form.

Using the Menu Bars and Menu Editors

The Menu Bars and Menu Editors are the two editors that you use to work with Menu Bar and Menu resources. Both of these editors are closely intertwined. The Menu Bars Editor allows you to create and edit Menu Bar resources.

A Menu Bar resource is simply a list of Menu resources. The Menu Editor allows you to create and edit Menu resources. A Menu resource consists of menu items that can be single items, sub-menus, or popups.

The functionality of both editors is virtually the same. The Menu Bar Editor is a means of accessing more than one menu in the same window. The advantage of using this editor is that you can work with more than one Menu resource at any given time. The disadvantage is that you cannot access a Menu resource's sub-menus. The Menu Editor is a means of accessing more than one menu item for a single menu.

In this section, we talk about: the Menu Bar Editor window, the Menu Editor window, and Menu Editor tasks. This section has some overlapping material because of the similarity in functionality of the editors. This makes it a breeze to whip through. Happy window sailing!

Menu Bar Editor window

The Menu Bar Editor window (shown in Figure 3-6) is the place where you create and edit the menu bars in your application.

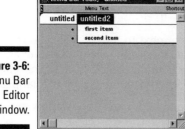

Figure 3-6:
Menu Bar
Editor
window.

The left side of the window shows the menu's title and the labels of its menu items. On the right side are the shortcuts (Graffiti command strokes) associated with each menu item. Because the Menu Bar Editor is a WYSIWYG (What You See Is What You Get) editor, its display shows the menu items in each menu and how they appear when a user pulls down the menu in a running application.

To open a Menu Bar Editor window for viewing or editing a specific menu bar, see the "Opening and Editing a resource" section in this chapter.

Menu Bar Editor tasks

To work with menu bars, you need to know how to create and edit them. This section shows you how to create and edit menu bars.

Creating a menu bar

To create a menu bar, follow the instructions in the "Creating a new resource" section.

Setting menu bar properties

The menu bar properties are its Resource ID and its Resource Name. You change these properties by using the Property Inspector window (refer to Figure 3-2). To change a menu bar's properties, do the following:

1. Select the Menu Bar resource in Constructor's project window (.rsrc file) for the project (refer to Figure 3-1).

2. Choose Property Inspector window (refer to Figure 3-2) from the Window menu. This causes the Property Inspector window to appear showing the menu bar's properties.

3. To change a particular property, click its value and enter the new value. Press the Tab key. Be sure to save the changes.

Adding menus to a menu bar

You can add a new or an existing menu to a Menu Bar resource. To add an existing menu, you just drag and drop the Menu resource from the Constructor's project window into the Menu Bar Editor window for the menu bar you want.

Adding a new menu isn't much harder. To add a new menu to a Menu Bar resource, do the following:

1. Open the Menu Bar Editor window for the Menu Bar resource.

2. Decide where you want the new menu to appear. To do this, select the menu after which you want the new menu to be added. If there aren't any menus, then the new menu appears as the first menu in the menu bar.

3. Choose New Menu from the Edit menu. This causes a new menu to appear. Enter the menu's name. Double-click the menu or select Property Inspector from the Window menu to access the Property Inspector. You can edit the menu's properties and also add menu items to it. See the section "Adding Menu Items to a Menu" to find out more about this. When you are finished, be sure to save the Menu Bar resource.

Performing the preceding steps not only creates a new Menu resource, it automatically associates this menu with a menu bar. You must manually associate menus created with the Menu Editor with a particular menu bar by using the dragging and dropping technique.

Changing a menu in a menu bar

To change a Menu resource in a menu bar, do the following:

1. Open the Menu Bar Editor window for the Menu Bar.

2. Select the menu you want to change and edit it. Use the Tab key to move around the menu items, their names, and their shortcut properties. Be sure to save the Menu Bar resource when you are finished.

Don't forget that you can also use the Property Inspector window to edit a Menu resource's properties.

Changing a Menu's resource ID corrupts the Menu Bar resources that refer to it. Don't do this. If you do, you'll find that when you attempt to edit the menu bar, it displays incorrectly in the Menu Bar Editor.

Arranging menus in a menu bar

To arrange the order of Menu resources in a Menu Bar resource, use the Menu Bar Editor window. Open the window for the menu bar you want to revise, and then select the menu you want to move. Drag and drop the menu to the right of the menu that it is supposed to appear after.

Deleting menus in a menu bar

To delete a Menu resource from a menu bar (not from a project), select the Menu resource and then choose Remove Menu from the Edit menu. To delete a Menu resource from the project, see the "Deleting a resource" section in this chapter.

Menu Editor window

The Menu Editor window is the place where you create and edit the menus in your application. Figure 3-7 shows the window.

Figure 3-7:
Menu Editor window.

The Menu Editor window is almost identical to the Menu Bar Editor window, but the Menu Editor window contains only a single menu whereas the Menu Bar Editor window contains more than one menu. On the left side of the window is the text that appears in a menu, such as the title and the labels of its menu items. On the right side are the shortcuts (Graffiti command strokes) associated with each menu item. This display shows the menu items in each menu and how they appear when a user pulls down the menu in a running application.

To open the Menu Editor window for a specific menu, use one of the techniques described in the section called "Opening and editing a resource." When you are finished editing the menu, be sure to save it.

Menu Editor tasks

In this section, we show you how to create and edit menus and add menu items to them.

Creating a menu

You can create a menu in two ways: by using the Menu Bar Editor or by using Constructor's project window. A menu created from the Menu Bar Editor is automatically associated with the Menu Bar being edited. See the section called "Adding Menus to a Menu Bar" for more information. A menu created from Constructor's project window is not associated with any menu bar. This is handy if you want to use the same menu in more than one menu bar. To create this kind of menu, follow the steps in the "Creating a new resource" section in this chapter.

Setting menu properties

Setting menu properties is the same as setting menu bar properties except that you select a Menu resource instead of a Menu Bar resource to change. To change a menu's properties, do the following:

1. Select the Menu resource in Constructor's project window.

2. Choose Property Inspector window from the Window menu. This causes the Property Inspector window to appear showing the menu's properties.

3. To change a particular property, click its value and enter the new value. Press the Tab key. Be sure to save the changes.

Adding menu items to a menu

The process for adding menu items to a menu is similar to the process for adding menus to a menu bar. See the "Adding menus to a menu bar" section in this chapter. The only difference is that you select a Menu resource instead of a Menu Bar resource, and you select Menu Items instead of Menus.

Changing a menu item in a menu

You can change a menu item in either the Menu Editor or in the Menu Bar Editor. To change a Menu Item resource in the Menu Bar Editor, follow the instructions given in the section called "Changing menus in a menu bar." To change a menu item by using the Menu Editor:

1. Open the Menu Editor window for the menu to which the menu item belongs.

2. Select the menu item you want to change, and edit it. Use the Tab key to move around the menu items, their names, and their shortcut properties. Be sure to save the Menu resource when you are finished.

Don't forget that you can also use the Property Inspector window to edit a menu's properties and its menu items' properties.

Changing a Menu or Menu Item resource ID corrupts the resources that refer to it. Don't do this. If you do, you'll find that when you attempt to edit the menu bar that was using the menu or menu item, it displays incorrectly in the Menu Bar Editor.

Arranging menu items in a menu

When inside the Menu Editor window, you can arrange the order of menu items in a menu by dragging and dropping the menu item's name within the menu. Also, you can drag and drop menu items from other menus.

Deleting menu items in a menu

To delete a Menu Item resource from a menu, follow the instructions in the "Deleting a resource" section.

Mac OS users can also drag and drop the offending items into the Trash.

Strings and Things

Constructor deals with more than simple characters. It deals with characters as Character String resources, String List resources, and Category Name resources. These resource types provide places to store string literals in the resource file rather than in your program code.

A string literal is just that, a constant string value, such as "hello", that appears in the C code of an application. If you use one of the string resources instead of a string literal, you can change it without having to change your program. This lets you localize your application (supporting different languages, or styles of interaction) simply by changing the string in the resource file.

A Character String resource holds a character string. This is the same as a single string literal in C. A String List resource holds a group of Character String resources. This is like an array of string literals in C. Category Names resources hold a group of category names for a database. A Category Name resource is also called an App Info String List resource. We discuss Categories in detail in Chapter 13.

As you might expect, each type of resource has an Editor window. However, there is only one String Editor. All three Editor windows are almost identical in appearance. All the editors consist of two sections. The top section lets you control how the text of the string is displayed in the editor, and the bottom section displays the text. The only thing that changes is the section displaying the text and the bar separating the top and bottom sections of the window.

The String resource uses a simple line to separate the top and bottom halves of the window. The String List and Category Names resources use a two column display for the text, so the line that separates the top and bottom halves of the window has two labels in it: Index and Text. For the String List resource, the index is the list name of the group of character strings that it holds. The text is an item in the list. For the Category Names resource, the text are the items in the category.

Because all the windows are virtually the same, we show only the String Editor window and its tasks. You can use these instructions to work with the other two types of resources. We also tell you anything special about a particular type of resource. So don't worry. You can create/edit all three resource types using these instructions. This section discusses the String Editor window and the String Editor tasks.

String Editor window

The String Editor window is the place where you create and edit Character String resources. It is here that you enter and edit the text and set the font used to display Character Strings. Figure 3-8 shows the String Editor window.

Figure 3-8:
The String
Editor
window.

At the top of the window, you see the resource's ID and name. The View As information specifies whether or not the text will be displayed as hexadecimal or in some other way, such as Standard or Bold. Beneath these options is a separator bar. Underneath that bar is the actual text that is stored in the Character String resource.

To open a String Editor window for viewing or editing, follow the instructions in the Opening/Editing a resource section under the Common Constructor Tasks section in this chapter.

The String List Editor window and App Info String List Editor window (Category Names window) are virtually identical to the String Editor window and therefore work in the same way.

String Editor tasks

The following sections discuss how you create and edit text that is stored in Character String, String List, and Category Names resources. We show you how to create, change, and delete these resources. We also talk a bit about creating help text.

Creating a character string, character string list, or app info string list

All three types of resources are created in the same way. The only difference is in the actual selection of the type of resource that is chosen in Constructor's project window. For example, to create a String List resource, you must select the String Lists resource and not the Strings resource. Also, the menu selections may change by a word or two. For example, instead of saying New String Resource it will say New String List Resource when you are editing lists. Keeping these minor differences in mind, follow these general steps:

1. In Constructor's project window (.rsrc file) for the project (refer to Figure 3-1), select the resource type you want to create.

2. Choose the New Resource item from the Edit menu. A new resource appears in the project window. The resource is selected for you.

3. Open the appropriate editor window by double-clicking the resource or pressing the Return or Enter key.

4. Enter the text you want for the String resource, and set its font. When you are finished editing the resource, be sure to save it.

Changing character strings, character string lists, and app info string lists

When changing any of these types of Character Strings, Character String Lists, or App Info String Lists resources, you can get an idea of what the text will look like on an actual Palm device by changing the font in the View As list in the top half of the editor window. This shows the text in the chosen font in the editor. The font information is not saved nor is it used in any way by your program, it's just there to let you see what the string will look like on the Palm device. To change a Character resource of any type:

1. Open the appropriate editor for the type of resource to be edited. Do this by using one of the techniques described in the Opening/Editing a resource section in this chapter.

2. When the resource appears, you can edit the text as you would in any standard Windows or Mac OS application. You can also change the text's font by making a selection from the View As popup appearing in the upper part of the editor's window.

3. When you are finished editing, close the editor and save the newly changed resources.

Changing the resource IDs of any of these resources will adversely affect other resources that refer to them. Be sure to update the properties of any forms, alerts, and other resources that may be involved.

Deleting character strings, character string lists, and app info string lists

To delete any of the types of Character String resources, follow the instructions in the "Deleting a resource" section in this chapter.

We also must discuss the need to remove a Character String resource within a String List resource or an App Info String List. To do this, open the appropriate editor. Next, select the desired item in the String List or App Info String List and then follow the instructions in the "Deleting a resource" section in this chapter.

Creating Help Text

Help text is actually stored in a Character String resource. Help text appears as an online tip in forms and alerts. To learn more about adding help to a form, see the section "Help I need somebody, Help!" To find out more about adding help to an alert, see the "Adding Help to an Alert" section found in the next part of this chapter.

Alerts

An Alert sounds pretty serious doesn't it? When we hear the word, we think of red flashing lights and buzzers sounding. We also think of late night TV docu-dramas. Fortunately, Palm Alerts aren't quite as showy. An Alert is a mild-mannered resource that probably will never have a TV show named after it.

An Alert resource is a lot like Form resource except that an Alert is not user-editable. Alert resources are modal and are used to display information that the user must address immediately. An Alert resource contains an icon, some text, and up to three buttons.

This section discusses the Alert Editor window and shows you how to use the Alert Editor to create and edit Alert resources.

Alert Layout window

The Alert Layout window is the place where you go to create and edit the Alert resources. Figure 3-9 shows the Alert Layout window.

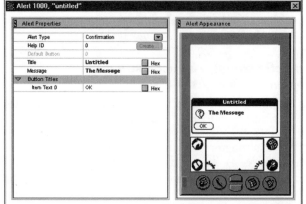

Figure 3-9:
The Alert
Editor
window.

Use this window to specify the text and buttons that appear in an alert. The window is very similar in appearance to the Form Editor in that both windows have Resource Properties listed on the left and an Appearance view on the right. The Form and Alert Editors are also very similar because an alert is essentially a modal dialog box. The major difference is that the Alert Appearance view cannot be used to select items and edit them or move/resize them. It is there just to show you a What You See Is What You Get (WYSIWYG) view.

To open the Alert Editor window for editing, see the "Opening and Editing a resource" section in this chapter.

Alert Editor tasks

In the following sections, we discuss how to create alerts, set their properties, set help messages, and add and delete buttons.

Creating an alert

To create an Alert resource, follow these steps:

1. Open the Constructor's project window (Figure 3-1) for the project file if it is not already open.

2. Select the Alert resource from the Resource Type and Name List.

3. Select New Alert Resource from the Edit menu. Edit the Alert and save it by selecting Save or Save As from the File menu.

This causes a new alert to appear in the Constructor's project window underneath the Alert resource item. The Alert resource item is in a gray bar and the new alert is in a white bar.

Setting alert properties

Every alert is a form. Therefore, like forms, alerts have properties. Properties are characteristics of the alert that affect its layout and behavior. To set these properties, follow the same instructions for setting a form's properties. See the "Setting form properties" section in this chapter.

Here's a brief look at each property:

- ✔ Alert Types: Specifies the type of the alert. Its values can be Information, Confirmation, Warning, or Error. Use Information when a situation has developed that the user should be aware of, but that won't cause problems. Use Confirmation when the application needs the user's affirmation or verification. Use Warning when the action that is about to be performed isn't reversible. Use Error when a problem has occurred that cannot be reversed or that cannot be recovered from.

- ✔ Help ID: Contains the resource ID of the help text or dialog box that appears when a user taps the help icon in an alert.

- ✔ Default button: Contains the resource ID of the default button associated with the form when the form is dismissed.

- ✔ Title: Specifies as text (in ASCII or hexadecimal) the name that appears in the title bar of the alert.

- ✔ Message: Contains the textual message that appears in the alert. Like the Title property, the message is ASCII or hexadecimal text.

- ✔ Button Titles: Specifies the names of the buttons that the alert contains. The button titles are either ASCII or hexadecimal text.

Adding Help to an Alert

When a user taps the Help icon appearing in the upper-right corner of the alert window, a modal form containing information that is helpful to the task at hand is displayed. To add help to an alert:

1. Open the alert to which you want to add Help. You can do this by selecting the Alert's resource from the Constructor's project window (refer to Figure 3-1) for the project (.rsrc file).

2. Enter a resource ID for the Help ID setting. If you have already created a character string to be used as Help, enter the resource ID for that character string; otherwise, enter a new ID.

3. Click the button that appears next to the Help ID setting in order to create and edit the Help text. Save the Alert.

Setting the Alert's message

To set the alert's message, follow these steps:

1. Open the Alert to which you want to add a message. Recall that you can do this by selecting the Alert's resource from the Constructor's project window (refer to Figure 3-1) for the project (.rsrc file).

2. Select the message text appearing in the Alert Properties side of the Alert Editor. When you are finished editing the text, you must click another property or use the Tab key. Using the Enter or Return keys causes the text to be deleted. Be sure to save the alert.

You can add parameters to an Alert's message by entering up to three variables that are substituted at runtime with real information. You use the Shift+6 key to create a caret and then you add to that caret the number 1, 2, or 3. For example, to create an alert that says `Sorry <userName>, you cannot edit record <recordName>`, you enter the Message property: `Sorry ^1, you cannot edit record ^2`. This kind of message can now display different values for these two parameters. Valid example are: `Sorry Kiera, you cannot edit record Over Due Bills`; `Sorry Ben, you cannot edit record Things to Do.`

Adding buttons to an alert

Adding a button to an alert is very similar to adding a message to an alert except that Step 2 involves selecting the Button Titles property and choosing New Button Title from the Edit menu.

If your application requires more than three buttons, you should use a modal form instead of an alert. That's because after three buttons, Constructor shoves additional buttons all over the place, including off the screen.

Deleting buttons in an alert

Deleting buttons in an alert involves little more than selecting the button in the Alert Properties part of the Alert Editor and then choosing Clear Button Title from the Edit menu.

Icons and Bitmaps

Pretty pictures are what icons and bitmaps are all about. Palm programs use pictures in many ways and for many reasons. This means that as a developer of Palm applications, you have to know what kinds of pictures you can create and how to go about messing with pixels to get them.

A pixel is one small dot on a screen. In Palm-speak, this translates to being the smallest unit that is used to form images on a video display. An icon is a picture on a screen that represents a specific command or application. Icons are used in the Palm OS to launch applications. Icons are used in the Bitmap Editor to represent various editing tools. When you create an application, you should create an icon for it that will appear in the Palm's Applications window. If you don't create an icon, a generic icon is used. A Bitmap is a picture composed of individual pixels that can be modified at the pixel level.

Drawing applications that work in a pixel by pixel manner are called Bitmap Editors. Constructor has such an editor. This Bitmap Editor is used to create/edit the following resource types:

- Black-and-white icons (ICON),
- Black-and-white bitmaps (PICT), and

Icons (cicn) and Bitmaps (PICT) can be black-and-white or multibit, 4-level grayscale. However, multibit, 4-level grayscale images are not currently supported by the Palm OS. Support for these images is scheduled for the near future.

Bitmap Editor window

Figure 3-10 shows the Bitmap Editor (for icons). Use this window to create/edit images.

Figure 3-10:
The Bitmap
Editor
window.

If you have ever used a Bitmap Editor before, then you pretty much know all that you need to know about this one.

To open the Bitmap Editor window for editing, see the Opening/Editing a resource section under the Common Constructor Tasks section. When choosing a resource type, you can choose either Icons or Bitmaps. There is a resource type of Multibit Icons, but this is only there for future support and currently doesn't work.

This window has three parts. The Tool Palette is on the left. This palette is a set of buttons that lets you access various tools that control drawing operations. These are the standard tools that most bitmap editors have. The Canvas is the middle part where you draw/edit the image. The third part is called Sample Views. This shows the actual size of the image.

To edit an image in the Canvas, you first select a tool from the Tool Palette and then you move the cursor over the Canvas. The cursor changes to look like the icon on the button of the tool that you selected. You can then click and move the cursor to apply the tool to the pixels of the image.

Here are some things you need to know about the Bitmap Editor:

✔ The Sample Views image is updated to be consistent with the changes that you make in the Canvas.

✔ Cut, Copy, and Paste, as well as drag and drop can be used to transfer images between windows and between applications.

✔ When an image is dropped on the Canvas, the image remains in its original scale and is not resized. If the image is larger than the Canvas, it is cropped to fit.

✔ Drag and drop also works with Sample Views that can be obtained from another Sample View in the same window or from another Constructor Bitmap Editor window.

Chapter 4

Better Editing

. . . .

. . . .

*Y*ou use CodeWarrior's Source Code Editor to create and edit your application's source code. It is a multi-featured editor that supplies among other things navigation tools and specific formatting options to help you create source code. In this chapter, you see how to:

✔ Use the Source Code Editor window

✔ Customize the Editor to meet the needs of your particular style of programming

✔ Navigate through the source code to find specific functions and keywords

Getting Around the Source Code Editor Window

To launch the Source Code Editor, double-click the .c file that you want to edit. When you do so, the contents of the file appear inside the Source Code Editor window. Figure 4-1 shows the Source Code Editor window.

Figure 4-1:
The Source
Code Editor
window.

The parts to this window are:

- ✔ Interface popup menu: Use this popup to open a header file that is referenced in the program file. The Touch and UnTouch commands are also here. Use them to control whether or not the file is to be recompiled again. This popup only works for files that are within a project file, and have successfully been compiled.

- ✔ Routine popup menu: This menu lists the functions in the file. The checked function indicates the location of the insertion point. This popup only works if the filename ends in .c, .cpp, or .h.

- ✔ Marker popup menu: Use this menu to add/remove markers in a file. Use markers to mark where you left off or to set a bookmark.

- ✔ Options popup menu: Use this menu to turn color syntax highlighting on/off. It is also used to set the format (Macintosh, DOS, or UNIX) for how to save the file.

- ✔ Permissions popup menu: This is the Version Control System popup. It indicates the read/write status of the file. Use it to get a new copy of the file, to check out the file for editing, and to make the file writable.

- ✔ File path: This is the file directory path of the file.

- ✔ Dirty File marker: This marker indicates if the file has been modified since the last time it was opened or saved. The file can be in one of two states: unchanged file, or modified and unsaved file.

- ✔ Popup Menu Disclosure button: When you click this button, you move the popup menu's buttons to the bottom of the screen and get rid of the display of the file's path. Use the Editor in this mode if you want an additional line of text displayed.

- ✔ Pane Splitter controls: There are controls on the right and bottom of the window to split the pane into horizontal and vertical panes.

- ✔ Line Number button: This is the line number of the line where the insertion point is currently located. You can also click this button to display a dialog box for going directly to a particular line in the source code.

- ✔ Text editing area: This is the area where you write/edit the source code.

Getting Customized

The Source Code Editor is like all program editors in that it has useful tools for performing editing tasks. You are already familiar with the standard tasks of adding, deleting, moving, and selecting text. As you would expect, you can also perform cut, copy, paste, and clear operations. In addition to these, the Source Code Editor provides facilities for the following:

✔ Balancing punctuation

✔ Shifting text left and right

✔ Syntax coloring

Balancing punctuation

Parentheses (()), braces ({}), and brackets ([]) come in pairs. It is easy to forget to add the ending punctuation mark when you are coding. If you forget to complete the pair, you get errors, or your program may not work as expected. To help you create completed pairs, the Source Code Editor provides a facility for balancing the punctuation. You can run this facility automatically (this is the default setting), or you can use it manually.

To manually check for balanced punctuation, place the insertion point in the text that you want to check. Then choose Balance from the Edit menu. Another way to do this is to double-click on a parenthesis, brace, or bracket. In either case, the editor searches starting from the insertion point until it finds a matching parenthesis, brace, or bracket. Then it searches in the opposite direction until it finds the matching half. When a match is found, the text between the pair of punctuation marks is selected. If no matching mark is found, a beep is sounded.

To automatically check for balanced punctuation as you type, check the Balance while typing preference in the Editor Settings Panel of the IDE Preference Panel. (For more information about editor preferences, see the next section in this chapter.) When the Balance while typing preference is checked and you type a right parenthesis, brace, or bracket, the editor searches for its left match. When it finds the match, the editor highlights it for a period of time known as the Flashing Delay. Highlighting the punctuation mark may require scrolling to it and then scrolling back to the right punctuation mark. The Flashing Delay is set in ticks equal to $\frac{1}{60}$ of a second in the Editor Settings Panel.

Shifting text left and right

The Source Code Editor can indent or outdent entire blocks of text by inserting one Tab stop to the right (using Shift Right) or one Tab stop to the left (using Shift Left) at the beginning of every line in the selection.

To shift blocks of text, select the text and then choose Shift Right or Shift Left from the Edit menu. The number of spaces in the Tab stop is determined in the Font & Tabs Preference Panel. To open this panel, choose Font and Tabs from the IDE Preferences Panel.

Syntax coloring

Coloring the names of functions, types, keywords, or anything else you may want is an easy way to quickly find these elements in source code. The Source Code Editor provides a facility whereby you can select what is colored and in what color it appears. To set your syntax coloring options, choose the Syntax Coloring Preferences Panel from the IDE Preferences Panel. You can also add customized keywords to be colored. To turn syntax coloring on/off for the current file, use the Options popup menu in the Source Code Editor window.

IDE Preferences Panel

The IDE Preferences Panel is where you set all the options for how all the files look and how the editor behaves. There are certain settings for CodeWarrior's integrated development environment (IDE) that can be set for all projects. These are found in the IDE Preferences panel. To open this panel, select Preferences from the Edit menu. The panel appears with two parts. The left side has a hierarchical list of the available preference panels. The right side shows the details of the chosen preference panel. The available preference panels vary depending on the type of CodeWarrior product you are using. Changes made to the right side of the dialog box are reflected in all projects created afterward.

You use three buttons to discard or save the IDE settings: Factory Settings, Revert Panel, and Save. Click the Factory Settings button to return the panel's contents to the settings provided when CodeWarrior was originally installed. Click the Revert Panel button to return the panel's contents to the settings that it had prior to this session's changes. Click the Save button to save the changes in the current panel. When you are finished, close the window by selecting the Close box or by selecting Close from the File menu.

CodeWarrior provides three categories of settings each with their own sub-categories:

- ✔ General settings
- ✔ Editor settings
- ✔ Debugger settings

General settings

The General settings include Build settings, IDE Extras, and Key Bindings.

Some of these panels have additional settings for the Mac OS. We focus on Windows and therefore don't discuss these extra settings here. To find out more information about these additional settings, see the CodeWarrior documentation on the CD-ROM.

Build Settings panel

The Build Settings panel is different for Windows and for the Mac OS. For Windows, the panel shows two settings: Build Before Running and Compiler Thread Stack (K). The values for Build Before Running can be Always, Never, or Ask. This tells IDE how to handle builds. The Compiler Thread Stack (K) setting specifies the upper limit of the stack size to be allocated for compiling and linking thread support. All builds are threaded. Normally, you don't change this setting. Only do so if your project is very big or complex.

IDE Extras Preference panel

The IDE Extras Preference panel is different for Windows and for the Mac OS. For Windows, the panel shows two settings: Recent Projects and Recent Documents. Enter the number of projects/documents to be shown when the Open Recent command in the File menu is selected.

Key Bindings panel

This panel enables you to customize the keys that are bound to any command in order to meet your programming style. The panel lists the menus in CodeWarrior's menu bar and allows you to view/change their keyboard shortcuts. To do this, click on the plus sign next to the name of the menu you want to change. The menu's contents appears with each menu option and its associated keyboard equivalent. Double-click the menu option you want to change. Change its keyboard equivalent. Save your changes.

Editor Settings

Editor Settings include Browser Colorings, Editor Settings, Font & Tabs, and Syntax Coloring.

Browser Colorings

Browser Colorings changes the colors used to highlight elements in the Browser.

CodeWarrior's Browser creates a database of all the symbols in your code and provides you with an interface to access the data. The Browser works with both procedural and object-oriented code and provides three perspectives: high-level architecture, functionality, and user interface. The easiest way to use the Browser is to select the Browser Catalog window from the Window menu. A window appears with a popup menu. Use this menu to select the type of elements you want to see, such as globals or function names. When a list is displayed, you can double-click an item and you will be taken to it.

If you want to learn more about the Browser, see CodeWarrior's documentation on the CD-ROM.

Editor Settings panel

The Editor Settings panel is the place where you specify how the editor behaves in order to make your text editing easier. The panel has three sections: Color Settings, Remember Settings, and Other Settings. The Color Settings section controls the color highlighting of the non-syntax portion of your code and the background color in the editor's window. The Remember settings section determines the state information that is saved for editor windows between editor sessions. The Other Settings section controls how the editor works including such things as the way it saves information and whether it allows drag and drop.

Font & Tabs Settings

The Font & Tabs Settings controls the font and tab information for the active editor window. To change the font and tab settings for a file make it the active file and then open this preferences panel. Make your changes. If no window is open at the time of editing this panel, the changes apply to the CodeWarrior defaults.

Syntax Coloring

See the section "Syntax coloring" under "Getting Customized" earlier in this chapter. Recall that syntax coloring applies colors to the names of functions, types, keywords, or anything else you may want in your source code.

Debugger Settings

Debugger Settings include Display Settings, Global Settings, and Palm Connection Settings. The Debugger is a CodeWarrior tool used to help you find the bugs and errors in your programs. It is a source-level debugger. The Debugger has facilities for setting break points, single stepping through a program, and examining variable contents. We cover the Debugger in Chapter 16.

Display Settings panel

The Display Settings panel has two sections: Color Settings and Other Settings. The Color Settings deal with selecting the color used to highlight the changes in variables and watchpoints. The Other Settings deal with a variety of topics including determining how variable values in source code are displayed; how task displays are toggled on/off; and how functions are sorted in the Browser window's Function pane.

Global Settings panel

The Global Settings panel applies to the Debugger and has two sections: A Cache section and Other Settings. The Cache section obviously deals with the cache used by the Debugger. The Other Settings deal with such things as confirming the termination of processes when quitting, and stopping at the beginning of applications while launching them. You can probably leave these settings as is.

Palm Connection settings panel

This panel provides a place where you can indicate the target for your application to run on such as a Palm device or the POSE emulator. It also provides popups and checkboxes to indicate how you would like certain things to be done. See Chapter 5 for more information on the emulator.

Navigating in a File

Several facilities are available for navigating in a file. You can:

- Use the Find dialog box
- Go to selected text
- Go to a particular routine
- Go to a particular line
- Use a marker

Using the Find dialog box

The Source Code Editor provides a multi-featured Find facility. The Find dialog box allows you to search in a single file, across multiple files, and to use batch searches. Find also allows you to replace text.

To open the Find dialog box, select Find from the Search menu. Enter text to find and click the Find button. You will be taken to the first occurrence of the text in the file and the selected text will be highlighted. You can also enter text to be found by first selecting text and then choosing Enter 'Find' String (Ctrl+E) from the Search menu. Next, open the Find dialog box and you'll see the text already entered in the Find portion of the box.

A batch search provides the results of a Find in a Search Results window. This window has two parts. The top part shows a list of all the occurrences of the text string. The bottom portion shows the place in the source code of the selected occurrence of the text string that is highlighted in top portion of the window. To perform a batch search, check the Batch checkbox in the Find dialog box. The search will be done as batch and the results are displayed in a Search Results window. Select an occurrence to view from the top part of the window. The location of the selected text is shown in the bottom part of the window with the text highlighted.

Going to selected text

You can go to selected text by selecting text and then choosing Find Selection (Ctrl+F3) from the Search menu. The next occurrence of the selected text is highlighted and displayed. This usually involves scrolling the file to get to the next occurrence. After you select text, you can also select Find Next (F3) from the Search menu.

Going to a routine

You can go directly to a particular routine (function) by selecting its name from the Routine Popup menu displayed at the top of the Source Code Editor window (refer to Figure 4-1). (See the "Getting Around the Source Code Editor Window" section at the beginning of this chapter.) Double-click the name of the routine, and you will be taken to it.

Going to a particular line

You can go directly to a particular line if you know its line number. Source code lines are numbered consecutively with the first line being numbered 1. There are two ways to go directly to a particular line. The first way to go to a particular line is to select Go To Line (Ctrl+G) from the Search menu. A Go To Line Number dialog box appears. Enter the number of the desired line and click OK. You are taken to that line in the source code. The second way to go to a particular line is to click the Line Number button at the bottom of the Source Code Editor window (refer to Figure 4-1). (See the "Getting Around the Source Code Editor Window" section at the beginning of this chapter.) Again, the Go To Line Number dialog box appears. Use it as previously instructed.

Using a marker

Markers are like bookmarks. You use them to set places in your files that you want to quickly jump to. To add a marker, choose Add Marker from the Marker popup menu.

You can select text and then choose Add Marker from the Marker popup menu to quickly add a function or line as a marker. The selected text appears as the new marker name.

For example, suppose that you want to be able to quickly jump to the three places in a file where the code adds, modifies, and deletes database records. Rather than have to search for these places every time, you can just add three markers in the appropriate locations in the file. Suppose that you named the markers AddRecord, ModifyRecord, and DeleteRecord. To jump to the marker named DeleteRecord, just select it in the Marker popup menu, and the source text is scrolled such that the location in the source code for the marker is displayed.

Chapter 5

Emulation Is the Sincerest Form of Flattery

CodeWarrior includes an emulator that you use to quickly and easily test your programs, without needing an actual Palm device. This emulator is called POSE (Palm Operating System Emulator.) POSE runs applications as if they were actually running on a real Palm device. POSE provides a "life-like" image of a Palm device that appears on your desktop's screen. You interact with POSE just as if it were a real device.

Emulation is the act of imitating the functions and behavior of another system so as to allow the imitating system to accept the same inputs, perform the same tasks, execute the same programs, achieve the same results, and produce the same outputs as the imitated system. It makes sense then that an *emulator* is the imitating system.

POSE runs on your desktop computer. You use the emulator once you have created an application that you need to test. You can test an application in two places: on the Palm device and on POSE. We talk about debugging and running a program on a Palm device in Chapters 2 and 16. We also talk a bit about testing an application on POSE in Chapter 2, but we didn't get into a great deal of detail. Our purpose there was to get through an example. Our purpose here is to show you how to get POSE started and how to get your applications on POSE for testing.

Emulators like POSE are good for the quality assurance part of your product development cycle. Instead of having to download the application to a device, run it, test it, make changes on the desktop's version and then download to start the process all over again, you can simply load the application into POSE and test it there. No docking of the device, no time-intensive downloading, no device needed at all!

The advantage of having an emulator is that you can test and re-test an application without tying up an actual Palm device. You can also have more than one person testing an application without requiring multiple devices. In addition, it is a great time saver. You can debug your application by using CodeWarrior's Debugger along with POSE. Because this is such a big advantage, we will show you how to start POSE and the Debugger simultaneously.

In this chapter you'll see how to:

✔ Get POSE up and running

✔ Launch POSE

✔ Load applications onto POSE

✔ Quit POSE

✔ Use the Serial Port and POSE

✔ Use the Simulator with the Mac OS

POSEing with Your Applications

Before we get into the business of getting POSE up and running, we thought it would be nice for you to see what POSE looks like. Figure 5-1 shows POSE with the application's window displayed.

Figure 5-1:
POSE.

Setting IDE Preferences

You must set certain IDE Preferences in order for POSE to work with your applications. Recall from previous chapters that IDE preferences are viewed/changed via the Preferences option on the Edit menu. When you choose this option, a Preferences Panel appears with a list of panels on the left and panel details on the right. When you select a panel on the left, its contents appears on the right.

To set the preferences you need to get POSE to work, follow these steps:

1. Select the Preferences option from CodeWarrior's Edit menu.

   The IDE Preferences window appears.

2. Select Palm Connection Settings, found under the Debugger group.

   Choosing this option causes the contents of this panel to appear on the right.

3. Set the Target setting to Palm OS Emulator.

4. Be sure that Always Download Application to Device and Show Palm OS menu are checked. Also, be sure the path name of the emulator is correct.

5. Click the Save button and close the window.

Installing POSE

If you installed everything when you installed CodeWarrior, POSE already exists on your desktop computer's hard drive. You can happily skip to the next section. If you didn't install the Full Monty, it's time for pay back. Don't worry, though; it's not so bad. If you aren't using CodeWarrior Lite, you can download the latest version of POSE from www.palm.com/devzone/pose/pose.html. After you download POSE, you need to unzip the archive into a folder (for example, POSE) on your hard drive, and then get a copy of the Palm OS ROMs (see the POSE Web site for details). Use it and the following directions to get POSE up and running on your system.

To load POSE, do the following:

1. Copy contents of POSE onto your hard drive.

2. Double-click Emulator.exe to launch POSE.

   A dialog box requesting a ROM image appears.

3. Click the Browse button to locate a file called `Palm 3.0 Debug.ROM`.

   (Doing this implies that when you copied POSE, you also copied the entire contents of the POSE folder. If you left out the ROM image and you would like to get another one, you can copy it from the CD or get one from `www.palm.com/devzone/pose/pose.html`.)

4. When `Palm 3.0 Debug.ROM` is found, select it and click the Open button. POSE starts up with the Preferences program displayed.

POSE is a hardware emulator. This means that it imitates the Palm device's hardware. So where does the software for POSE come from? The answer is the ROM image. A ROM image is the operating system, the memory, and the pre-installed group of applications that are collectively placed into a single file. Basically, everything that a real, physical ROM has in an actual Palm device is put into this file.

Launching POSE

You can start POSE in two ways:

- ✔ Launch it without selecting an application first
- ✔ Launch it by selecting an existing application to open with it

Launching POSE without an application

You can launch POSE without an application in two ways. The first way is to double-click `Emulator.exe` from wherever you put it on your hard drive. The second way is to follow these steps:

1. Be sure that CodeWarrior is running and the IDE preferences have been correctly set. Also, be sure you have installed POSE on your hard drive.

2. Select Launch Palm OS Emulator from CodeWarrior's Palm OS menu. This causes POSE to appear with the Preferences window displayed.

Launching POSE with an application

Launching POSE with an application is really loading an application into POSE while it is being launched. So instead of repeating ourselves, we are sending you to the next section called Loading an application into POSE.

Loading an Application into POSE

You can load an application into POSE in two ways. The method you choose depends upon what you want to do with your application. The methods are:

✔ Loading an application into POSE without using the Debugger

✔ Loading an application into POSE along with the Debugger

If you want to test your application while using the Debugger, choose the second method; otherwise, you should use the first method.

If the screen that shows the Application Icons in POSE is visible when you're loading an application, crazy things happen. Be sure that another application like Preferences is showing and then load your application.

Loading without using the Debugger

To launch POSE without selecting the Debugger:

1. Be sure that CodeWarrior is running and you have set the IDE preferences. Also, be sure that you have installed POSE on your hard drive.

2. Select Launch Palm OS Emulator from CodeWarrior's Palm OS menu.

   POSE appears with the Preferences window displayed.

3. Right-click anywhere over POSE.

   A popup menu appears.

4. Select Load app/<full path name of application's .prc file>.

   To complete this action, you may need to select Other and use the Open dialog box to locate the desired application's .prc file.

If this seems like a lot of work, you can simply drag the .prc file for the application and drop it onto the POSE window, once POSE is open. This installs the application for you.

Loading with the Debugger

To launch POSE with an application and the Debugger:

1. Be sure that CodeWarrior is running and you have correctly set the IDE preferences. Also, be sure that you have installed POSE on your hard drive.

2. Select Launch Palm OS Emulator from CodeWarrior's Palm OS menu.

   POSE appears with the Preferences window displayed.

3. Open the application's project window (the .mcp file).

   You are in CodeWarrior not the Constructor.

4. Select Debug from the Project menu.

   The application downloads into POSE. Also, the Debugger window appears.

5. Click the Run button in the upper-left corner. It looks like a right-pointing arrow. Or you can select Run from the Project menu.

   The application appears in POSE.

6. When you are finished, click the X button in the Debugger to quit the application. Or you can select Kill from the Debug menu.

Quitting POSE

To quit POSE, right-click anywhere on it and select Exit from the popup menu.

Debugging Serial & Network Applications

If you've written a wonderful application that uses serial communications or network communications, how do you debug it on a Palm device? It's impossible, since you'd need to use the serial port for debugging. Can you guess the answer? POSE! That's right, the POSE emulator can use your desktop serial port as if it were the real Palm device serial port. Anything you want to plug into that serial port is accessible from the emulated Palm device in POSE, so you can debug to your heart's content.

Here are just a couple of the things you can do:

✔ Hook two PCs together with a serial cable, run POSE on one, and the HotSync application on the other, and debug Conduits

✔ Plug a modem into the desktop serial port and debug modem communications applications

To enable serial communications in POSE, follow these steps:

1. Launch POSE.

2. Right-click anywhere in the POSE window and select Preferences from the popup menu.

3. Select the desired serial port from the Serial Port pull down list.

If you use the 2.1 version of POSE, you gain these features, as well:

✔ Automatic loop back for the serial port. If nothing is plugged into the selected desktop port, POSE just sends everything you spit out of the serial port right back into it, so your application sees it as serial input. This is handy for testing some serial applications.

✔ Mapping of Palm OS network function calls to the desktop PC network connection. This is amazingly valuable for debugging network applications. All you need is a working network connection on your desktop PC, and POSE will do the rest.

To redirect network calls to the desktop network connection in POSE, follow these steps:

1. Launch the 2.1 version of POSE.

2. Right-click anywhere in the POSE window and select Preferences from the popup menu.

3. Check the Redirect Netlib calls to Host TCP/IP checkbox.

The 2.1 version of POSE is still in beta testing as we are writing this book. Check the Palm Web site at `www.palm.com/devzone/pose/pose.html` to see if the final 2.1 version has been released.

Using the Palm Simulator for Macintosh

If you're using a Macintosh, you get an extra toy surprise in the Metrowerks CodeWarrior toolbox. It's called the Palm Simulator, and it's only available for Macintosh.

You non-Macintosh users can read this paragraph and then skip the rest of this section. The Macintosh uses a very similar CPU as is used in Palm devices. That makes it possible to compile a Palm application and link it with special libraries, such that it actually runs directly on the Macintosh. It's not running on an emulator; it's a special version of the application. So it simulates what your application will do when run on a Palm device. In the dim past, this was the only way to debug and test applications other than using a Palm device, but POSE has more than made up for this.

Simulating versus emulating

Why would you ever want to use the Palm Simulator, when POSE is available for Macintosh? We asked ourselves that question and drew a blank, but only for a moment. Then the answers revealed themselves and we were content. The simulator:

✔ Is faster than the emulator, especially when you use the Gremlins automated testing tool.

✔ Provides a very cool event trace window that shows events as they happen.

✔ Can record and playback events, which makes debugging a little easier.

✔ Has a console window where you can perform special actions, like changing the date or time, which does not work under POSE.

The Simulator has a lot of problems, not the least of which is that an application may work quite well when simulated, yet crash horribly when run on POSE or a Palm Device.

These are the things you can do on the Simulator that won't work on a real Palm device or POSE:

✔ You can allocate more stack memory for local variables.

✔ You can directly access storage memory instead of using the Data Manager routines.

✔ You can allocate more dynamic memory.

✔ You can link a large program for the Simulator that may not link for the Palm device, since the device does not support function calls that are farther than 32KB away.

✔ You can call standard C runtime functions that don't exist on the Palm device but do exist on the Macintosh.

Also, be aware that the Simulator does not send all possible launch codes.

If you're not discouraged by this list, all you need to do is add a new Target to your project for the Simulator. To find out how to do this, see the Metrowerks documentation file named `CookBookMac.eps` on the CD-ROM in the PalmDocs folder.

Striking a POSE

Before we end this chapter, we want to tie up just a few loose ends. We thought you should know:

The Web is a great place to get more information about POSE. See `www.palm.com/devzone` and sign up for developer support. It's free, and it's a great way to get lots of development information.

You can't reliably change the time with POSE's Preferences application. The time is synched with the host PC time.

In the Macintosh simulator, the function keys F9 through F12 simulate the four application buttons of the device.

Just in case you didn't read this the first time: When you load an application onto POSE, the screen showing the Application Icons can't be visible, or crazy things happen. Be sure that another application like Preferences is showing and then load your application. If you really want to be sure POSE is ready to load your application, reset POSE. You do this by right-clicking anywhere in the POSE window and selecting Reset from the popup menu. After POSE completes the reset, it's ready to load an application.

POSE and the Simulator are nice places to test your applications, but don't use them as a complete substitute for testing your applications on a real Palm device. Always, and we mean always, test your applications on a real device before shipping.

Chapter 6

Do You GNU?

• •

In This Chapter

▶ Feeling free

▶ Getting the tools

▶ Using the tools

• •

*O*ne of the reasons the Palm is so successful is the availability of a heavy duty, professional, and totally free development environment. This environment is built off of the GNU C/C++ compiler and associated tools. That means it's industrial strength, rock solid, and totally UNIX-like.

We had you right up to that last bit, didn't we? Totally UNIX-like is either a blessing or a curse, depending on your background. For those of us old enough to remember when the raging debate was the C Shell versus the Bourne Shell, UNIX is like an old friend. In case you can't tell, we're that old. Anyway, lots of people happen to think that UNIX-like is good. There are those who might not even be using a MacOS or Windows operating system. There are those who might not want to shell out the dollars for CodeWarrior. If you find yourself in any of these camps or if you'd like to know more about those of us in these camps, read on.

Freeing Yourself from the Corporation

So where did this GNU thing come from, you ask? It came from the idle hands of youth, mostly. You see, a long time ago in a galaxy far far away, there lived a young farmer named Luke. Fast forward a while and you get the whole GNU project off the ground. Lots of software freedom fighters write programs, compilers, operating systems, and just about anything else they can think of, mostly for the sheer joy of it, and partly to get Master's degrees and Ph.Ds. What you end up with, sometime in the mid 1990s, is a fully functional set of development tools that compiles C and C++ code into working programs for lots of different hardware and operating systems. One of the CPUs supported by gcc (the compiler bit of GNU) happens to be the same (or close enough) as the CPU used by a Palm device, as it was called back then. You can see where this is going, can't you?

So a bunch of clever people took the GNU source code and, after lots of hard work, they made a version of it that works with the Palm OS. Because they started with GNU, which is free and designed to always stay that way, the result of their labors must also be free. This means that we now have access to the finest set of compilers and associated tools ever written for no money down, no cash payable on receipt.

Grabbing the Freebies

You can download the full GNU package for the Palm OS from a lot of different places. Versions are available for the following operating systems:

- Windows (95, 98, NT4.0)
- Linux
- Other UNIXes

You knew this was coming, didn't you. We've got all the GNU stuff right on the CD-ROM. This is a good thing, because the basic GNU package runs about 15MB, and downloading that over a modem is not pretty. You'll find the Windows package in the GNU directory.

If you're running some UNIX variant, chances are that you've got a fast network connection. In this case, you'll need to download it from `ftp://ryeham.ee.ryerson.ca/pub/PalmOS`.

Establishing a baseline

The GNU package for Windows includes the following tools:

- emacs: One wacky program editor
- bash & shell tools: Now your Windows PC can really look like UNIX
- make: The granddaddy of all software build tools
- gcc: One of the finest compilers ever written
- pilrc: A resource compiler that works well enough to get the job done
- gdb: A source level debugger from the past
- copilot: An older version of the POSE emulator

The packages for Linux and other UNIXes are similar.

The emulator that's included with the GNU Windows distribution is quite out-of-date. It's the predecessor of POSE, the Palm OS emulator that 3Com gives away for free. You can download POSE from www.palm.com/devzone/pose/pose.html, and you should use it, even if you use GNU. We show you how to use the Debugger with POSE a little later in this chapter and also in Chapter 2.

Filling in the blanks

The GNU package has a ton of stuff, but some of it is a bit out-of-date. Actually, it's all a tad out-of-date, since it hasn't been updated since mid-1997. It's a testament to the quality of the original job that it's stood the test of time, but some things have happened in the intervening years. Fortunately, we're on top of it and can bring you up-to-date, too.

Posing for debuggers

One of the biggest changes is that 3Com has taken over development of copilot, the emulator that was part of the GNU tools. Needless to say, they're doing a fine job updating it. They call it POSE now, and it comes with CodeWarrior. It's pretty darn handy, but alas it does not work with the GNU Debugger, gdb. But wait! There is hope in the form of the latest, "seed" version of POSE.

You can find the seed version of POSE on the POSE homepage — www.palm.com/devzone/pose/pose.html. The download for release and seed versions is here: www.palm.com/devzone/pose/pose.html#downloads.

When you use gdb and POSE, you must have TCP/IP networking installed on your Windows machine. If you can surf the Web with your Windows machine, you're all set.

Making modern resources

There have been a few changes to the Palm resource world, and not surprisingly there's a new version of pilrc that understands them. The latest version, by Wes Cherry, updates pilrc to support the latest Palm OS 3.0 features. It also includes the pilrcui utility. This utility draws an approximation of the forms you create, so you can check them out as you make changes in the resource file.

You can find the latest pilrc- on the CD-ROM in the Tools/pilrc folder. Follow the instructions in the readme.txt file to use pilrc. You can simply copy the pilrc.exe and pilrcui.exe files into your GNU bin folder, so you're sure to be using the latest tools.

Seeing triple

You probably noticed by now that the Palm OS is numbered and that they're up to 3.0. Back in '97 they were still at 2.0, so all the libraries and header files in the GNU distribution aren't exactly up-to-date. They work just fine for all the pre-3.0 stuff, which it turns out is about 95 percent of the functions you'll use. Ah, but if you need one of the new functions, you're out of luck.

But wait! There is the Palm 3.0 SDK to save the day. You can download the Palm 3.0 SDK and its documentation for free from `www.palm.com/devzone/tools/sdk30.html`.

Going Retro with GNU

You've got the GNU package installed, and you're ready to code. So you might be wondering how to pull that off now. It's really not all that hard.

Here are the steps you follow to create an application with GNU:

1. Define your interface by editing a text file. Be sure to name the file with an extension of .rcp.

2. Create a header file (ending in .h) that defines all the resource IDs used in the resource file.

3. Create a C source file (ending in .c) that contains your program code.

4. Create a make file (usually just named makefile) that contains the rules needed to compile your application.

5. Make your application.

6. Load your application into POSE.

7. Run your application.

The following sections dig into each step so that you can see how the tools work.

Defining resources

The GNU tool uses a tool named pilrc (for PILot Resource Compiler) to translate a textual description of a program's resources into the actual binary resources included in the application file.

A Palm application file (a file ending in .prc) is just a series of binary resources assembled in a specific way. Palm application files include your forms, menus, alerts, strings, and other goodies, along with the compiled program code. The pilrc tool takes your text file and compiles the various descriptions you make for the resources into many different files, one per resource type. These files are combined with the output of the code compiler to "link" your application.

Unlike CodeWarrior, when you use GNU you're not able to use a what you see is what you get (or WYSIWYG — pronounced wizzy-wig) editor to draw your application's interface. At first, this seem like a horrendous burden, but in fact it's not all that difficult to create an application interface using pilrc. Here's a simple resource file that pilrc understands:

```
#include "helloworld.h"
VERSION 1 "0.0.0"
FORM ID Main_Form 0 0 160 160
NOFRAME
USABLE
MENUID About_Menu
BEGIN
    TITLE "Hello, World!"
    LABEL "Hello there, world!" ID 1 20 20 USABLE FONT 2
END
MENU ID About_Menu
BEGIN
   PULLDOWN "Options"
   BEGIN
      MENUITEM "About Hello World  " ID About_AboutHelloWorld
             "A"
   END
END
STRING ID 1000 "This is an example."
ALERT ID About_Alert
HELPID 1000
INFORMATION
BEGIN
   TITLE "About Hello World"
   MESSAGE "Hello World, the easy way!"
   BUTTONS "OK"
END
ICON "hello.bmp"
```

Right off the bat, you can see a few things from this file:

- ✔ pilrc files can include other files, using the standard C language #include statement.

- ✔ The files has a bunch of keywords, one for each resource type.

- ✔ pilrc understands C++ style (//) comments, but only outside of all keyword blocks. In other words, use comments outside of ALERT, MENU, and FORM definitions.

Only slightly apparent from this example is that pilrc understands the C #define directive, and will correctly substitute the defined value where appropriate. The rule here is to keep it simple. Just use #define <name> <resource id>, and pilrc is happy.

Here's the header file for the resource file:

```
#define Main_Form 1000
#define About_Menu 3000
#define About_AboutHelloWorld 3001
#define About_Alert 1000
```

There is really no excuse for hard coding resource ID in your program. Not only does it make for a hard-to-read program, but it also leads to errors. Always create a header file and assign resource IDs there, by including a #define statement for each resource ID you need to use in your program.

We're not going to repeat the excellent manual that comes with pilrc; instead we suggest that you read it. It's an HTML document named Pilrc.html, on the CD-ROM in the Tools/Pilrc folder.

In the next sections we give you a brief overview of the keywords you use to build your application resources with pilrc.

Creating forms

You use the FORM keyword to define each form and all the controls, fields, lists, and other items it contains. The general structure of the FORM keyword is:

```
FORM ID formId AT (left, top, right, bottom)
NOFRAME
USABLE
MENUID menuResourceId
BEGIN
    objects on the Form
END
```

To create a dialog box, include the FRAME, MODAL, SAVEBEHIND, and HELPID keywords.

Inside the BEGIN/END keywords, you use several different keywords to define the form's contents. Unless otherwise noted below, you may use any number of each of these keywords as needed to create your form.

The keyword for each item in a form, listed alphabetically, are:

✔ BUTTON: This keyword makes a Palm button.

✔ CHECKBOX: This keyword makes a Palm checkbox.

   To create a group of checkboxes, make as many CHECKBOX items as needed. Specify the same left position and group ID in each of them.

✔ FIELD: This keyword creates a Palm field. You must always use the MAXCHARS keyword with FIELD.

✔ FORMBITMAP: This keyword defines a bitmap image on the form.

✔ GADGET: This keyword defines a region on the form that processes pen taps.

✔ GRAFFITISTATEINDICATOR: This keyword defines an icon that indicates the Graffiti shift state. You should have at most one of these keywords in a form.

✔ LABEL: This keyword creates a Palm label.

✔ LIST: This keyword makes a Palm list, or a popup list when associated with a POPUPTRIGGER.

✔ POPUPLIST: This keyword associates a POPUPTRIGGER with a LIST, yielding the complete popup list control item.

✔ POPUPTRIGGER: This keyword makes a Palm popup trigger. To make a functional popup, you must have a POPUPTRIGGER and LIST, as well as a POPUPLIST keyword that associates the two.

✔ PUSHBUTTON: This keyword makes a Palm push button.

   To create a row of push buttons, make as many PUSHBUTTON items as needed. Specify the same height and group ID in each of them, and give the same top position to all of them.

✔ REPEATBUTTON: This keyword makes a Palm button that sends the ctlRepeatEvent event every half second, as long as the user continues to press it.

✔ SCROLLBAR: This keyword defines a Palm scroll bar.

✔ SELECTORTRIGGER: This keyword creates a Palm selector trigger.

✔ TABLE: This keyword defines a lovely pool table. No seriously, it really defines a Palm table.

✔ TITLE: This keyword defines the title of the form. There should be at most, one of these keywords in a form.

Creating menus

You use the MENU keyword to define each menu bar and all the menus and menu items in it. The general structure of the MENU keyword is:

```
MENU ID menuId
BEGIN
   menus
END
```

Each menu in a menu bar is represented by menus and has this structure:

```
PULLDOWN title
BEGIN
   menu items
END
```

All the menu items in a menu are either of the following:

```
MENUITEM itemName ID menuItemId acceleratorChar
MENUITEM SEPARATOR
```

The `acceleratorChar` is the uppercase character to use as the menu accelerator. The `SEPARATOR` menu item is the menu separator, much as you would expect.

Creating alerts

You use the `ALERT` keyword to define each alert. The general structure of the `ALERT` keyword is:

```
ALERT ID alertId
HELPID helpId
alertType
BEGIN
   TITLE title
   MESSAGE message
   BUTTONS button1 buttonN
END
```

The `alertType` is one of `INFORMATION`, `CONFIRMATION`, `WARNING`, or `ERROR`, and determines the icon displayed with the alert. The `BUTTONS` keyword is followed by one or more strings. Each string is the title of a button on the alert.

You must have at least one button on an alert. In addition, there is a practical limit of three buttons on an alert. If you need more than three buttons, you have to use a dialog box. Chapter 9 discusses dialog boxes.

Creating other resources

You can create every possible resource via pilrc. Here are the rest of the resource keywords, listed alphabetically:

- ✔ APPLICATIONICONNAME ID appId appNameString: **Creates the Application name shown in the launcher.**

- ✔ BITMAP ID bitmapId bitmapFileName: **Converts Windows .bmp, .xbm, or .pbm files into Palm Bitmap ('Tbmp') resources.**

- ✔ BITMAPGREY ID bitmapId bitmapFileName: **Converts Windows .bmp, .xbm, or .pbm files into 2-bit grayscale Palm Bitmap ('Tbmp') resources.**

- ✔ ICON iconFileName.bmp: **Converts a Windows-style bitmap into the Application Icon (resource ID 1000) shown in the launcher.**

- ✔ SMALLICON iconFileName.bmp: **Converts a Windows-style bitmap into the Application Icon (resource ID 1001) shown in the launcher when in List view.**

- ✔ STRING ID stringId stringValue: **Creates a string ('tSTR') resource.**

- ✔ VERSION ID versionId versionString: **Creates the application version.**

Taking a quick look with pilrcui

You can view the forms you define by using the pilrcui utility. Just enter:

```
pilrcui resfile.rcp
```

At the bash shell prompt, and you'll get a crude approximation of the form you've defined. If you have multiple forms in a resource file, you can select which form to display by using the Form menu.

Bash is the Born Again Shell. It's like the MS-DOS prompt window, in that it gives you a command line interface to run programs. Unlike the MS-DOS window, however, bash implements the same commands as you would find in the UNIX shell program sh.

A file named pilrc.html is on the CD-ROM in the Tools/Pilrc folder. This file explains in more detail how to define resources when using pilrc.

Writing code

Step 2 in the step-by-step process to creating an application with the GNU tools is to write the header file for your resources. When you created the resource file, you made up a bunch of names for the resource IDs. Now you create a header file and use #define to define a resource ID for each name.

You should be aware of some rules for resource IDs:

- Resource IDs for each type usually begin with the number 1000.
- Resource IDs within each resource type (form, menu, and so on) must be unique.

  This means every button, field, and so on must have a unique resource ID. You should leave plenty of room between each form resource ID.

- The exception to this rule is for menu items. Two menu items in different menus (PULLDOWN as it is called in pilrc) may have the same ID, if they really mean the same thing. For example, you may have multiple Edit menus, each with a Cut menu item. It's okay for each of these menu items to have the same resource IDs.

- Within a form, the resource IDs of items in the form determines the back-to-front ordering. For example, a button with resource ID 1010 is drawn before a field with resource ID 1011.

Editing with whatever you want

Step 3 in the step-by-step process is to write the C source files. You may choose to create a single source file or many source files. The process is no different than with any other C program. In fact, you can use C++ if you prefer, although there isn't much of an advantage in doing so.

The GNU distribution comes with emacs, a full-featured program editor. This editor is very powerful, but true to its UNIX heritage, it is somewhat difficult to learn and use. It's a lot like a Ginsu knife — sharp and powerful, and it makes great julienne fries, but you can also cut yourself with it!

If you want to dig in and use emacs, you'll have to learn how on your own. Whole books have been written on this subject, so you might want to stay away from it. We've had good success using the Windows NotePad to write programs. It's hardly fancy, but it works well enough.

Most Windows programs create text files with what is known as DOS line breaks. This means that each line in your program ends with both a carriage return and line feed character. The GNU tools are designed to work with UNIX text files, which have UNIX line breaks. This is just the line feed character. If you want to use the GNU gdb debugger, you'll need to make sure that your file has UNIX line breaks.

We've found a great freeware program that converts text files from DOS to UNIX style. Called cvret-e.exe, it's on the CD-ROM in the Tools/Conv folder. To convert a file named program.c to UNIX style line breaks, just use this command:

```
cvret-e /du program.c
```

Dealing with one glaring gcc *bug*

There really is only one "gotcha" to compiling programs with gcc, the GNU compiler. It has to do with the way gcc compiles functions, and it's pretty obscure.

You need to do two simple things to work around this bug. You need not understand what it is and why these things fix it. Just do them, and you'll be fine.

A very bright fellow named Ian Goldberg created a small include file, named Callback.h, that defines two macros. These macros are named CALLBACK_PROLOGUE and CALLBACK_EPILOGUE. You must place these two macros at the beginning and end of every function you write that is called as a callback.

A callback is a function that's called directly from the Palm OS, not from within your code. You can tell you're writing a callback if your program never explicitly calls the function.

Which functions are called as callbacks? There's a simple rule for this. First, every form event handler function you write is called as a callback. That's pretty obvious, since your program doesn't directly call these functions. The only other callback is PilotMain() and only some of the time. When the Palm OS calls PilotMain() to launch your program, everything is fine. When it calls PilotMain() with the sysAppLaunchFlagSubCall launch flag, that's the program's way of saying "this is a callback!" In those cases, you're going to need to use the two macros. We explain launch flags in detail in Chapter 12.

A typical Palm program that compiles with gcc starts out like this:

```
#include <Pilot.h>
#ifdef __GNUC__
#include "Callback.h"
#endif
```

If you never intend to compile the program with CodeWarrior, you don't need to bother with the #ifdef/#endif statements around the #include statement. These statements are compiler directives. They tell the compiler to ignore the enclosed statements when __GNUC__ isn't defined. (The GNU compiler defines this value; CodeWarrior does not.)

In every form event handler, you use the two macros, like so:

```
static Boolean MyFormHandleEvent(EventPtr event) {
    Boolean handled = false;
#ifdef __GNUC__
CALLBACK_PROLOGUE
```

(continued)

(continued)

```
#endif
    switch (event->eType) {
    // stuff you do for each event
    }
#ifdef __GNUC__
CALLBACK_EPILOGUE
#endif
    return handled;
}
```

All you do is put the two macros at the beginning and end of the function.

You cannot use the `return` statement in the middle of the function. If you do, the program skips the last macro, and bad things happen. Really bad things. You must include a single `return` statement, and it must come just after the last macro.

In `PilotMain()` you use the two macros only around those code blocks that are executed as callbacks. Here's a typical example:

```
DWord PilotMain(Word cmd, Ptr cmdPBP, Word launchFlags)
{
    Err error = 0;
    Boolean launched = false;
    switch (cmd) {
    case sysAppLaunchCmdNormalLaunch:
        // No GNU problems here
    case sysAppLaunchCmdSaveData: {
#ifdef __GNUC__
        CALLBACK_PROLOGUE
#endif
        // Always a Callback!
#ifdef __GNUC__
        CALLBACK_EPILOGUE
#endif
        }
        break;
    case sysAppLaunchCmdFind:
        launched = launchFlags & sysAppLaunchFlagSubCall;
        if (!launched) {
            // Not a Callback
        }
        else {
#ifdef __GNUC__
            CALLBACK_PROLOGUE
#endif
            // Is a Callback
#ifdef __GNUC__
```

```
            CALLBACK_EPILOGUE
  #endif
        }
      break;
    // Other cases
    }
    return error;
}
```

From this example, you can see that as far as this GNU bug is concerned, there are three types of launch codes:

- ✔ sysAppLaunchCmdNormalLaunch: **Never a callback.**
- ✔ sysAppLaunchCmdSaveData: **Always a callback.**
- ✔ All others: **Only a callback if** launchFlags & sysAppLaunchFlagSubCall **is not** 0.

You can also see in the code example that the two macros must be inside of a set of braces in order to work. That's because the first macro actually defines a variable, and in C, that must happen within a set of braces, before the first executable statement. If you get a weird compiler error, add a set of braces just before and after the macros.

Making the makefile

Steps 4 and 5 in the step-by-step process for building applications with the GNU tools is to create a makefile and use it to build the application. The GNU tools use an old UNIX standby to build applications. The make utility is incredibly powerful, yet somewhat cryptic for the novice programmer. We suggest you use common sense here — start out by modifying our basic makefile provided in the upcoming example. If you find you need more power, then you'll need to explore make in one of the many UNIX programming books, Web sites, or even the GNU documentation provided with the Palm distribution.

You can find a sample makefile on the CD-ROM in the Examples/Chap06 folder. This makefile is ready to customize for your application. The first four lines of the makefile are shown in the following example, with the parts you need to change italicized:

```
TARGET = hellowld
ICONTEXT = "Hello World"
APPID = PFDe
OBJS = $(TARGET).o
```

This makefile is designed to work with just one C file. It also assumes that your resource file (.rcp), program file (.c), and final Application Name (.prc) are all the same. Just change the TARGET value (hellowld) to the name you use for your files, and you're ready to build the application.

Change the ICONTEXT to the text you want displayed in the Palm launcher, and change the APPID to the creator ID for the application. That's all there is to it!

The creator ID (also known as the creator code) is the four-character code that's unique for your Palm application. Visit the Palm developer Web site at www.palm.com/devzone/crid/cridsub.html to register a unique creator ID with 3Com.

To actually build the application, follow these steps:

1. Open a bash window by selecting Start⇨Programs⇨PalmPilot-GNU, and then double-click the bash icon in the window that opens.

2. Use the cd command to open the directory your makefile and source files are in.

   This is bash, so don't forget to use UNIX style directory slashes (/). If the files are on a different drive, just cd to the drive letter first. For example: cd "e:/my stuff/examples/GCC/Chap06".

3. Build the application by using the make command. Simply enter make and press Return.

4. If you get compile errors, go back and edit the files with the errors.

Loading and running

Steps 6 and 7 in the step-by-step process for building applications with the GNU tools concern loading and running your application in POSE.

This is simply a matter of launching POSE and then right-clicking on the POSE window. Choose Load App from the popup menu and then select Other from the next popup menu. Navigate to your application within the window that appears. The application is loaded into POSE. You run it inside POSE just as if you were running it on a real Palm device. Tap Applications and then tap your application's icon. That's it!

Debugging your application is much more involved. To debug your application with gdb, you use version 2.1 or later of POSE. You can either run gdb from a bash window in command line mode, or you can run gdb from within emacs. Running gdb inside of emacs is challenging to get right, but once you get it you'll never go back. We cover debugging with gdb (both ways) in Chapter 21.

Part II
Building blocks

The 5th Wave   By Rich Tennant

"You can do a lot with a Palm device, and I guess dressing one up in G.I. Joe clothes and calling it your little desk commander is okay, too."

In this part . . .

Part II is where you see how to use the building blocks supplied by the Palm OS to create your applications. You discover how to use forms, menus, and other user interface elements to quickly create powerful applications that look and behave like standard Palm OS programs. We also show you how to take advantage of the inherent characteristics of the Palm device such as its memory and screen size. To round off this part, we talk about the managers that you use to provide the desired functionality in your applications.

You get everything you need to create professional-looking and acting Palm OS programs.

Chapter 7

Living in a Small World

In This Chapter

- Making the most of a tiny screen
- Living life 64KB at a time
- Getting input in
- Being kind to the batteries

No doubt about it, the Palm OS and Palm Devices are the embodiment of the phrase, "less is more." You have probably already discovered a lot of the "more" part by either using a Palm device or by writing a program for it. Now we're going to tell you the "less" part and how it impacts your programs.

In fact, things aren't as bad as you might think. Once you get used to the miniscule screen, microscopic memory, and puny power capacity of a pair of AA batteries, you won't even notice the incredibly slow (by today's desktop PC standards) CPU. In this chapter, we take a look at these issues and how to deal with them.

Squeezing Information into a Tiny Box

Take a deep breath and then repeat these words, "My entire interface must fit into 160x160 pixels." Figure 7-1 shows a popular desktop word processor sized to 160x160 pixels.

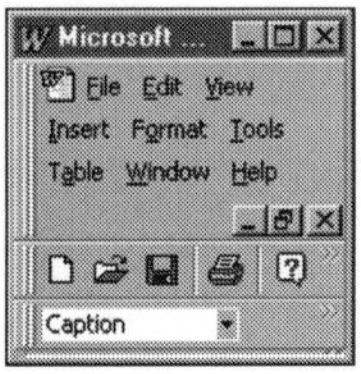

Figure 7-1: A puny little screen.

As you can see, the title bar, menu, and other controls fill the screen, leaving no room at all for the actual word processing document. This is obviously not an appropriate use of such a little display, so what's a programmer to do?

These are the things that the Palm OS does to help you out:

✔ Menus are only shown when the user taps the Menu silkscreen button

✔ Forms don't have borders, and they fill the screen

✔ Overlapping windows aren't supported

✔ Toolbars aren't supported

✔ Status lines aren't supported

✔ User elements that aren't valid at a given moment are not "grayed out" — they should be hidden if not available

✔ Forms have small title areas

In addition to these things, you're responsible for creating usable application interfaces. The folks at Palm have detailed user interface guidelines, which you should read. They specify the standard way to organize your interface so that it is both consistent with other Palm OS applications and usable.

You can find the Palm OS user interface guidelines on the Web at `www.palm.com/devzone/docs/CookBookWin.zip`. We suggest that you read them, but we'll summarize what they say here.

Here is our summary of the Palm OS user interface guidelines:

✔ Don't require a lot of navigation between forms.

✔ Don't nest many dialog boxes, especially modal ones.

✔ Make your application as fast as possible when retrieving and displaying information.

✔ The more often a command or setting is used, the easier it must be to find and the faster it needs to execute. Something used very often must only require one tap on the screen from the user.

✔ Provide a button to initiate or execute common commands and functions.

✔ Use the best Control for the task, but balance the suitability of a Control against its need for screen space.

Buttons are great since they do a single function with one tap, but they take a lot of screen space. If you have ten functions to perform, you cannot use ten separate buttons. You'll need to provide menus and/or popup lists if there are many choices or commands.

✔ Always create an application icon and give your application a descriptive but short application icon name.

✔ Provide an overview form that displays a summary of the information the application holds and that allows selection of individual records or items of information.

✔ Support the hardware navigation buttons (the up and down buttons in the center of the Palm device button array) and Graffiti next field gestures and previous field gestures.

✔ Support Categories and the Private Records features for applications that include a database. Categories are the way users can group related records. For example, in the Memo Pad built-in application you can see the Categories available in the popup menu located in the upper-right corner of the screen. Private Records allow the user to mark a record private, and then either show or hide all private records via a Preference selection.

✔ Don't ever require a double-tap to perform an action.

✔ Command buttons go at the bottom of the screen.

✔ Support HotSync and desktop editing and entry of information by writing a Conduit. A Conduit is a program you write that works with HotSync, and allows HotSync to correctly synchronize data in your application with the desktop computer. Conduits are discussed in Chapter 17.

In addition to this list, we've found the following guidelines to be helpful when dealing with a very small screen:

✔ Follow the Keep It Simple Silly (KISS) principle. Your application and its interface should do one thing and do it well, without a lot of excess features.

✔ Be consistent. Do things the same way as the built-in applications, and do things the same way on every form and dialog of your application.

✔ Provide feedback. Let the user know that the application is working, if it must do something that takes a long time. Use alerts and dialogs to confirm data removing operations.

✔ Reduce what users must remember. For every form, dialog, and alert the user must know where they are, what their options are, and what the results of their actions will be.

Squeezing into Very Small Memory

It's time for another mental exercise. Are you old enough to remember which computers had 1KB of program accessible memory and 128KB floppies? How about 64KB of memory and 241KB floppy disks? Or how about the IBM PC/XT, with 640KB of memory and a 5MB hard drive? Most Palm devices fall into the second category, with slightly more storage space. Unless you're as old as we are, you may be used to much more when it comes to both memory and storage space.

Knowing the limitations

The Palm OS does everything it can to squeeze into one heck of a tight memory footprint, but you've got to do your part as well. The Palm OS and the devices it runs on limit your program size and memory usage in the following ways:

✔ The local variable memory is limited to between 2KB and 4KB. You cannot allocate large local variables, and you cannot use a lot of recursion in your program. Recursion is the act of a function calling itself, and as you might expect, it uses a lot of stack memory.

✔ The dynamic memory your program can allocate, and the memory for global variables comes from the same place. The total available global and dynamic memory is between 12KB and 60KB. You cannot declare very large globals or allocate very large amounts of dynamic memory.

✔ On Palm OS 2.0 and earlier devices, no single database record can be larger than 64KB in size. This restriction is lifted in Palm OS 3.0 or later.

✔ Palm devices have as little as 64KB and as much as several megabytes of storage memory. The most popular model is still the 512kb version, with about 448KB of usable storage memory.

✔ Program executable code is limited to 32KB in size. There are ways to create larger programs in both CodeWarrior and with the GNU tools, but once your application's compiled code size exceeds 32KB, you have to get actively involved.

When we say executable code is limited to 32KB in size, what we really mean is that your program cannot call a function that's more than 32KB away, in the executable image, from itself. It's a limitation of the CPU used in Palm devices. We can all bemoan this throwback to the dark ages of computers, or we can just deal with it.

When we look at the preceding list, we think of one word. Ouch. The good news is that, even with these limitations, programmers around the world have created literally thousands of useful and interesting applications for the Palm OS. We talk about memory allocation (both dynamic and storage) in Chapter 13. That's where you'll find all the details for working with (and around) the tight memory of the Palm OS.

Dealing with limited memory

Here is our list of things to keep in mind, memory-wise, with the Palm OS:

- ✔ Know how much memory you're allocating and where it's allocated.

- ✔ If you must have a large local variable, either declare it `static` in the function, or allocate it from dynamic memory and then free it when you're done.

- ✔ If you must have a huge variable that exceeds the dynamic memory limits, create a database with one or more records in it and use them to hold the value. Delete the database when you're done.

- ✔ Know how deep your function call stack is. Try to keep it as shallow as reasonable, which just means try not to have many nested function calls or deep recursion in your program.

- ✔ Test the return values of your dynamic memory allocations to make sure that they succeed and include code that notifies the user if you run out of dynamic memory.

  On Palm devices, running out of dynamic memory is considered a bug in your program. You can use the Palm OS Emulator to test your application with several different memory configurations. Chapter 20 discusses debugging in detail.

- ✔ Test the return values of your storage memory allocations to make sure that they succeed and include code that notifies the user if the storage memory is full.

  It's not a bug if the Palm device that your program is running on happens to run out of storage space. Your application must leave things in a stable, usable state even if this happens.

- ✔ Pack the data in records as tightly as possible. Don't use fixed widths for strings stored in records.

- ✔ Edit the information in a record in place. Don't copy the contents of a record into local or dynamic memory.

- ✔ If your application is larger than 32KB, use the appropriate workaround. See the sidebar "Bigger than 32KB" for suggestions.

Bigger than 32KB

How can you tell when your application has crossed the line, size-wise? Whether you're using CodeWarrior or the GNU tools, the linker will let you know.

With CodeWarror, you get a Link error that says `16-bit reference out of range` should your compiled program result in a function call that's more than 32KB away. At this point, you have several options, ranging from rearranging your source code so that the functions are closer to changing the project preferences to use the "Smart code model." Refer to the Metrowerks documentation Acrobat file named Targeting Palm OS.pdf for more information.

With the GNU tools, you get a Link error that says `relocation truncated to fit: DISP16` followed by a function name including `bhook`. The name printed is the target of the call, not the caller, so you will need to examine your code to find the calling location. Unfortunately, with the current version of the GNU tools, you don't have a choice but to try and rearrange your source files to see if you can move the offending function closer to its caller, or to reduce your overall executable size below 32KB. You can use what are known as *shared libraries* to create separate packages that contain commonly used functions, which can reduce your overall code size.

Getting Text In

We like Palm devices, but frankly we're not big fans of Graffiti. We fall into the group of users who will never be able to do more than slowly scratch out the occasional entry, and who resort to using the popup keyboard most of the time. On the other hand, there are Graffiti lovers out there who are so used to it they find themselves writing it even on paper. At any rate, you can do certain things in your application that make using Graffiti, or entering text in general, a better experience for the user.

These are our tips for improving text entry in your application. On any form that has text entry fields:

✔ Include a Graffiti shift indicator somewhere on the form. The standard location is in the lower-right corner of the form.

✔ Set each field's numeric property appropriately, enabling it if the field should only hold numbers.

✔ Use the `GrfGetState()` and `GrfSetState()` Palm OS functions to disable the initial automatic capitalization of the first letter of a Field when you don't want that behavior. If you're using CodeWarrior, you can control this behavior by setting or clearing the Auto Shift property of a field in Constructor.

✔ Support the standard Edit menu, which includes the Undo, Cut, Copy, Paste, Select All, Keyboard, and Graffiti Help menu items.

✔ Support the Next/Previous Field Graffiti shortcuts.

✔ Set the focus for the form onto the first editable field on the form in your form initialization function by using the `FrmSetFocus()` Palm OS function.

Sipping Juice

Is your application a power guzzler? Believe it or not, eating the batteries of a Palm device is easier than you'd think. All it takes is some innocent but deadly code on your part, and your application will eat batteries like a toddler eats candy. Palm devices have three power modes:

✔ Sleep mode, where the unit appears powered off, but is in a very low power state. It wakes from this state when the user presses a hardware button or an alarm goes off.

✔ Doze mode, where the unit appears powered on, but is in a reduced power state since the CPU is halted. It wakes from this state when the user or system generates an event. Your goal as a programmer is to write your programs such that the Palm device can get into this state as often as possible.

✔ Running mode, where the CPU is actually executing program or operating system instructions. This mode uses the most power.

If you follow the general structure of a standard Palm OS application, as we outline in Chapter 8, then you're already a long way toward being kind to the batteries, since your application will be in doze mode whenever it is waiting for an event in the event loop. Even so, there are things you sometimes have to do that can be electron hogs. The sections that follow show you the right way to do some typical battery-consuming tasks.

Waiting a little while

When you want to pause execution for a second or so, without returning to the main event loop, you may be tempted to code what's known as a delay loop. This is usually a `for()` loop that executes several hundred or thousand times doing nothing, or worse yet checking the system tick count to see if enough ticks have passed. It's death for the batteries!

Replace code like this:

```
// delay 1 second
ULong startTicks;
for (startTicks = TimGetTicks();
       (TimGetTicks()-startTicks) < SysTicksPerSecond(); )
   ;
```

With this:

```
// delay one second
SysTaskDelay(SysTicksPerSecond());
```

The former version keeps the system in full power mode, and the latter puts the CPU into doze mode for the specified number of ticks.

Doing periodic and frequent updates

When you're writing a communications program or game, you often need to perform actions on a regular basis. This can include checking the serial port to see if any input is ready, moving the monster in your arcade game, computing the next move in your chess game, or doing a background recalculation in your spreadsheet.

When you need to do this, the best approach is to supply a timeout value in your event loop for the EvtGetEvent() Palm OS function. When you do this, your application receives a nilEvent event when no event occurs within the number of ticks specified by your timeout value. That way the CPU can spend as much time in doze mode as possible, yet still wake up and do whatever it needs to do periodically.

The system does not guarantee that your application will get a nilEvent event after exactly the specified number of ticks. It may send the event a few ticks sooner. Also, if some other event is sent (such as the user tapping a Control), then that event is sent, and the "countdown" for the next nilEvent is reset.)

This means that you should check the system tick counter to see whether enough ticks have passed before you do whatever you want to do on a periodic basis. The best place to do this is in your form event handler function:

```
static Boolean MyFormHandleEvent(EventPtr eventP)
{
   if (checkTime())
      DoPeriodicFunction()
   // rest of the handler
}

static Boolean checkTime() {
   static ULong lastTicks;
   ULong ticksNow;
   ticksNow = TimGetTicks();
   if (lastTicks == 0) {
      lastTicks = ticksNow;
      return false;
   }
   else if ((lastTicks + SysTicksPerSecond())
         <= ticksNow) {
      lastTicks = ticksNow;
      return true;
   }
   return false;
}
```

The event handler function calls checkTime() to check if enough time has passed since the last event to do the periodic function. The checkTime() function keeps a static local variable containing the tick count when the last periodic function was performed. It returns true if at least one second has passed since the last time it returned true.

Chapter 8

It's All in the Events

In This Chapter

▶ Following the flow of events

▶ Determining which events are triggered

▶ Categorizing events

*P*alm programs come in many forms, and for all but the most specialized of applications, every program has one thing in common. That thing is as plain as the nose on your face . . . it's the interface. If you've somehow managed to avoid looking at your Palm up till now, go ahead and take a peek at it. You'll see that whatever program is running has a graphical user interface, or GUI.

A *GUI* is a graphical representation of the commands available in a program, as well as the data currently being displayed or edited. It's called *graphical* because it uses windows, buttons, icons, and other modern conveniences to get the job done. Unless you live in a cave, you've used and probably even written programs that use GUIs.

Palm applications, like most applications that use GUIs, are event-based. An event-based program is a little different than old-style command and menu-based programs.

An *event* is a small bit of information that's generated whenever a user does just about anything with a GUI-based program. Events are the language of GUIs — they communicate the user's desires to your program.

Event-based programs are reactive in nature. Your program displays its GUI and then reacts to the events generated by the user. Events are put in a pipe of sorts, called the *event queue*, by the operating system, or by Palm functions.

In this chapter, we're going to look at every aspect of events you need to write Palm programs. As you go through it, you see:

✔ How event-based programs differ from traditional programs

✔ How to structure a Palm program to handle events

✔ How to handle specific events

Getting Events

In the dim past, the programmer decided exactly when each part of a program would run. That's because in the pre-GUI days of computing, programs relied on command lines, much like the dreaded DOS prompt or the retro-but-cool UNIX shell prompt. Then, in the Mesozoic computing era, users were given limited freedom when programmers started creating menu-based programs. There were still just a few choices at any given point in a program, but at least it was a start.

A really odd thing happened next. Users were given complete freedom by the advent of the GUI. Suddenly users could do just about anything! They could click (or in the case of the Palm, tap) anywhere, do anything! That's great for users, but for you, the programmer, it means switching to a whole new model of programming.

Event-based programs have to be ready for just about anything. Once your program displays a GUI screen, the user is free to interact with any part of it at any time. Sure, your program still controls what's on any given screen. It can even provide a menu, just like the good old days. But in general, your program needs to be ready for any events that may come its way.

In general, an event-based program has three parts:

✔ Initialization

✔ Event loop

✔ Clean up

The initialization portion sets up the first screen the program displays. The Palm folks call screens forms. We cover forms in detail in Chapter 9. All you need to know about forms right now is that they can contain zero or more controls. A control is pretty much what it sounds like, something the user can manipulate to control the program. Things like buttons, fields, and lists are all controls. You can read all about controls in Chapter 10.

What's important to know now is that when the user does something with a control (such as tapping a button), it generates an event. In addition to Control Events, the operating system generates a variety of events so that your program can respond to things like forms displaying and hardware buttons getting pressed.

The event loop is the engine of an event-based program. It does what it says. It loops around and around, reading the next event and then processing it. For example, a button-press event is received in the event loop, and after the program looks it over and figures out which button generated it, it calls the correct function to process the event and perform the function associated with the button. The whole process repeats until a specific event is received, indicating that the user is done using the program. That's when the event loop ends.

When the program is done looping around looking for events, all that's left to do is clean up. This step varies depending on what the program did while it ran, but typical functions include freeing up allocated memory and saving information.

The little engine that could

Regardless of what you want your program to actually do, if it has any kind of interface at all, it has to use events. This means your program must do the following things:

1. Load the initial form.
2. Enter an event loop.
3. Perform the final cleanup.

When your application is launched on a Palm device, the first function that's called is named `PilotMain()`. C and C++ programmers will instantly grasp the similarity of this function to the `main()` function, which traditionally gets called when you run your program. Technically speaking, you can code your entire program within `PilotMain()`. However, years of experience have shown that it makes a whole lot more sense to create several functions to handle the details of each step. This makes the purpose and structure of each function much more obvious.

Throughout this chapter, we present a very basic example program that displays a screen that displays `Hello there, world!` It has a Menu with one menu item. When this menu item is selected, an alert is displayed. Figure 8-1 shows three views of the `Hello World` program running on a Palm device.

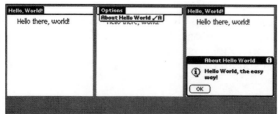

Figure 8-1:
Three views
of the Hello
World pro-
gram.

The complete source code for the Hello World example is on the CD-ROM that accompanies this book in the Examples\Chap08 folder. We're not going to show all of the code or resource files in this chapter, but rather just the relevant portions from the helloworld.c program source file.

The PilotMain() calls three functions that correspond to the three steps:

```
DWord PilotMain(Word launchCode, Ptr cmdPBP,
    Word launchFlags) {
    Err err;
    if (launchCode == sysAppLaunchCmdNormalLaunch) {
        if ((err = StartApplication()) == 0) {
            EventLoop();
            StopApplication();
        }
    }
    return err;
}
```

When PilotMain() is called, it is supplied with several parameters. The most important one is LaunchFlags, which contains the launch code, indicating why the application was launched. Chapter 13 discusses launch codes in detail, but for now the important thing to know is that LaunchFlags is sysAppLaunchCmdNormalLaunch when the user taps the application icon to run your program. Our PilotMain() function checks for this, and if it is true, we perform the following step-by-step process:

1. We call StartApplication() to perform the initialization of the program.

2. We call EventLoop() to enter the Event loop.

3. Finally, we call StopApplication() to perform the final cleanup.

Starting the application

People have been debating how the universe was created since the beginning of time. Fortunately, the question of how events begin to flow into a Palm program is not only knowable, it's quite simple.

About function names

A program has three types of functions: those you write, those that are part of the Palm library, and those that the operating system expects you to have, like `PilotMain()`. The functions you write can obviously have any name you want. You could call your event loop function `Fred()` for example. Common sense suggests that you should pick function names that describe what the function does, so that you or someone else reading your code can at least guess what a function does just by reading the name.

We take this convention one step further. Other than this book, a huge body of Palm programs and technical documentation is available. This includes code freely available on the Web (see `www.palm.com`) and Palm's own programming documentation. This code and documentation is pretty consistent in both how programs are structured and how functions are named. For example, the three functions `StartApplication()`, `EventLoop()`, and `StopApplication()` could be called by many other names, but almost always have these names within Palm's documentation and a huge number of other programs. We figure it makes more sense to be consistent rather than clever with these and other user-defined functions, so you'll be able to more quickly read and understand other people's code and documentation.

Before any events are generated, your program must display something on the screen.

You've got to do something when your application starts to get the ball rolling. That's what Step 1 of our step-by-step process is all about. For most applications this means that they need to:

1. Restore the saved state of the program.

2. Get your first form displayed on the screen.

3. Select which form to display, if your application has multiple forms.

Let's get the ball rolling by displaying the same form each time our application starts:

```
static Err StartApplication(void) {
    FrmGotoForm(Main_Form);
    return 0;
}
```

This startup code does not restore any state information. All it does is load the same form each time the program is run by using the `FrmGotoForm()` Palm function and supplying the resource ID of the form to load. We discuss form definitions and resource IDs in Chapter 3. After we load the form, we `return 0` to indicate the application has started successfully. Note that if, for some reason, an application cannot or does not want to start, it needs to return a non-zero value. That will cause the Palm OS to return to the previously running application.

Let there be light! You've now set into motion the generation of events.

Going with the Flow

The first event your application receives is `frmOpenEvent`, but that's not important here. That's just one event that you'll be looking for in your event loop. In fact, so many events are possible that they're broken down into four categories:

- System events
- Menu events
- Application events
- Form events

In the following sections, we take a look at these event types in more detail.

Running the loop

Step 2 of the step-by-step process is to sit in a loop, getting Events and processing them. Since many possible types of Events are available, this step is usually implemented as a cascaded group of function calls within a loop:

```
static void EventLoop(void) {
    EventType event;
    Word error;
    do {
        EvtGetEvent(&event, evtWaitForever);
        if (! SysHandleEvent(&event))
            if (! MenuHandleEvent(0, &event, &error))
                if (! ApplicationHandleEvent(&event))
                    FrmDispatchEvent(&event);
    } while (event.eType != appStopEvent);
}
```

The `do while` loop repeatedly gets the next Event by calling `EvtGet Event()`. This function takes two parameters. The first parameter is a pointer to an `EventType` structure and is filled in with the details of the specific Event that's sent to the program. The second parameter is a `Long` integer that tells the function how long to wait for an Event, in system ticks.

A system tick is a measure of time in the Palm OS. It's a heartbeat, of sorts, and among other things makes sure that everything works when it is supposed to. In the Palm OS, a system tick is usually ¹⁄₁₀₀ of a second, but this can vary based on the actual hardware device. To get the actual number of system ticks for the current system use `SysTicksPerSecond()`.

If you want to wait forever and also save battery power, use the constant `evtWaitForever`, which is defined to be `-1`. That means the Palm OS can put the hardware into a state that uses far less power. When an event is generated, the hardware powers up, and you get the event.

If you are creating a program that updates the display even when the user has done nothing, you cannot use the `evtWaitForever` value, because this value means that the `EvtGetEvent()` call waits forever for the next event. Instead, you need to supply some number so that your program will have a chance to do the update. If that's the case, then if no event is received within the specified number of ticks, the call to `EvtGetEvent()` returns with an `event.eType` of `nilEvent`.

Assuming that you actually get an event, you need to process it. Processing events is a four-step process:

1. Let the system try to handle the event by calling the Palm function `SysHandleEvent()` and passing in a pointer to the `EventType` you received from `EvtGetEvent()`.

   If that function handles the event, it returns `true` and you're all done with this event. If not, then you know it's not a system event.

2. Give the Menu system a shot at the event by calling the Palm function `MenuHandleEvent()`, again passing in a pointer to the `EventType` you received from `EvtGetEvent()`.

   If that function handles the event, it returns `true` and you're all done. If not, then you know it's not a menu event.

3. Call your `ApplicationHandleEvent()` function, passing in a pointer to the `EventType` you received from `EvtGetEvent()`.

   If that function handles the event, it returns `true` and you're all done. If not, then you know it's not a application event.

4. Call the Palm function `FrmDispatchEvent()`, passing in a pointer to the `EventType` you received from `EvtGetEvent()`.

   This function is a little different than the other Palm Event handling functions in that it first calls your registered form event function for the particular form that generated the event, and if you don't handle the event there it then does the default processing for the event. We haven't shown you when you register the form event function just yet, but we will in just a few moments.

Figure 8-2 shows the flow of events through these functions.

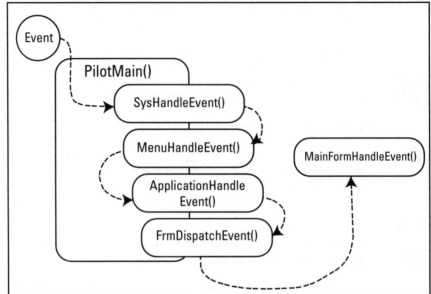

Figure 8-2:
Event flow
in a
program.

Processing system and menu events

System and menu events have to be processed by something, but fortunately for us, Palm supplies default handler functions. You can process system and menu events yourself if you have a need to, but generally you just call the default function and let it go at that.

Consider the penDownEvent, which is sent whenever the user puts the pen down while your application is running. Depending on where the user puts the pen down, the SysHandleEvent() Palm function works very hard to figure out just what the user is really trying to do. If it happens to be in the Graffiti area, then the user's pen stroke is converted into a keyDownEvent event. The MenuHandleEvent() does the same type of thing, converting pen taps and drags into menuEvent events.

Clearly you don't need to deal with these events in most cases. However, if you're writing a game application, you sure do want to get hold of these events before the sysEventHandler() eats them. That's why you get to decide how events are handled.

Processing application events

If an event isn't a system or menu event, then it's either an application event (something general to do with your application) or an event specific to the form currently displayed.

Application events include things like form loading and unloading events. Consider the `ApplicationHandleEvent()` function for the Hello World application:

```
static Boolean ApplicationHandleEvent(EventPtr event) {
    FormPtr frm;
    Word formId;
    Boolean handled = false;
    if (event->eType == frmLoadEvent) {
        formId = event->data.frmLoad.formID;
        frm = FrmInitForm(formId);
        FrmSetActiveForm(frm);
        switch (formId) {
            case Main_Form:
            FrmSetEventHandler(frm, MainFormHandleEvent);
            break;
        }
        handled = true;
    }
    return handled;
}
```

When the program loaded the initial Form in the `StartApplication()` function, it did so by calling the `FrmGotoForm()` Palm function. That function inserts a `frmLoadEvent` event into the event queue. When your program finally got around to looking for events in the `EventLoop()` function, it found this event waiting. Since `frmLoadEvent` is neither a system or menu event, the `sysHandleEvent()` and `menuHandelEvent()` functions don't do anything with it. That means it gets passed to the `ApplicationHandleEvent()` function, where we finally get to do something. The `FrmGotoForm()` function also puts a `frmOpenEvent` event into the event queue, which we process later in the Form Event handler.

Although this function handles only this one event, and this application has only one form, we're showing a more general implementation. That way, you'll be able to see how to make a more powerful program with multiple forms.

There's a very real possibility that the `ApplicationHandleEvent()` function will be called with other events destined to be handled by a form event function, so we set a `Boolean` named `handled` to `false`. We'll return this `Boolean` at the end of this function, and we want to return `false` if we don't end up doing anything.

Next, we test the event type. If it is, in fact, a `frmLoadEvent`, our function springs into action. It retrieves the `Form Id` from the Event, and then it calls two Palm functions that get the Form ready to display. The `FrmInitForm()` function takes a `Form Id` and loads the Form information from the program's resources.

We describe resources in detail in Chapter 3, but recall that a Palm program is more than just your program code. It also contains one or more resources, which consist of information describing the forms, menus, and other non-program bits of information needed while it executes.

The `FrmInitForm()` Palm function returns a pointer to the information about the Form loaded from the program's resources. You pass this pointer to the `FrmSetActiveForm()` Palm function, which tells the Palm OS which Form is the currently active form.

All that's left to do is register the correct form event handling function with the Palm OS. You do this by using the `FrmSetEventHandler()` Palm function. That function takes two parameters: the pointer to the loaded form information and a pointer to the form event handler function.

If your program uses more than one form, you need to use a `switch` statement, as we did here, to register the appropriate form event handler function based on the form ID of the loaded form.

You will always use these same three Palm functions (`FrmInitForm()`, `FrmSetActiveForm()`, and `FrmSetEventHandler()`) to handle a `frmLoadForm` event.

Now that the form has been loaded and set as the active form, and the correct form event handler is loaded, your program is prepared to handle form events as they are generated.

Processing form events

After you've checked all the other types of events possible, the only other type of event is a form event.

Because you might have several forms in a program, it makes sense that you'd want to group the entire related event handling code for a specific form within a single function. You may well have additional functions that do the actual actions associated with a particular form, but the form event handler is where you determine what a form event means and what your program should do to process it.

Generally speaking, your form event handler processes these types of events:

- ✔ `frmOpenEvent` events, which indicate the opening of the form.

- ✔ `frmCloseEvent` **and/or** `frmSaveEvent` events, which indicate that you need to save any changes on a form.

- ✔ `menuEvent` events, which indicate a user selection from a menu associated with a form.

- ✔ `ctlSelectEvent` events, which indicate that the user tapped on a control of the form.

Consider the `MainFormHandleEvent()` function for the Hello World application:

```
static Boolean MainFormHandleEvent(EventPtr event) {
    Boolean handled = false;

#ifdef __GNUC__
    CALLBACK_PROLOGUE
#endif

    switch (event->eType) {
        case frmOpenEvent:
            FrmDrawForm(FrmGetActiveForm());
            handled = true;
            break;
        case menuEvent:
            switch (event->data.menu.itemID) {
            case About_AboutHelloWorld:
                FrmAlert(About_Alert);
                break;
            // process other menu items
            }
            handled = true;
            break;
        case ctlSelectEvent:
            switch(event->data.ctlSelect.controlID) {
            // process control selections
            }
            handled = true;
            break;
    }

#ifdef __GNUC__
    CALLBACK_EPILOGUE
#endif

    return handled;
}
```

The first thing you'll notice is that there is a pair of #ifdef __GNUC__ statements wrapped around this function. We talk about using the GNU C compiler in Chapter 6, but all you need to know here is that you always need to wrap your Form Event handler code with these statements if you want to compile the program using the GNU compiler. If you never intend to use GNU C, then you need not bother with these #ifdef statements.

Events contain much more information that just the event type. For each event type, additional data is provided that sheds more light on exactly what happened to generate the event. The event structure includes the following fields:

- ✔ eType: An enumerated type describing the type of event.

- ✔ penDown: A Boolean indicating if the pen was down when the event was generated.

- ✔ screenX: The x-coordinate of the point where the event was generated, if appropriate.

- ✔ screenY: The y-coordinate of the point where the event was generated, if appropriate.

- ✔ data: a union of structures, one per event type. The data union contains overlaid structures with the same names as the various event types, minus the trailing "event." For example, the menuEvent has a data union member structure named menu.

When processing the specific event, you will find the extra information included with the event very helpful. You can find out what information is included in each event type in the last section of this chapter.

The MainFormHandleEvent() function consists of a single switch statement. There is a case block for each event type we're interested in. Since this program doesn't have any information to save, we don't bother handling frmCloseEvent or frmSaveEvent event types.

The first case block processes the frmOpenEvent event. When this event is received, we draw the form by using the frmDrawForm() Palm function, which finally gets the Form GUI displayed. Note that we don't need to hard-code the Form Id in this call, rather we use the FrmGetActiveForm() Palm function to retrieve a pointer to the currently active form.

The frmOpenEvent event is generated when you open a form by using the FrmGotoForm() Palm function. That function generates two events, frmLoadEvent and frmOpenEvent, in that order. When you handle the frmLoadEvent in your ApplicationHandleEvent() function, you set the loaded form as the active form by using the FrmSetActiveForm() Palm function. That's why, when you handle the frmOpenEvent event here, you can simply retrieve the form pointer by using the FrmGetActiveForm() Palm function.

The next `case` block processes the `menuEvent` event, which signals that the user has made a selection from the form's menu. The Hello World program has a single menu, with one menu item. That means we could just assume that any time we get the `menuEvent` event we do the action associated with the single menu item, but our code is a bit more general.

Use a `switch` statement to select the operations to perform based on the ID of the menu item that is selected. The menu item ID is retrieved from the event by using `event->data.menu.itemId`. The actual operations may be within the form event handler, or may be a call to a separate function in your program. Using a separate function makes a lot of sense when the user has several different ways (such as a menu and a button) of initiating the same operation.

All we do when the user selects the menu item is to display an alert by using the `FrmAlert()` Palm function and supply it with the resource ID of the Alert resource we want displayed.

The last case doesn't do anything in the application, but in many ways it is similar to the `menu case block`. All controls (buttons, checkboxes, and so on) on a form, when tapped, generate some form of `SelectEvent`. Controls generate a `ctrSelectEvent` event; lists generate a `lstSelectEvent`; and so on.

As in the case of the `menuEvent` event, use a `switch` statement to select the operations to perform based on the ID of the Control that is selected. The control Id is retrieved from the event by using `event->data.ctlSelect.controlId`.

Winding down

There's one last way your program may get an event, and it goes against everything we've said up until now. We can only assume that Palm did things this way to get around a thorny little problem as your program shuts down. We look at a typical program clean up function to see this problem, and its solution, in action.

Recall that in your `EventLoop()` function, the last event you receive from `EvtGetEvent()` is `appStopEvent`. Once you get that one, you return from `EventLoop()` and then, in `PilotMain()`, you call your `StopApplication()` function to clean up all the loose ends.

The Hello World program has a fairly simple `StopApplication()` function:

```
static void StopApplication(void) {
    FrmSaveAllForms();
}
```

All we do is call the FrmSaveAllForms() Palm function, which sends the frmSaveEvent Event to all open Forms in the program. What's wrong with this picture, you ask? Well, at this point, you've exited the event loop and can't receive any new events from the event queue.

The solution is simple — the FrmSaveEvent event isn't sent to the event queue at all! In fact, the event handlers for each loaded form are called directly from within FrmSaveAllForms() and are handed a frmSaveEvent event. You don't need to do anything special to handle this event differently from any other event. It's just important to know that events aren't always delivered via the event queue.

FrmSaveAllForms() and FrmCloseAllForms() are intended to be used in your application's clean up function, so these functions send their events (frmSaveEvent and frmCloseEvent) directly to the form handlers of all loaded forms. That's because these functions need to deliver their events even if you've already exited from your EventLoop().

Grasping the Big Picture

The Hello World application is very simplistic, yet it still deals with several events and fully reveals the flow of events in a typical Palm program. There are, however, many more events you will need to deal with as you create more complex applications. Rather than try and come up with a super-whiz-bang example that uses all the possible events, this section gives you a roadmap of the events, when they're generated, and what you should do with them in your programs.

Thirty-four events exist. They are grouped into four broad types:

- ✔ System, generated by the hardware or Palm OS
- ✔ Menu, generated by a menu
- ✔ Application, generated by Palm functions called from your program
- ✔ Form, generated by the user interacting with a form

The following sections explore the events in each broad type in more detail.

System events

System events are the lowest-level events possible. Unless you're writing a special program such as a system utility, game program, or drawing program, you will probably not need to deal with any of these events. In fact, the standard system, menu, and form event handlers often handle system events and in turn generate more meaningful events, as you'll see a bit later on.

Seven system events exist. In this section, we describe each event, tell you the things that generate it, and tell you what extra information is provided with the event.

Three events communicate basic information about the user tapping the screen with the pen:

- ✔ The penDownEvent event is generated when pen touches the digitizer (any part of the Palm screen).
- ✔ The penUpEvent event is generated when pen is lifted from the digitizer.
- ✔ The penMoveEvent event is generated multiple times as pen moves (is dragged) on the digitizer.

Your program does not see penMoveEvent events when an event handler tracks pen motion following a penDownEvent event. Of these three related events, only the penUpEvent event includes additional information. The event->penUp structure includes two fields:

- ✔ start, a variable of type PointType, that contains the x- and y-coordinates of where the stroke started
- ✔ end, a variable of type PointType, that contains the x- and y-coordinates of where the stroke ended

The keyDownEvent event is generated when the user makes a Graffiti stroke, taps on a silk screen button, or presses a hardware button. The event->keyDown structure includes three fields:

- ✔ chr, a variable of type Word, that contains the ASCII code for the key, or 0
- ✔ keyCode, a variable of type Word, that contains the key code for the key, or 0
- ✔ modifiers, a variable of type Word; that contains a flag value indicating any special state of the key

The list of modifiers is defined in the Palm header file Events.h, and includes shiftKeyMask (shift key is also down) and controlKeyMask (control key is also down)

Event conversion in action

When the user taps on a silk screen button, your program sees a simple `penDownEvent` event. When the `SysHandleEvent()` function sees this event, it figures out that the pen tap started in the bound of one of the silk screened buttons, and it tracks the pen to see where it is when it is lifted. If it's still in the bounds of the silk screen button, then `SysHandleEvent()` creates a new `keyDownEvent` event and adds it to the event queue. If you're feeling devious, you can process `penDownEvent` events before calling `SysHandleEvent()`, and discard all events that originate in the silk screen area. Of course,

then you'll effectively disable all the silk screen buttons, which is bad, since the user won't be able to launch any other applications and will be forced to reset their Palm.

A similar conversion happens when the user makes a Graffiti stroke. The first `penDownEvent` event within the Graffiti area is delivered to your program, and `SysHandleEvent()` detects where it starts and decides to get Graffiti involved. Once the Graffiti routine figures out what the pen stroke means, it adds a `keyDownEvent` event to the event queue.

The Palm documentation for the `keyDownEvent` is incorrect. It says that when `chr` is 0, `keyCode` will be one of a set of virtual key codes. You'll find the definition of these codes in the Palm header file named Chars.h, but they include `findChr` (sent when the user taps the Find icon) and `menuChr` (sent when the user taps the Menu icon). For these and all other command key codes, the value is provided in `chr`, `keyCode` is 0, and `modifiers` is `commandKeyMask`.

The `daySelectEvent` event is generated by, and used within, the day selector user interface element. You won't need to deal with this event.

The `winEnterEvent` event is generated when a window becomes the active window, and the `winExitEvent` event is generated when the active windows is deactivated and another window becomes the active window. Each event supplies the same detailed information (in `event->winEnter` and `event->winExit`) in two fields:

- ✔ `enterWindow`, a variable of type `WinHandle`, that is the handle of the window that became the active window

- ✔ `exitWindow`, a variable of type `WinHandle`, that is the handle of the window that is no longer the active window

Menu events

The `menuEvent` event is generated by the menu handler `MenuHandleEvent()` when the user makes a selection from a pull-down menu, or when the user enters a menu item command shortcut by using Graffiti. The extra information in `event->menu` is a single field, `itemId`. It is a variable of type `Word`, that is the `resource ID` of the selected menu item.

Application events

The last event you'll ever see from the `evtGetEvent()` Palm function is the `appStopEvent` event. You generally look for this event within your `EventLoop()` function and stop processing events once you see it.

The `frmLoadEvent` event is generated by the `FrmGotoForm()` and `FrmPopupForm()` Palm functions. This event includes the `FormId` (resource ID) of the relevant form in its detailed event information.

You can send yourself the `frmGotoEvent` event when you open a form in response to a launch code. We cover launch codes in detail in Chapter 12, but for now all you need to know is that they tell your program why it was launched. This might be because the user performed a Find operation and matched a record in your application's database. The `frmGotoEvent` event includes several fields in its `event->frmGoto` variable that you can use to pass additional information on to your form event handler. These are:

- ✔ `formID`: A variable of type `Word`, that is the resource Id of the Form to display
- ✔ `recordNum`: A variable of type `Word`, that is the index of the record containing a match
- ✔ `matchPos`: A variable of type `Word`, that is the position inside the record of the match
- ✔ `matchLen`: A variable of type `Word`, that is the length of the match
- ✔ `matchFieldNum`: A variable of type `Word`, that is the field number the match was found in
- ✔ `matchCustom`: A variable of type `DWord`, that you can use to pass in application-specific information

Form events

Form events are the most plentiful of all events, but fortunately for you and us, they can be clumped into a smaller number of sets. The enter events are:

- ✔ ctlEnterEvent
- ✔ lstEnterEvent
- ✔ fldEnterEvent
- ✔ tblEnterEvent
- ✔ frmTitleEnterEvent
- ✔ sclEnterEvent

These events are sent when the form event handler receives a penDownEvent event and the pen is down inside a control, list, field, table, the form title, or a scroll bar. Each event includes detailed information in event->ctlEnter, event->lstEnter, and so on, as follows:

- ✔ controlID, listID, fieldID, tableID, formID, or scrollID: A variable of type Word, that is the resource Id of the Control, List, Field, Table, Form, or Scroll Bar entered
- ✔ pControl, pList, pField, pTable, or pScrollBar: A variable of type pointer to ControlType, ListType, FieldType, TableType, or ScrollBarType, that is a pointer to detailed item information

The exit Events are:

- ✔ ctlExitEvent
- ✔ lstExitEvent
- ✔ fldExitEvent
- ✔ tblExitEvent
- ✔ sclExitEvent

These events are sent when the Form Event handler receives a penUpEvent event and the pen is not lifted inside the same control, list, field, table cell, or scroll bar it was originally placed down in. This only happens when the user taps an item, drags the pen outside of the item, and then lifts the pen. Each event includes detailed information in event->ctlExit, event->lstExit, and so on as follows:

- ✔ controlID, listID, fieldID, tableID, or scrollID: A variable of type Word, that is the resource ID of the control, list, field, table, form, or scroll bar exited.

✔ For the scroll bar, two additional variables of type `Short` are provided: `value` is the position of the scroll bar before the user dragged it, and `newvalue` is the new position of the scroll bar when the user lifts the pen. You can manually scroll something with a scroll bar by using these two values.

✔ For the table, two additional variables of type `Word` are provided: `row` is the row the pen was on when it was lifted, and `column` is the column the pen was on when it was lifted.

✔ `pControl`, `pList`, `pField`, `pTable`, or `pScrollBar`, a variable of type pointer to `ControlType`, `ListType`, `FieldType`, `TableType`, or `ScrollBarType`, that is a pointer to detailed item information.

The select events are the ones your programs process directly. These are sent when the user taps a control, makes a selection from a list or popup menu, taps the form title, or taps on a cell in a table.

The select events are:

✔ `ctlSelectEvent`

✔ `lstSelectEvent`

✔ `popSelectEvent`

✔ `frmTitleSelectEvent`

✔ `tblSelectEvent`

These events are sent when the form event handler is tracking the pen and the pen is lifted inside the same control, list, popup list, form title, or table cell it was originally placed down in. Each event includes detailed information in `event->ctlSelect`, `event->lstSelect`, and so on as follows:

✔ `controlID`, `listID`, `formID`, or `tableID`: A variable of type `Word`, that is the resource Id of the control, list, form, or table selected. For popup lists, both `controlID` and `listID` are provided.

✔ For the table, two additional variables of type `Word` are provided: `row` is the row the pen was on when it was lifted, and `column` is the column the pen was on when it was lifted.

✔ For the popup list, two additional variables of type `Word` are provided: `selection` is the item number (counting from zero for the first item) of the item chosen in the Popup List, and `priorselection` is the zero-based item number of the previous selection in the popup list.

✔ `pControl`, `pList`, `pForm`, or `pTable`, a variable of type pointer to `ControlType`, `ListType`, `FormType`, or `TableType`, that is a pointer to detailed item information. For popup lists, both `pControl` and `pList` are provided.

Special controls and scroll bars send the repeat events. Repeating buttons send the `ctlRepeatEvent` every half second as long as the user continues to hold the pen down in the control, while scroll bars send `sclRepeatEvent` as the user drags the pen in the scroll bar. Each event includes detailed information in `event->ctlRepeat` or `event->sclRepeat` as follows:

- `controlID` or `scrollID`: A variable of type `Word`, that is the resource Id of the control or scroll bar still being pressed.

- `time`: A variable of type `Long`, that is the system tick count when the event is generated. You can test this to decide if enough time has elapsed and you should process the event.

- For the scroll bar, two additional variables of type `Short` are provided: `value` is the position of the scroll bar before the user dragged it, and `newvalue` is the new position of the scroll bar as the user drags the pen. You can manually scroll something with a scroll bar by using these two values.

- `pControl` or `pScrollBar`, a variable of type pointer to `ControlType` or `ScrollBarType`, that is a pointer to detailed item information.

Fields generate two events when they change in response to user actions. If you create a resizable Field that changes its height as text is added or removed, then it sends the `fldHeightChangedEvent` event when this happens. You don't normally need to deal with this event. Likewise, fields send the `fldChangedEvent` event when the text of a field scrolls due to the user dragging the pen and making a selection within the field. This one is hardly ever processed by applications, either.

There are several form-related events having to do with the entire form. These events are sent by Palm functions, or by your own program, as forms are opened, closed, or redrawn.

The `frmOpenEvent` event is generated by the `FrmGotoForm()` and `FrmPopupForm()` Palm functions. It includes the resource ID of the opened form in its `event->frmOpen.formID` variable.

The `frmSaveEvent` event is generated by the `FrmSaveAllForms()` Palm function, while the `frmCloseEvent` event is sent by the `FrmGotoForm()` and `FrmCloseAllForms()` Palm functions. The `frmCloseEvent` event includes the `formID` resource ID of the relevant form in its detailed event information.

Finally, the `frmUpdateEvent` event is sent by the `FrmUpdateForm()` Palm function, and sometimes by the `FrmEraseForm()` Palm function. Handling this event can be a little tricky, so we cover it in detail in Chapter 9.

Chapter 9

A Form for All Seasons

*A*t the heart of most Palm programs is the form. This simple idea really goes a long way: Most programs present information one screen at a time. That means that you generally work quite hard to come up with a useful, interesting screen that the user works with for a while. The user may move from one screen to another by selecting an item, pressing a button, or making a menu selection. In the Palm world, "screen" is translated into "form." The stuff on a form is divided into two kinds of information: static and dynamic.

Static information does not change. It's like the pre-printed forms we've all gotten so used to filling out. *Dynamic information* is what you supply when you fill in the blanks on a form. It changes based on who is filling out the form.

The clever folks at Palm use Form resources to capture the static information about a form. When you want to display a form, all you need to do is call a Palm function with that form's resource ID, and like magic it appears on the Palm device. Actually, you're responsible for doing some of that magic, but it's not like making the Statue of Liberty disappear. Now all you need to do is take care of the dynamic part, and you're all set.

Unlike paper forms, Forms on the Palm can also have associated menus. A menu bar containing one or more drop down menus may be associated with a form. This menu bar and its menus provide another means for the user to perform actions in your application. Because forms and menus are so closely associated, we cover menus in this chapter, as well.

Remembering the PIN Example

Unless you want us to do a lot of hand waving, we're going to need an actual example project to explain how forms and menus work. Forms and menus rely heavily on events and on event processing in your application. We described events and a general approach to structuring an application that deals with events in Chapter 8. We use that same application structure for the example in this chapter.

The example we've created is named Simple Pin. It is a simple application that stores up to ten PIN numbers (personal identification numbers) for you.

The Simple Pin application is not meant for actual use, since the PINs are not password protected. It's just an example program, we don't intend for you to rely on it in your real life. Don't use it; just learn from it.

Simple Pin:

- Has two forms, each with its own menu bar
- Has an overview form that shows the names of each of your PINs
- Has a detail form that displays and edits a particular PIN
- Supports Find, so you can search for PINs

Simple Pin actually has a lot of code that we don't discuss in this chapter because it deals with implementing Find, as well as managing the intricacies of fields. The full source code to the example is on the CD-ROM that accompanies this book in the Examples\Chap09 folder. If you're using CodeWarrior, just open the project file named simplepin.mcp. If you're using GCC, the Src subfolder contains all the necessary files, along with a makefile. In either case, all the program code is in the SimplePin.c file.

Making Forms Work

Like most things in life, forms are both easy and hard to deal with. Forms are merely containers for both the static and dynamic information that they display. The things in charge of handling that dynamic dirty work are the controls, fields, lists, tables, and other interface elements you put on a form. We talk about editing form and menu resources in Chapter 3 and about programming controls and other form elements in Chapter 10. You might think that leaves little to do in this chapter, but fear not! We've got plenty to deal with just getting these forms displayed correctly.

To display any form, you need to follow these steps:

1. Load the form from the program's resources.

2. Open the form.

3. Register the form's event handler.

4. Tie the editable fields of the form to some memory.

5. Draw the form.

That looks like a lot of work, but in fact it goes by pretty quickly.

These steps are concerned with getting the form displayed on the Palm device, ready for the user to actually do something with it. There are several scenarios where you'll find you need to display a form:

✔ When the application is launched with a sysAppLaunchCmdFind launch code, it displays an initial form showing either detailed information for an item, an overview of all items, or a blank form for a new item.

✔ When the application is launched with a sysAppLaunchCmdGoTo launch code, it displays a specific form pre-loaded with dynamic information for a specific item found using Find.

✔ When the user selects an item on one form, a second form showing more detailed information for that item is displayed.

✔ When the user completes work on a detailed information form and returns to the overview form.

All these scenarios have several things in common, as far as our step-by-step approach is concerned. They just begin the process and end the process a little differently.

Loading the form on launch

When your application is launched, you get a single clue about what it should do from the Palm OS. This clue, called the launch code, is described in detail in Chapter 13. We're going to focus here on the three most common launch codes, since they effect what form your program loads when it's launched.

If you're only going to handle three launch codes, these are the three you should handle in your PilotMain() function:

✔ sysAppLaunchCmdNormalLaunch is the normal launch code sent when the user selects your application for running.

- ✔ `sysAppLaunchCmdFind` is the launch code your application receives to locate matches in response to the user doing a Find.
- ✔ `sysAppLaunchCmdGoTo` is the launch code your application receives when the user selects some matching Item you returned from a `sysAppLaunchCmdFind` launch code.

Of these launch codes, only the first and last are requests for your program to actually display a form. Let's look at how these two launch codes affect the initial form load.

Doing a normal launch

The `sysAppLaunchCmdNormalLaunch` launch code means your application should open normally, displaying whatever it was displaying when the user closed it. This implies that you've remembered where the user left off using your application.

The saved state of the application isn't somewhere in the sun belt; it's the information you need to know in order to recall the precise Form, exactly as the user left it, data and all, when the user quit the program. That seems like a tall order, but it's not all that difficult. All you really need to know is the:

- ✔ Form ID
- ✔ Dynamic information the form was displaying
- ✔ Field that had the focus, if any
- ✔ Cursor location for the Field that had the focus, if appropriate
- ✔ Scroll position of all scrollable items

Don't you just love it when we say things like "all you need to know" and then follow that with five things to keep track of? At least we're not writing software for nuclear reactors; we'd hate to think of what you need to keep track of there.

Every form keeps track of the focus. This is the thing on the form that is currently displaying the text cursor. A form may have many fields, but at most only one field has the focus. When you first open a form, no field has the focus.

You don't really need to save all the information in that list! In many cases, you can just save enough information so that the application can restore the right form and data, without keeping the exact details of where the user was when they exited. For example, the Palm Note Pad takes you right back to the particular note, scrolled to the same spot as where you left it, and the Palm Prefs application only returns you to the same Form. Do as little or as much as makes sense.

The Palm OS has a handy-dandy way for you to save and retrieve state information. They call it the application preferences, and they give you two functions to get and set it:

Registering unique Creator IDs: It's the law

Creator IDs are used for a couple of things in the Palm OS. They're used to associate an application to its preferences, its databases, and event to figure out what resources it should load.

You need to make up a unique Creator ID for each application you write. You do this by

visiting the Palm Web site at `www.palm.com/devzone/crid/cridsub.html` and trying to register an ID. If the ID you choose is already taken, you have to try and come up with another one.

- ✔ `PrefGetAppPreferences()` gets the application preferences, using your unique Creator ID.
- ✔ `PrefSetAppPreferences()` sets the application preferences, using your unique Creator ID.

An application Creator ID is a four-character code that's supposed to be unique for every Palm application. You can use any old set of four characters while you're learning how to program the Palm, but once you're ready to unleash your creation on the world you must visit the Palm developer Web site at `www.palm.com/devzone/crid/cridsub.html` to register a unique Creator ID with Palm. We registered `PFDe` as a Creator ID for our example programs.

You load your application preferences when your application starts. These preferences are in the form of a block of memory with some meaningful information in it. In C, the usual way of organizing a chunk of memory in a meaningful form is to use a structure, or C `struct`.

The simplest way to deal with preferences is to define a C `struct` and then create a global variable of that `struct` type. Then you can just load your preferences into the global variable in `StartApplication()` and have access to it throughout your program.

For Simple Pin, we use the following structure and global variable:

```
typedef struct {
    struct PinDetail {
        Char Name[17];
        Char PIN[17];
        Boolean Used;
    } PinDetail[10];
    int editPinNo;
} SimplePinPreferenceType;

static SimplePinPreferenceType prefs;
```

The `PinDetail` array defines ten slots, each holding a `Name` and a `PIN` string.

Each slot also has a Used flag that indicates if the slot holds valid information. That's where all the application's data is stored. The editPinNo integer is the only state information we actually store in our preferences. It holds the index of the PIN slot the user was displaying in the detail view when the application closed, or -1 if the user was viewing the overview when the application closed.

Your preference data can contain anything you want. If your application doesn't need to store a whole lot of information, you can just store it as the preference data, as we do in Simple Pin.

We create a function named StartApplication() that we call to load our preferences when the application is launched:

```
static Err StartApplication(void) {
    Word prefsSize;
    prefsSize = sizeof(SimplePinPreferenceType);
    if (PrefGetAppPreferences(appFileCreator,
            appPrefID, &prefs, &prefsSize, true) ==
                noPreferenceFound)
        CreateDefaultPrefs();
    return 0;
}
```

This function calls the PrefGetAppPreferences() Palm function to load the preferences into a C struct. We pass in our Creator ID, and a preference ID, which uniquely identifies our preferences. We also pass in a pointer to some memory so that the system can return our preference data. We tell the system how large this memory area is and indicate that we'd like to get the saved preferences.

If the system does not find the specified preference, it returns noPreferenceFound. That's going to happen the first time you run your program, so you need to create some default values. We call the CreateDefaultPrefs() function to do that for Simple Pin.

Once you know the state the application was last in when it closed, you're ready to open the correct form. This happens in the PilotMain() function, a portion of which is shown in the following code listing:

```
DWord PilotMain(Word cmd, Ptr cmdPBP, Word launchFlags)
{
    Err error;
    switch (cmd) {
    case sysAppLaunchCmdNormalLaunch:
        error = StartApplication();
        if (error) return error;
        if (prefs.editPinNo == -1)
```

```
        FrmGotoForm(Overview_Form);
        else
        FrmGotoForm(Detail_Form);
    EventLoop();
    StopApplication();
    break;
  // other cases
  }
  return error;
}
```

We check the launch code passed in via the cmd parameter, and if it is sysAppLaunchCmdNormalLaunch, then we load our application preferences into the prefs global variable by calling StartApplication(). At that point, prefs.editPinNo will either be -1 or a number from 0 to 9.

If prefs.editPinNo is -1, then the user last left Simple Pin in the overview Form, or this is the first time the user has launched Simple Pin. In either case, we use the FrmGotoForm() Palm function to begin the process of displaying the overview Form by supplying the resource ID Overview_Form.

We cover resources in detail in Chapter 3, but recall that every form you create in CodeWarrior's Constructor tool, or define in a resource file with GCC, has an associated resource ID. This ID is actually an integer, but it's easier to remember (and understand) an identifier such as Overview_Form rather than an integer like 1100. CodeWarrior lets you assign identifiers in Constructor, and it then generates a header file that you include in your program.

If prefs.editPinNo isn't -1, we know the user was looking at a specific PIN in the detail Form, and prefs.editPinNo specifies the index of the PIN slot in the prefs.PinDetail array. You'll see how that gets used later on in this chapter. We use the FrmGotoForm() Palm function to begin the process of displaying the detail Form by supplying the resource ID Detail_Form.

In either case, we use FrmGotoForm() to load a form from the program's resources, which is part of Step 1 of the step-by-step process for dealing with forms.

Doing a go to launch

There are times in life when you just need to drop everything and handle a request, like when your baby needs a new diaper. The sysAppLaunchCmdGoTo launch code is a bit like that. It's the system's way of telling you to forget about any grand ideas you had about selecting what to display when you're launched. In fact, it tells you exactly what to display, explicitly.

Chapter 13 is the place to go for the nitty-gritty details on launch codes; in this chapter, we're just focusing on how they impact form handling.

You handle the `sysAppLaunchCmdGoTo` launch code in `PilotMain()`, just like all the other launch codes. Let's look at the `case` block that handles it for Simple Pin:

```
case sysAppLaunchCmdGoTo:
    launched = launchFlags &
        sysAppLaunchFlagNewGlobals;
    if (launched) {
        error = StartApplication();
        if (error) return (error):
            GoToItem((GoToParamsPtr) cmdPBP, launched);
        EventLoop();
        StopApplication();
        break;
    }
    else {
#ifdef __GNUC__
    CALLBACK_PROLOGUE
#endif
        GoToItem((GoToParamsPtr) cmdPBP, launched);
#ifdef __GNUC__
    CALLBACK_EPILOGUE
#endif
    }
    break;
```

We'll admit this looks a little intimidating, but hang in there. There are basically two different versions of the same thing here, and the important bit, form-wise, is the call to the `GoToItem()` function. All the rest of the stuff has to do with doing the right thing for this launch code.

If you'd rather not think about what this code is doing, then you can safely treat it as black magic and forget about it. Always do this exact same thing in all your programs and just worry about writing the `GoToItem()` function.

The `GoToItem()` function has to do three things, based on the supplied information in the `GoToParamsPtr` parameter. It needs to:

- Display the correct form
- Load the correct data into the form
- Select the matching bit of text in the correct field of the form

As usual, the code to do this is spread all over the place. We're still following the trail that gets the form loaded, so let's look at the `GoToItem()` function for Simple Pin:

```
static void GoToItem (GoToParamsPtr goToParams,
    Boolean launchingApp) {
  EventType event;

  if (!launchingApp) FrmCloseAllForms();
  prefs.editPinNo = goToParams->recordNum;
  FrmGotoForm(Detail_Form);

  MemSet (&event, sizeof(event), 0);
  event.eType = frmGotoEvent;
  event.data.frmGoto.formID = Detail_Form;
  event.data.frmGoto.recordNum = goToParams->recordNum;
  event.data.frmGoto.matchPos = goToParams->matchPos;
  event.data.frmGoto.matchLen =
    goToParams->searchStrLen;
  event.data.frmGoto.matchFieldNum =
    goToParams->matchFieldNum;
  event.data.frmGoto.matchCustom =
    goToParams->matchCustom;
  EvtAddEventToQueue(&event);
}
```

New Globals? What Happened to the Old Globals?

Here's what's going on in the `sysAppLaunchCmdGoTo case` block. First, we figure out if launch flags has the `sysAppLaunchFlagNewGlobals` flag set. If it does, that means the Palm OS figured out that this application was not already running before it called `PilotMain()`. That happens when the user taps the Find icon with some other application open, and then the user selects a match from this application's list of matches. In this case, your program needs to start up just as if it had received the normal `sysAppLaunchCmdNormalLaunch` launch code, except it still needs to do the special Form processing as commanded by the `GoTo` launch code.

If your program is the currently open application when the user taps Find, it does not need to re-do all the stuff it did already. Instead it's as if `PilotMain()` was called a second time, with a different launch code. In fact, that's exactly what happens, which is why we include the `#ifdef __GNUC__` stuff around the code that we execute when launch flags does not have the `sysAppLaunchFlagNewGlobals` flag set. The GNU compiler needs a little help dealing with these types of function calls, which is what the pair of `CALLBACK_` macros provide. Refer to Chapter 6 for more details on GNU and callbacks.

Look at the first few lines of this function; they're the heart of the matter. We begin by cleaning up the rest of the mess we're in, when we get called to display something and we're already running. How do we do that? Simple, we pretend like the application is closing. When we call `FrmCloseAllForms()`, we know that every open Form's Event Handling function gets called directly and is supplied with a `frmCloseEvent`. The Form Event Handler will, if coded correctly, clean up everything it needs to, and whichever Form was open will close.

We then fudge our `prefs.editPinNo` to point to the supplied `goToParams->recordNum`. That's the record number of the matching item to display. In our case, it's the index of the PIN slot in the `prefs.PinDetail` array. When we put that value into `prefs.editPinNo` and then use `FrmGotoForm(Detail_Form)`, it's exactly as if we're re-launching the program and restoring our saved state. Pretty nifty!

Notice that we use `FrmGotoForm()` to load a Form from the program's resources, which is Step 1 of our step-by-step process for dealing with Forms. However, there's a little twist here, with all this extra code. We still need to set the focus of the form on the right field and select the matching text, but this isn't really the right time to do it. So what we do is create a `frmGotoEvent` event, stuff in all the information we got from the `goToParams` parameter, and then add the event to the event queue by calling the `EvtAddEventToQueue()` Palm function. Much later in this chapter we'll see the handler for this event.

Loading a different form

There really isn't anything particularly special about loading a new form. You can do it just about any time you need to in your program, including when the user:

- ✔ Selects a menu item
- ✔ Taps a silk screen button or presses a hardware button
- ✔ Selects an item in a list or table
- ✔ Taps a button or other control

In all cases, the actual thing that kicks off the Form display is our old friend `FrmGotoForm()`. Just pass it the resource ID of the form you want, and you're done with Step 1 of the step-by-step process for dealing with forms.

If you look at the checklist above, you'll notice that it implies that some form is already displayed. Since we haven't quite made it that far, let's press on. We'll point out later on in the chapter when we're displaying a different form in this way.

Getting the form displayed

Step 2 in the step-by-step process for dealing with forms is to open the form. It's pretty simple to do, since you always do the same thing. In your `ApplicationHandleEvent()` function, which you're calling inside your `EventLoop()`, you just include a `case` block for the `frmLoadEvent` event.

The `frmGotoForm()` Palm function always inserts the `frmLoadEvent` event into the event queue after it loads a form's resources.

You also do Step 3 at this time, since you're about to unleash a form. Also, it makes it possible to handle the next event waiting in the event queue within the form event handler.

Really loading the form

Let's look at how Simple Pin handles the `frmLoadEvent` event:

```
static Boolean ApplicationHandleEvent(EventPtr eventP) {
    Word formId;
    FormPtr frmP;
    Boolean handled = false;

    switch (eventP->eType) {
    case frmLoadEvent:
        formId = eventP->data.frmLoad.formID;
        frmP = FrmInitForm(formId);
        FrmSetActiveForm(frmP);
        switch (formId)    {
        case Overview_Form:
            FrmSetEventHandler(frmP,
                OverviewFormHandleEvent);
            break;
        case Detail_Form:
            FrmSetEventHandler(frmP,
                DetailFormHandleEvent);
            break;
        }
        handled = true;
        break;
    }
    return handled;
}
```

This function is pretty general. All it does is get the Form ID from the `frmLoadEvent` event data area and then pass that into the `FrmInitForm()` Palm function. The result is that the form is actually loaded into memory at this time, and we get back a form pointer. We're still not quite done yet. Next, we make the just initialized form into the active form by passing in the new form pointer into the `FrmSetActiveForm()` Palm function.

The last bit is where we register the form event handler. There isn't any way to do this other than to use a `switch` statement, with `case` blocks for every form we ever need to load in the program. Each `case` block calls `FrmSetEventHandler()` Palm function, and passes in a function pointer to the desired function in our program. Since we have two forms, we have two `case` blocks and two different form event handling functions.

Always write a different event handling function for every form. It makes coding each handler easier, since you know the handler is only called if the event has something to do with the particular form.

That takes care of Step 2 and Step 3 of the step-by-step process for dealing with forms. One last event is still waiting in the event queue from the `frmGotoForm()` Palm function we called in Step 1, and it's the last thing you need to process before the form finally appears on the Palm display.

Drawing the form

Steps 4 and 5 of the step-by-step process happen inside the form event handler. They happen when we process the `frmOpenEvent` event.

The `frmGotoForm()` Palm function always inserts the `frmOpenEvent` event into the event queue after the `frmLoadEvent` event. Since we register our form event handler when we process the `frmLoadEvent` event, we can handle the `frmOpenEvent` event there instead of in the `ApplicationHandleEvent()` function.

Inside a form event handler, doing Steps 4 and 5 usually looks like this:

```
case frmOpenEvent:
    FrmDrawForm (FrmGetActiveForm());
    InitThisForm();
    handled = true;
    break;
```

First, just call the `FrmDrawForm()` Palm function and pass in a pointer to the active form. You can get the active form by using the `FrmGetActiveForm()` Palm function. This draws the form on the device screen.

Next, you do the actual work of Step 4 in some other function, just to keep the event handler small. That's where you load the form with the dynamic data you've saved, or the default data you use when it is a new form.

Simple Pin has two forms, which means it has two form event handlers. Each form has different dynamic information, so there are two different form initialization functions. The `frmOpenEvent case` block in the `OverviewFormHandleEvent()` form event handler handles the opening of the overview form:

```
    case frmOpenEvent:
        FrmDrawForm (FrmGetActiveForm());
        InitOverviewForm();
        handled = true;
        break;
```

This looks very normal. The overview form contains just one list. This list has 10 list items, which correspond to the Name values of the 10 PinDetail slots we have in our global prefs variable. The InitOverviewForm() function's job is to simply stuff the current values of the 10 Names into the list and get everything ready for the user to interact with the overview:

```
static void InitOverviewForm() {
    ListPtr lstPtr;
    int i;

    for ( i = 0: i < 10: i++)
        listValPtrs[i] = prefs.PinDetail[i].Name;
    lstPtr = (ListPtr)GetObjectPtr(Overview_PinList);
    LstSetListChoices(lstPtr, listValPtrs, 10);
    LstSetSelection(lstPtr, -1);
    prefs.editPinNo = -1;
}
```

We cover lists in detail in Chapter 10, but you can probably figure out what's going on here anyway. We build an array of 10 string pointers and get a pointer to our list. Then we call the LstSetListChoices() Palm function to set the list up, and then we call the LstSetSelection() Palm function with a -1 parameter to set the list selection to none. Finally, we set the prefs.editPinNo global variable to -1, indicating that we're not editing any PINs.

Taking all this into account, we see that every time we load the overview form, it displays a list with the current 10 Names from the prefs.PinDetail global array.

The other form is the detail form. The frmOpenEvent case block in the DetailFormHandleEvent() form event handler handles the opening of the detail form:

```
    case frmOpenEvent:
        FrmDrawForm (frmP);
        InitDetailForm();
        handled = true;
        break;
```

This also looks pretty normal. The detail form contains two editable fields. These fields correspond to the Name and PIN values of the selected PinDetail slot in our global prefs variable the user is editing. The InitDetailForm() function's job is to simply stuff the current values of the Name and PIN values of the selected PinDetail slot into the two fields, and get everything ready for the user to interact with the detail form:

```
static void InitDetailForm(FormPtr frmP) {
   FormPtr frmP;
   frmP = FrmGetActiveForm();
   if (prefs.PinDetail[prefs.editPinNo].Used) {
      SetFieldText(frmP, Detail_PIN_NameField,
         prefs.PinDetail[prefs.editPinNo].Name);
      SetFieldText(frmP, Detail_PINField,
         prefs.PinDetail[prefs.editPinNo].PIN);
   }
   else {
      SetFieldText(frmP, Detail_PIN_NameField, "");
      SetFieldText(frmP, Detail_PINField, "");
   }
FrmSetFocus(frmP,FrmGetObjectIndex(frmP,
      Detail_PIN_NameField));
   doSave = true;
}
```

When we want to display the detail form with the data from a particular PIN slot, we set prefs.editPinNo to the index of the slot we want and then call the FrmGotoForm() Palm function. When we get to the InitDetailForm() function, all we need to do is load the correct information into the two fields. We check the Used variable of the selected PIN slot, and if it's true, we load the current values of the Name and PIN variables for the slot from our global prefs variable, and place them into the fields. If the Used value is false, we load empty strings into the fields.

We wrote the SetFieldText() function to stuff a string value into an editable field. We cover fields in detail in Chapter 10, so we're not going to look at that function here. You can just assume it works.

Juggling Forms and Menus

Your program has to deal with a form's entire life span. By life span, we mean the progression from opening the form, displaying it, and then finally closing it. Each of these life moments can happen at any time, much like real life's little ups and downs. Once your application has started, and has a form displayed, it's in the mid-life crisis mode. It has a form event handler, it has some data loaded, and it even might have a menu. It's time to consider how to juggle all these needs in the mid-life form.

For a lot of applications, you have two kinds of forms:

- ✔ Overview, showing a summary of all the information available
- ✔ Detailed, showing and editing one item of information

This is typical of database applications such as the Note Pad, the Address List, and even the Calendar application. Each type of form has different needs, so it's helpful to look at them separately.

Riding herd on the little ones

Overview forms are generally presented as lists or tables. Each list item or table row presents a summary of the total information contained in the corresponding record. Again, consider the Address List application in the Palm. When you launch it, you get a list of names. Each name corresponds to an entry in the address database. Tap one, and a detailed view appears.

From this description, we can determine that the overview forms need to:

1. Load information into the list or table of the form.
2. Handle a selection event within the list or table they contain, and from their menu.
3. Figure out which bit of saved data they need to retrieve to display the details of the selection.
4. Load the detailed form.

Overview forms have menus. These menus often provide options to create new items. When a user selects any menu option from the menu, your form event handler function receives a `MenuEvent` event.

When you create the resources for a program, you define the forms and menus your program displays. When you define a form, you can also associate one menu bar with that form. Whenever your program loads one of these forms, the associated menu bar is also loaded for you.

All this stuff happens in the form event handling function. Here's the complete overview form event handler function for Simple Pin:

```
static Boolean OverviewFormHandleEvent(EventPtr eventP){
   Boolean handled = false;

#ifdef __GNUC__
   CALLBACK_PROLOGUE
#endif

   switch (eventP->eType) {
   case frmOpenEvent:
      FrmDrawForm (FrmGetActiveForm());
      InitOverviewForm();
      handled = true;
      break;
   case MenuEvent:
      handled = OverviewFormDoCommand(
            eventP->data.Menu.itemID);
      break;
   case lstSelectEvent:
      EditPin(eventP->data.lstSelect.selection);
      handled = true;
      break;
   }

#ifdef __GNUC__
   CALLBACK_EPILOGUE
#endif

   return handled;
}
```

In the preceding section, we describe what the frmOpenEvent Event case
block is doing. That's Step 1 in the step-by-step process. Steps 2, 3, and 4 are
handled in the OverviewFormHandleEvent() function by the MenuEvent
and lstSelectEvent Event case blocks.

The MenuEvent event case block calls the OverviewFormDoCommand()
function and passes in the selected Menu Item resource ID. That function is
responsible for processing the menu selection.

The lstSelectEvent event case block does its magic when the user taps
an item in the list within the overview form. We call the EditPin() function,
supplying it with the selected list item index. Since the list shows 10 items,
and our internal prefs.PinDetail array has 10 slots, we can use the list
item index to select the PinDetail item to edit directly.

Here's the menu processing:

```
static Boolean OverviewFormDoCommand(Word command) {
   Boolean handled = false;

   switch (command) {
   case Options_AboutSimplePin:
      FrmAlert(About_Alert);
      handled = true;
      break;
   case Pins_New:
      EditNewPin();
      handled = true;
      break;
   }
   return handled;
}
```

No big surprises here. Two menus are located in the Overview Form menu bar, but each menu only has one menu item on it. That means we need two `case` blocks in this function. The first block handles the Options_About SimplePin menu option and simply displays an alert. We cover alerts a little later in the chapter, so we'll skip this for now. The second `case` block handles the Pins_New menu option. That's a request by the user to edit a new PIN, so we call the `EditNewPin()` function.

The `EditNewPin()` function needs to locate an unused slot in our `prefs.PinDetail` array. If it finds one, it switches to the detail form, editing that slot. If no slots are free, we have a problem. Here's how that works:

```
static void EditNewPin() {
   int freeSlot;
   Word i;

   freeSlot = -1;
for (i = 0; i < 10; i++)
      if ((!prefs.PinDetail[i].Used) &&
         (i != prefs.editPinNo)) {
         freeSlot = i;
         break;
      }
   if (freeSlot != -1) {
      EditPin(freeSlot);
   }
   else
      FrmAlert(NoneFree_Alert);
}
```

We scan the `prefs.PinDetail` array, looking for a slot that is not used. This function might be called from within the detail form, as well (as you'll see a little later on) so we also need to make sure that the unused slot isn't already

Smarter menus

The Simple Pin application does something that's considered bad by most interface design standards. It allows the user to make a menu selection that isn't valid, and it then displays an error alert. You can see this in action by editing and saving all 10 PINs, and then selecting the New menu option from the PINs menu. Instead of getting a nice detail form, you get an error alert. This is not unheard of in the Palm, as the built-in To Do application has a Record menu with a Delete Item option. Open To Do, make sure that no To Do item is selected, and then choose this menu option. Look! An error alert!

So what's a better way, you ask? On desktop computers, invalid menu items are usually shown grayed out, or are sometimes even removed from menus. Because you cannot change a Palm menu bar at all (no graying out, no adding or deleting menus or menu items) from a running program, you only have one alternative: You create a separate menu bar containing the subset of menus and menu items needed for each possible state of your application.

For our Simple Pin example, we could have an overview menu bar that doesn't have a PINs menu. Then when we determine that no free slots are available, we simply switch to this menu bar. The place to do this is in the overview form Initialization function. In that function, call this routine:

```
static void
    InitOverviewFormMenu() {
    int i;
    for ( i = 0; i < 10; i++)
        if
    (!prefs.PinDetail[i].Used)
            break;
    if (i == 10)
    FrmSetMenu(FrmGetActiveForm
    (),

        Overview_NoNew_MenuBar);
}
```

This function just looks for an unused slot. If it doesn't find one, then the PIN's menu isn't valid, so we override the default menu for the overview form by using the `FrmSetMenu()` Palm function. You can try this version out by adding this line to the top of SimplePin.c:

```
#define NO_ALERT_ON_FULL
```

Make the application, and when you run it, you'll see that it appears to remove the PINs menu from the menu bar of the overview form when you've filled all 10 PIN slots. If you remove a PIN (tap the Forget button in the detail form for any PIN), you see the PIN's menu in the menu bar of the overview form again. The program is simply switching menu bars as needed.

being displayed in the detail form. We do that by checking to see if the unused slot we've found isn't the same slot in `prefs.editPinNo`.

When we find a really free slot, we just call our `EditPin()` function and hand it the index of the free slot, and it takes care of getting the detail form displayed. If we don't find any free slots, we display an alert that tells the user they can only have 10 PINs. Notice that in this case, we don't change the current form at all, so we don't need to do anything else.

The EditPin() function is where we do the form switcharoo. Here's a look at it:

```
static void EditPin(Word pinIdx) {
    FormPtr frmP;

    if (FrmGetActiveFormID() == Detail_Form) {
        SaveDetailForm(frmP);
        prefs.editPinNo = pinIdx;
        InitDetailForm(frmP);
    }
    else {
        prefs.editPinNo = pinIdx;
        FrmGotoForm(Detail_Form);
    }
}
```

We call EditPin() from several places in the program, so it needs to be able to do the right thing regardless of which form is currently active. It starts out by determining whether the detail form is already the active form. If it is, then it saves the current data in the form, changes the prefs.editPinNo value to the new PIN slot to edit, and then reinitializes the detail form, which loads the new PIN slot's data into the form.

If the detail form isn't the active form, it doesn't need to worry about saving anything. It just sets the prefs.editPinNo value to the new PIN slot to edit and then uses the FrmGotoForm() Palm function to load the detail form.

Bedeviling the details

Detail forms are generally presented as a series of label and field pairs. Each field corresponds to some individual item of information, and the whole set of fields represents some cohesive group. There is usually one or more buttons on the bottom and a menu bar. Again, consider the Address List application in the Palm, where you find a detail form (Address Edit) consisting of a series of labels and fields, all of which represent single address records.

From this description, we can summarize that detail forms need to:

1. Load existing information into the fields of the form, or default information if editing a new record.

2. Support standard Palm editing commands on the fields of the form.

3. Support whatever commands are needed by the application to perform its actions.

4. Load a "Found" record and correctly set the insertion point and selection, if the application supports Find.

5. Correctly save the information on the Form as it closes, and save the state information needed to redisplay the same record if the user exits the application in the detail form.

All this stuff happens in the form event handling function. Let's look at the complete detail form event handler function for Simple Pin:

```
static Boolean
DetailFormHandleEvent(EventPtr eventP) {
    Boolean handled = false;
    FormPtr frmP;
    FieldPtr fldPtr;
    Word fldIdx;

#ifdef __GNUC__
    CALLBACK_PROLOGUE
#endif

    switch (eventP->eType) {
    case frmOpenEvent:
        FrmDrawForm (FrmGetActiveForm());
        InitDetailForm();
        handled = true;
        break;
    case MenuEvent:
handled = DetailFormDoCommand(
        eventP->data.Menu.itemID);
        break
    case frmGotoEvent:
        frmP = FrmGetActiveForm();
        fldIdx = FrmGetObjectIndex(frmP,
            eventP->data.frmGoto.matchFieldNum);
        FrmSetFocus(frmP, fldIdx);
        fldPtr = (FieldPtr)FrmGetObjectPtr(frmP, fldIdx);
        FldSetSelection (fldPtr,
            eventP->data.frmGoto.matchPos,
            eventP->data.frmGoto.matchPos +
                eventP->data.frmGoto.matchLen);
        handled = true;
        break;

    case frmCloseEvent:
        SaveDetailForm(FrmGetActiveForm());
        handled = false;
        break;
    case keyDownEvent:
        handled = FieldMove(eventP);
        break;
    case ctlSelectEvent:
        DoDetailButton(eventP->data.ctlSelect.controlID);
```

```
        handled = true;
        break;
    }

#ifdef __GNUC__
    CALLBACK_EPILOGUE
#endif

    return handled;
}
```

We describe the `frmOpenEvent` Event `case` block is doing in the previous section. That's Step 1 in the step-by-step process. Steps 2 and 3 are handled in the `DetailFormHandleEvent()` function by the `MenuEvent`, `keyDownEvent`, and `ctlSelectEvent` event `case` blocks.

The `MenuEvent` event `case` block calls our `DetailFormDoCommand()` function and passes in the selected menu item resource ID. That function is responsible for processing the menu selection.

The `keyDownEvent` event `case` block processes the event sent whenever a key is pressed. We're interested in two special keys, the `NextField` and `PrevField` keys. We call our `FieldMove()` function to move the focus, if either of these keys is generated via Graffiti.

The `ctlSelectEvent` event `case` block does its magic when the user taps either of the buttons on the form. Because these buttons also have corresponding menu items in the Detail PIN's menu, we just call the `DoDetailButton()` function and pass in the resource ID of the selected button here. We describe that function a little later.

The `frmGotoEvent` event `case` block processes the event sent when Simple Pin is sent the `GoTo` launch code, which is Step 4 of the step-by-step process. This event specifies which field should have the focus, and what area of that field we need to select. We extract that information from the event data and then use the `FrmSetFocus()` and `FrmSetSelection()` Palm functions to set the focus and selection correctly.

The last step is to save information as the form closes. The `frmCloseEvent` event `case` block processes the event sent when the form is closing. We just call our `SaveDetailForm()` function, which does the right things.

Here's the menu processing:

```
static Boolean DetailFormDoCommand(Word command) {
    Boolean handled = false;
    Word focusFldId;
FormPtr frmP;
```

(continued)

(continued)

```
    FieldPtr fldPtr;
switch (command) {
   case Options_AboutSimplePin:
      FrmAlert(About_Alert);
      handled = true;
      break;
   case Pins_Detail_New:
      EditNewPin();
      handled = true;
      break;
   case Pins_Detail_Done:
      DoDetailButton(Detail_DoneButton);
      break;
   case Pins_Detail_Forget:
      DoDetailButton(Detail_ForgetButton);
      break;
   case Edit_GraffitiHelp:
      SysGraffitiReferenceDialog(referenceDefault);
      break;
   case Edit_Keyboard:
      SysKeyboardDialog(kbdDefault);
      break;
   case Edit_SelectAll:
      frmP = FrmGetActiveForm();
      focusFldId = FrmGetFocus(frmP);
      if (focusFldId != noFocus) {
         fldPtr = (FieldPtr)FrmGetObjectPtr(frmP,
            focusFldId);
         FldSetSelection (fldPtr, 0,
            FldGetTextLength(fldPtr));
      }
      break;
   case Edit_Undo:
   case Edit_Cut:
   case Edit_Copy:
   case Edit_Paste:
      frmP = FrmGetActiveForm();
      focusFldId = FrmGetFocus(frmP);
      if (focusFldId != noFocus) {
         fldPtr = (FieldPtr)FrmGetObjectPtr(frmP,
            focusFldId);
         switch (command) {
         case Edit_Undo:
            FldUndo(fldPtr);
            break;
         case Edit_Cut:
            FldCut(fldPtr);
            break;
         case Edit_Copy:
            FldCopy(fldPtr);
            break;
         case Edit_Paste:
```

```
            FldPaste(fldPtr);
            break;
        }
        FldDrawField(fldPtr);
    }
    break;
}
return handled;
}
```

This function has two `case` blocks that are similar to the overview form menu function, because it has two options also found on that menu. The Options_AboutSimplePin and PINs_Detail_New menu items mean the same thing here as they do in the overview form, so the code to handle them is the same.

The next two `case` blocks handle the PINs_Detail_Done and PINs_Detail_Forget menu items. These are just menu options that perform the same functions as the Done and Forget buttons on the form, so we call our `DoDetailButton()` function and pass in the button resource ID of the corresponding button when these menu items are selected.

The rest of the function deals with the Edit menu. As you can see, dealing with this menu is tedious but not very difficult. The Edit_SelectAll menu handler tests to see if any field has the focus. Since the form has only two fields, you know that if anything has a focus, it's a field. If something has the focus, you select all its text by using the `FldSetSelection()` Palm function.

The `Edit_GraffitiHelp` and `Edit_Keyboard` case blocks just call the standard Palm functions for displaying the Graffiti Help dialog and the System Keyboard.

The other four Edit operations (Undo, Cut, Copy, and Paste) have Palm functions that support them for fields. All we need to do is call the right function. We figure out if any Field has the focus, and if one does, we call the Palm function that corresponds to the Edit menu operation. We redraw the field by calling the `FldDrawField()` Palm function, so any changes to the field will be visible.

Next we take a look at how the Done and Forget buttons/Menu choices are handled:

```
static void DoDetailButton(Word button) {
    if (button == Detail_DoneButton)
        doSave = true;
    else {
        if (prefs.PinDetail[prefs.editPinNo].Used) {
            CharPtr alrTxt =
```

(continued)

(continued)

```
            FldGetTextPtr((FieldPtr)GetObjectPtr(
                Detail_PIN_NameField));
        if (FrmCustomAlert(Delete_Alert, alrTxt, " ", " ")
            == Delete_Cancel)
            return;
        }
    doSave = false;
    }
    FrmGotoForm(Overview_Form
}
```

If the user taps the Done button or the PINs, Done menu option, we set the global Boolean doSave to true. If not, then the user must have tapped the Forget button or PINs, Forget menu option. We check to see if the user is editing an existing PIN by examining the Used variable of the slot currently being edited. If it is true, we display an alert asking the user to confirm the Forget action. If the user taps Cancel in this Alert, we just return from this function, which avoids doing anything at all. Otherwise, we set doSave to false. After all this, we use the FrmGotoForm() Palm function to load the overview form. That call will also close the detail form, so the DetailFormHandleEvent() function will get a frmCloseEvent event before the form closes. That's where we do the actual save of the contents of the form.

Next, here's a look at how the Field contents are saved:

```
static void SaveDetailForm(FormPtr frmP) {
    if (doSave) {
        CharPtr namePtr,
                pinPtr;

        if (FormChanged(frmP)) {
            namePtr = FldGetTextPtr((FieldPtr)GetObjectPtr(
                Detail_PIN_NameField));
            pinPtr  = FldGetTextPtr((FieldPtr)GetObjectPtr(
                Detail_PINField));
            prefs.PinDetail[prefs.editPinNo].Used = true;
            StrCopy(prefs.PinDetail[prefs.editPinNo].Name,
                namePtr ? namePtr : "");
            StrCopy(prefs.PinDetail[prefs.editPinNo].PIN,
                pinPtr ? pinPtr : "");
        }
    }
    else {
        prefs.PinDetail[prefs.editPinNo].Used = false;
        StrCopy(prefs.PinDetail[prefs.editPinNo].Name,
            "  - unused -");
        prefs.PinDetail[prefs.editPinNo].PIN[0] = '\0';
    }
}
```

Resource or literal string?

When you write any C program, you often use string literals in your code. The Simple Pin example, as shown in this chapter, uses string literals in a few places. You have another option with a Palm program, and that's to use a string resource. When you use a string resource, your code becomes a little more complex, but you gain a valuable advantage: All your string literals are now resources and can be changed without changing your program code at all. Then the job of editing the literals becomes easier. Here's a code block for the `SaveDetailForm()` function that uses a string resource instead of the literal " - unused -":

```
Handle strHandle;
CharPtr unused;
prefs.PinDetail[prefs.editPinNo
  ].Used = false;
strHandle = (Handle)
  DmGetResource('tSTR',
  Empty_String);
unused = (CharPtr)
  MemHandleLock(
  (VoidHand)strHandle);
StrCopy(prefs.PinDetail[prefs.e
  ditPinNo].Name,
  unused);
prefs.PinDetail[prefs.editPinNo
  ].PIN[0] = '\0';
MemHandleUnlock((VoidHand)strHa
  ndle);
DmReleaseResource((VoidHand)str
  Handle);
```

To use this resource, you must first get a handle to the resource by using the `DmGetResource()` Palm function. You pass in the resource type (`'tSTR'` for strings) and the resource ID of the desired string. Next, you need to lock the handle to get an actual string pointer, by using the `MemHandleLock()` Palm function. Then you can use the string pointer just like any other. When you're all done, you need to unlock the pointer by using the `MemHandleUnlock()` Palm function, and finally release the resource by using the `DmReleaseResource()` Palm function. The source code on the CD-ROM uses the `Empty_String` string resource instead a string literal.

This function begins by testing the global Boolean `doSave`. If the user tapped the Done button or PIN's Done menu item, or if the user closed the application with the detail form open, this variable is `true` and you need to save the contents of the Form. Next, we test to see if the contents of the form have changed, by calling our `FormChanged()` function. If it has, we get a pointer to the strings in each field, set the `Used` variable of the PIN slot to `true`, and then copy the field value strings into the `Name` and `PIN` variable of the slot.

Notice that the string pointers from the fields may be `NULL`. If this is the case, we copy in an empty string. If we didn't do that, `StrCopy()` would cause an error when it tried to copy from the `NULL` string pointer.

If the user tapped the Forget button or PINs, Forget Menu Item, then doSave is false. We set the Used variable of the PIN slot to false, and then copy our default values for an unused slot into the Name and PIN variable of the slot.

That's the bulk of the example, and also of dealing with forms. One small detail is left, and that's saving the preferences when the application ends.

Saving preferences

You probably think that saving applications is like loading them, only in reverse. You are correct! We create a function named StopApplication() that we call to save our preferences in Simple Pin when the application ends:

```
static void StopApplication(void) {
    FrmCloseAllForms();
    PrefSetAppPreferences (appFileCreator, appPrefID,
        appPrefVersionNum, &prefs,
        sizeof (SimplePinPreferenceType), true);
}
```

All we need to do is call the PrefSetAppPreferences() Palm function, after we've called the FrmCloseAllForms() Palm function. Recall that all our forms save their changes into the prefs global variable whenever they close. This means we can simply write the prefs global variable to the application preferences after we close the forms.

Alerting Developments

Let's face it, sometimes things happen in your program that are difficult to deal with. These things require what we in the software business like to call user intervention.

User intervention is simply the act of telling the user what has happened and allowing them to indicate what they want to do about it. You give two kinds of alerts to the user in this case:

- **Information-only:** Tell them what happened, but don't provide a way they can do anything about it.

- **Feedback:** Tell them what happened and give them a choice, via two or more buttons, to decide what to do about it.

Telling the user some information

For information-only alerts, you design your Alert resource so that it contains a message and a single OK button. You display the alert by using code like this:

```
FrmAlert(My_Alert);
```

This code displays the alert with the resource ID My_Alert, and it waits for the user to tap any of the buttons on the alert.

Because an information-only alert has only one button, you don't really care what the FrmAlert() Palm function returns. You only need to know that your program waits right at this statement for the user to tap the button on the alert.

Getting feedback from the user

For feedback alerts, you design your Alert resource so that it contains a message and two or more buttons. You display the alert by using code like this:

```
Word selection;
selection = FrmAlert(My_Feedback_Alert);
```

This code displays the Alert with the resource Id My_Feedback_Alert, and it waits for the user to tap any of the buttons on the alert. When the user taps one of the buttons, that button's index is saved in selection. Buttons are numbered left to right, starting with 0.

Because a feedback alert has multiple buttons, you do something with the value the FrmAlert() Palm function returns. You use the returned value in an if or case statement to perform different actions based on the user's choice.

Making personalized alerts

No matter what type of alert you need to use, you can make it a personalized alert message by using the FrmCustomAlert() Palm function. This works only if you create a special type of Alert resource. The Alert resource's message value must contain the special strings ^1, ^2, and ^3. For example, assume that you have an Alert resource named ConfirmDelete with this message string:

```
"Say, ^1, did you really mean to delete the ^2 record of the
        ^3 account?"
```

When you want to display this event, you supply three strings, which the Palm OS will substitute for the ^1, ^2, and ^3 markers in your message:

```
Word selection;
selection = FrmCustomAlert(ConfirmDelete_Alert,
    "Bob", "June Billing", "Penski");
```

When this code executes, the alert message is:

```
"Say, Bob, did you really mean to delete the June Billing
            record of the Penski account?"
```

You can use any string pointer for the various markers in your message. If you don't use all the markers, simply supply the empty string (" ") for that position.

Your alert message does not need to contain all three makers (^1 ^2 or ^3) but the FrmCustomAlert() Palm function always requires three substitution strings. Always use empty strings when you call this function, for the unused markers.

The Gray Area of Dialogs

When is a form not a form? When is an alert more than an alert? The answer is "when it's a dialog." There are times when you need to show the user more information than you can fit on an Alert resource, yet you want to maintain the control that an alert affords. That control is seductive: You know the user cannot do anything else in your program until they finish using the alert, by tapping one of its buttons.

The way around this dilemma is the dialog. A dialog is simply a form with an attitude. You can see an example of a dialog form in the To Do Palm application. Tap a To Do item, and a dialog form with the title To Do Item Details opens. Notice that your taps on any To Do item still visible behind the dialog are ignored. You can interact with all the stuff in the dialog. Once you tap on any of the buttons in the dialog, it closes. That's the way they work.

Because a dialog form is just a form, you use basic form techniques to deal with it:

1. **Initialize the Form.**

2. **Set the form as the active form (saving old active form first).**

3. **Set the form's event handling function.**

4. **Load the Form's contents as desired.**

5. **Call** FrmDoDialog() **to display the form.**

6. **Process Form Events in your form event handler.**

7. **Save the return value from** FrmDoDialog( ).

8. **Extract any values from the contents of the form.**

9. **Restore the old active form, if any.**

10. **Delete the dialog form.**

The difference is, you do all these things together, not in response to various events. Also, with regular forms, you don't worry about the old active form, nor do you explicitly delete a form. One other difference is that your dialog form event handler function won't receive the frmOpenEvent and frmCloseEvent events. That's why you do Step 4 and Step 8 (the form loading and saving operations) before and after you call FrmDoDialog( ).

You display a dialog by using code like this:

```
Word selection;
FrmPtr oldFrm, dlgFrm;

dlgFrm = FrmInitForm(MyForm);
oldFrm = FrmGetActiveForm();
FrmSetActiveForm(dlgFrm);
FrmSetEventHandler(dlgFrm, MyFormEventHandler);
LoadMyForm(dlgFrm);
selection = FrmDoDialog(dlgFrm);
SaveFormValues(dlgFrm);
if (oldFrm)
    FrmSetActiveForm(oldFrm);
FrmDeleteForm(frm);
```

This code displays the Form MyDialogForm as a dialog, and it waits for the user to tap any of the buttons on the form. When the user taps one of the buttons, that button's resource ID is saved in selection.

The FrmDoDialog( ) Palm function returns the resource ID of the tapped button, not the index of the button! This is different from the alert functions, and also from the Palm documentation. The documentation is wrong.

You don't need to use a Form Event handler at all, if your dialog form doesn't need to do anything special with form events. In that case, just omit the call to FrmSetEventHandler( ).

Now you know everything you always wanted to know about forms but were afraid to ask.

Chapter 10

Controls Freak

● ●

In This Chapter

▶ Understanding controls

▶ Dealing with text

▶ Making lists and checking them twice

▶ Setting the table

▶ Making a meal with leftovers

● ●

Attention: Following is a paid advertisement by "Special Give-Aways, Inc.":

Congratulations! You are the 1,000th person to read this chapter. Just because you are so lucky, we are giving you a brand new special television! That's right, this TV is special because it produces the world's best picture and audio of any TV found on the market today!

Sound too good to be true? Well sure, we can't fool you. The reason why this TV is so special is that there is no means of changing the channel or increasing/decreasing the volume. It's just a pretty face (with a mouth) and nothing more.

Sounds pretty dumb doesn't it? Well, take this general idea and transfer it to Palm OS applications. You can have pretty forms and pictures, but without any means of interacting with them, the application is just another pretty face. It might as well become part of our special give-away sweepstakes. To avoid this dreaded fate, you as an application developer must learn what CodeWarrior offers in terms of ways to interact with forms and what you can do with them programmatically.

Gathering the Resources

In previous chapters, we talk about resources as the components of an application. Many kinds of resources exist. Now, for the purposes of this chapter, we'll group resources into two high-level categories: Project and Catalog.

Project resources are forms, menu bars, menus, alerts, icons, bitmaps, strings, string lists, and app info string lists. We discussed these kinds of resources in great detail in Chapter 3. We talk about Catalog resources in this chapter. *Catalog resources* are those resources that can be found in Constructor's Catalog window. These are the user interface elements and controls that appear on forms to provide the display of data and to permit user interaction with an application.

You add Catalog resources to the user interface by dragging and dropping the desired resource's icon from the Catalog window to a form in the Form Editor. Figure 10-1 shows the Catalog window and its contents of resources.

Figure 10-1:
The Catalog
window.

If you're using the GNU distribution, the Catalog resources correspond to the special keywords you use within the FORM block when writing your pilrc interface definition file.

In order to add user interface elements to your forms and code, you must know some basic information. For the remainder of this chapter, we look at the resources and provide the following information:

- ✔ Brief description of resource
- ✔ Names of any associated resources and their four-character resource types
- ✔ Attributes of resource
- ✔ UI structure and explanations of fields
- ✔ Code examples

The Palm OS maintains an internal data structure (a C struct) for each Catalog resource in the active form. This data structure holds all the relevant information for the resource, such as its position and internal state. You usually access this information via Palm OS functions, but you can also directly access the value when you have a pointer to the resource.

Controlling Your Destiny

Controls are resources that allow for user interaction in an application. All controls are associated with the ControlType UI structure. These resources are:

- **Button (tBTN):** A clickable user interface element used to trigger events in an application. A button displays a text label in a rounded rectangle (default style).

- **Check box (tCBX):** Displays a toggle setting of either on (checked) or off (unchecked).

- **Popup trigger (tPUT):** Displays a text label followed by a graphic element that signifies that a popup list will appear when selected.

- **Push button (tPBN):** Looks like a button but always has square corners. Tapping a push button inverts the bounds. Releasing within the bounds causes the button to remain inverted.

- **Repeating button(tREP):** Looks like a button. Repeatedly sends the select event until the pen is lifted.

- **Selector trigger (tSLT):** A selectable rectangle with text inside. When selected, a dialog appears.

Control's UI structure

The user interface structure for controls is ControlType. You can find the type definition in the header file Control.h, in the PalmOS 3.0 Support\Incs\UI folder within the Metrowerks install folder, or the \Incs\UI folder within the GNU install folder.

When you get a pointer to a control, it's a ControlPtr. This is just a typedef to a ControlType*. There is also a ControlAttrType that defines a struct containing the attributes of a control. The fields of the ControlType structure are described in Table 10-1.

Table 10-1	Fields for `ControlType` structure
Field	*Description*
`id`	ID of the control, assigned by Constructor.
`bounds`	The coordinates of the outside bounds of the control, relative to the top-left corner of the form. The structure contains:
	`Left Origin`: Left side of the control. Valid values are 0-159.
	`Top Origin`: Top of the control. Valid values are 0-159.
	`Width`: Width of the control in pixels. Valid values are 0–160.
	`Height`: Height of the control in pixels. Valid values are 1–160.
`text`	The pointer to the resource's label. If `text` is NULL, then the resource has no label. Only buttons and push buttons have text labels.
`attr`	Resource attributes. The `attr` field is a bit field that contains:
	`usable`: When set the resource appears on the screen. A nonusable resource is not drawn. Nonusable resources can be programmatically set to `usable`.
	`enable`: When not set the resource doesn't respond to pen taps. Some controls, such as the scroll arrows, appear grayed-out when not enabled.
	`visible`: Set/cleared internally when the resource is drawn/erased.
	`leftAnchor`: When set, fixes the left bound of resources that expand and contract their width when their labels change.
	`frame`: Specifies the type of frame drawn around the button controls. Only button controls use this attribute. All other controls use `ControlStyle` to determine the frame.
`style`	The style of the resource. See `ControlStyles` enum in the header file.
`font`	The font used to draw the resource's label.
`group`	The group ID of a push button or a check box that is part of an exclusive group. The resource routines don't automatically turn one resource off when another is selected. The application must do this.

A controlling example

Most of what you do with controls is simply respond to the event sent when they're tapped. We discuss control events in detail in Chapter 8. You need to do a few other common things with controls:

✔ Enable and disable controls

✔ Retrieve or change the label of a button or popup trigger

✔ Get or set the check mark of a check box

✔ Manage a group of push buttons

The following sections look at examples of each of these activities.

Enabling and disabling controls

You may have one or more controls on a form that are only valid in specific situations. You can either disable or hide a control when it's not valid for the user to use it. The Palm OS interface guidelines suggest hiding, rather than disabling, non-usable controls.

To hide a control, use the `CtlHideControl()` Palm OS function; to show it, use `CtlShowControl()`. To disable a control, use `CtlSetEnabled()`, passing in `false`. To enable a control, pass in `true`. All these functions take a `ControlPtr` as their first parameter.

Instead of calling these functions directly, use the form functions `FrmHideObject()` and `FrmShowObject()` to hide and show a control. These functions take a pointer to a form, and the index of the interface element to hide or show. You can get the index for an interface element if you know its ID, by using the `FrmGetObjectIndex()` function, passing in a form pointer and the object's ID.

Changing a control's label

Chapter 16 includes an example program that changes a button's label. Initially, the button label is `"GET"`, but once the user taps it, it changes to `"Stop"`. Tapping it again changes it back to `"GET"`. Here's how that's done:

```
CtlSetLabel(GetObjectPtr(TextBrowser_SendButton), "Stop");
```

That seems simple enough. The button is resized based on the size of the label. If the button's `leftAnchor` attribute is `true`, the button grows or shrinks its right side; otherwise, its left side grows or shrinks as needed.

You need to know two important things about changing a label. First, you cannot change the label text to be larger than the initially defined label text length. Second, if you do change a label, the new text you pass in must either be a static text string, or it must be allocated in a global variable, because the pointer you pass in will be used as long as the label is displayed on the form.

Because popup triggers are just another type of control, you change their label the same way. If you're implementing a category trigger, you don't use this function at all. Refer to the section titled "Categorizing Records" in Chapter 13.

You can get the current text of a Control by calling the `CtrlGetLable()` function. Pass in a `ControlPtr`, and you receive a `CharPtr` back.

Getting and setting the check mark

Check boxes know when they're checked. This is handy for your programs, too. Chapter 13 includes an example program that uses a modal dialog form to allow the user to indicate, via a check box, if a deleted record should be archived. The following Palm OS function retrieves the state of that check box:

```
archive = FrmGetControlValue(alert, ctlIndex);
```

The value returned is 0 for unchecked and 1 for checked. You can also use the more direct `CtlGetValue()` Palm OS function, passing in the appropriate `ControlPtr`.

The example program also sets the check box on the dialog form:

```
FrmSetControlValue(alert, ctlIndex, SaveBackup);
```

As you might guess, you can also use the `CtlSetValue()` Palm OS function, supplying a `ControlPtr`, and 0 or 1, to have the check box unchecked or checked.

Managing a group of push buttons

If you've used a computer other than a Palm device, you're no doubt familiar with the concept of radio buttons that are grouped together. Only one radio button in a group can be selected at any time. The Palm OS calls radio buttons *push buttons*. When you create your UI, you indicate which push buttons belong together by assigning them to the same Group ID.

There is a pair of Form functions that manage the selection of just one push button in a group. You call `FrmSetControlGroupSelection()` and pass in a form pointer, group number, and specific Radio Button ID to select just that button and deselect all others in the group. Calling `FrmGetControl-`

GroupSelection() and passing in a form pointer and group number returns the ID of the currently selected radio button, or 255 if none are selected.

Text: Getting It in and Out and All About

Text resources allow users to enter, edit, and display text. Several Catalog resources can be grouped under the general "text" heading. These are Field, Label, and Scrollbar. We look at each of these resources in this section.

Field

The Field resource (tFLD) represents a field on a screen. Such a field contains one or more lines of editable text.

Fields have a number of features, including:

- ✔ Support for cut, copy, and paste using the Clipboard
- ✔ Drag-selection
- ✔ Expandable field height
- ✔ Insertion point positioning with pen
- ✔ Maximum character limit
- ✔ Scrolling for multiple line fields

The Field resource does not support character filters, horizontal scrolling, numeric formatting, overstrike input mode, special keys for page up/down, left/right word, home, end, left/right margin, and backspace, or word selection.

Field's UI structure

The User Interface structure for fields is FieldType. You can find the type definition in the header file, Field.h, in the PalmOS 3.0 Support\Incs\UI folder within the Metrowerks install folder, or the Incs\UI folder within the GNU install folder.

When you get a pointer to a field, it's a FieldPtr. This is just a typedef to a FieldType*. There is also a FieldAttrType that defines a struct containing the attributes of a field and a LineInfoType that defines a struct containing line information for multiple-line fields. Table 10-2 describes the fields of the FieldType structure.

Table 10-2	Fields of `FieldType` structure
Field	*Description*
`id`	ID of the Field, assigned by Constructor.
`rect`	Position and size of the Field. The structure contains: `Left Origin`, `Top Origin`, `Width`, and `Height`. These mean the same thing as they do for controls.
`attr`	Field attributes. The `attr` field is a bit field that contains:
	`usable`, `visible`: These attributes mean the same thing as they do for Controls.
	`editable`: When set the field accepts Graffiti input/edit com mands and the insertion point can be positioned with the pen.
	`singleLine`: When set, the Field's height only displays one line.
	`hasFocus`: Set internally when the Field has the current focus.
	`dynamicSize`: When set, the height of the Field changes as characters are entered into it.
	`insPtVisible`: Set internally. When this is set, the insertion point is scrolled into view.
	`dirty`: When set, indicates that the Field has been modified.
	`underlined`: When set all lines of a Field are underlined.
	`justification`: Specifies either left or right justification.
	`autoShift`: If set this means that the Palm OS 2.0 and later auto-shift rules are applied. The system uses an uppercase letter after an empty Field, after a sentence terminator, or after two spaces.
	`hasScrollBar`: If set, a scroll bar is attached to the Field and the system sends frequent `fldHeightChangedEvents` so that the application can adjust the scroll bar.
`text`	Pointer to the `NULL`-terminated string that is shown in the Field.
`textHandle`	Handle to the text stored in the Field.

Field	Description
lines	Pointer to an array of LineInfoType structures. Each visible line of text has one entry in this array.
LineInfoType	Structure containing the character position of the first character shown by a line and the number of characters shown.
textLen	Current number of characters in the displayed string. The NULL terminator is excluded.
textBlockSize	Allocated size of memory block that holds the Field's text.
maxChars	Maximum number of characters the Field accepts. Valid values are: 0–32767.
selFirstPos	Starting character position of the current selection.
selLastPos	Ending character position of the current selection. (Note that when selFirstPos equals selLastPos, there is no selection.)
insPtXPos	Column position of the insertion point.
insPtYPos	Display line where the insertion point is positioned. The first display line is zero.
fontID	Font ID for the Field.

Fielding an example

You can use a field in two ways: Either you leave everything up to the Palm OS, or you take matters into your own hands. This is because each field contains a pointer to a memory handle. If you do nothing, the Palm OS will allocate and free this handle, as well as manage its size. Alternatively, you can allocate the handle yourself and tell the field to use the handle you allocate. Doing the latter gives you greater control and access to the contents of the field, but then you've got to take the additional responsibility of managing the memory. Memory handles are the way the Palm OS manages allocated memory. Chapter 13 describes them in detail.

You need to do a few common things with fields:

✔ Get a pointer to the field's text

✔ Update the field's text by using the field editing functions

✔ Update the field's text by changing the memory handle directly

✔ Manage the scroll bar associated with a field

The following sections provide examples of each of these activities.

Getting a pointer to the field's text

There are two ways to get a pointer to a field's text string. The simplest way is to call the FldGetTextPtr() Palm OS function, passing in a FieldPtr for the desired field, as shown in the following code. We do this in several of the examples in this book, including the Simple Pin example in Chapter 13.

```
CharPtr namePtr,
namePtr = FldGetTextPtr((FieldPtr)GetObjectPtr(
    Detail_PIN_NameField));
```

This is fine when you just need to copy the text or save it to a database record. The other way to get the text is to retrieve the handle to the memory holding the text and then lock the handle. Doing this is important if you need to update the text, so we show you how to do this a little later in the chapter.

Updating the field's text by using the field editing functions

The Palm OS provides several functions that edit field text. These functions mimic the typical cut, copy, paste, and undo functions performed via the Edit menu.

These functions don't work for non-editable fields. If you need to manipulate these types of fields, you need to use the techniques described in the next section.

To undo, cut, copy, or paste text with a field and the Clipboard, use the FldUndo(), FldCut(), FldCopy(), and FldPaste() Palm OS functions, passing in a FieldPtr for the desired field. The Simple Pin example in Chapter 9 implements an Edit menu that uses these functions. See that chapter for a description of their use.

You can also use the FldInsert() Palm OS function, passing in a FieldPtr and a CharPtr, to insert new text into an editable Field. We use this function in our SetFieldText() function to update an editable field's text:

```
static void
SetFieldText(Word fldId, CharPtr text) {
    FieldPtr fldP;
    fldP = GetObjectPtr(fldId);
    FldSetSelection (fldP, 0, 0);
    FldFreeMemory(fldP);
    FldInsert(fldP, text, StrLen(text));
    FldSetDirty(fldP, false);
    FldDrawField(fldP);
}
```

This function begins by getting a `FieldPtr` for the supplied Field ID. It then clears the selection of the field and frees its current memory handle. Then it uses the `FldInsert()` function to insert the next text into the field, which also allocates a new handle. It clears the `dirty` flag for the field so that you can later detect if the user edits it. Then it redraws the field.

Updating the field's text by changing the memory handle

When you really want to make wholesale changes to a field's text, there's nothing like directly accessing its handle. The Chat example in Chapter 14 uses a single Field to hold up to 2KB of text received via the Serial Port. The field is non-editable and has a scroll bar. Because the field is non-editable, we can't use the `FldInsert()` Palm OS function to add new text to the end of the field. Instead, we directly access the memory handle of the field. Before we can do this, we need to allocate the handle and give it to the field, which we do in the `InitChatForm()` function:

```
static void InitChatForm() {
    CharPtr fldTxt;
    FormPtr frmP;
    FieldPtr fldPtr;
    txtHandle = MemHandleNew(MAX_CHAT_BUFF);
    fldTxt= MemHandleLock(txtHandle);
    *fldTxt = '\0';
    MemHandleUnlock(txtHandle);
    fldPtr = GetObjectPtr(Chat_HostField);
    FldSetTextHandle(fldPtr, (Handle)txtHandle);
    FldSetTextAllocatedSize(fldPtr, MAX_CHAT_BUFF);
    FldSetMaxChars(fldPtr, MAX_CHAT_BUFF);
    frmP = FrmGetActiveForm();
    FrmSetFocus(frmP,
        FrmGetObjectIndex(frmP, Chat_SendField));
}
```

This function begins by allocating a new memory handle of the desired size, and storing it in a global variable named `txtHandle`. It then locks the handle to get a `CharPtr` and sets the first character to be 0, thus `NULL` terminating the string. Then it unlocks the handle. It gets the `FieldPtr` for the field and sets the field's text handle to the allocated handle. Then it updates the field's `Text Allocated Size` and `Max Chars` values to correspond to the size of the allocated handler. Finally, it sets the form focus to the field.

When new characters arrive via the serial port, they're appended to the field. This occurs in the `PasteFieldText()` function. That function also manages a scroll bar associated with the field, so we discuss it in the next section.

Managing the scroll bar associated with a field

Fields can have scroll bars, which is quite handy. When you create your interface in Constructor, or in a text file for pilrc if you are using the GNU tools, create a scroll bar with the same height as the field and a width of 7. Place it directly to the right of the field. Your program needs to manage the scroll bar as the field's contents change. One such change happens if you directly update the field text, as we do in the Chat example of Chapter 14. This occurs in the PasteFieldText() function. That function does a bit of extra work to handle end of line conversions, which we've removed in the code that follows:

```
static void
PasteFieldText(CharPtr text, UInt textLen) {
    FieldPtr fldP;
    ScrollBarPtr sclP;
    Word scrollPos, textHeight, fieldHeight;
    CharPtr fldTxt, appendTxt;
    UInt fldTxtLen;
    UInt i;
    fldP = GetObjectPtr(Chat_HostField);
    sclP = GetObjectPtr(Chat_HostScrollBar);
    FldSetTextHandle(fldP, NULL);
    fldTxt= MemHandleLock(txtHandle);
    fldTxtLen = StrLen(fldTxt);
    if (fldTxtLen + textLen >
            MemHandleSize((VoidHand)txtHandle)) {
        fldTxtLen -= textLen;
        MemMove(fldTxt, fldTxt+textLen, fldTxtLen);
    }
    appendTxt = fldTxt+fldTxtLen;
    for (i = 0; i < textLen; i++) {
        *appendTxt++ = text[i];
    }
    *appendTxt = '\0';
    MemHandleUnlock(txtHandle);
    FldSetTextHandle(fldP, (Handle)txtHandle);
    FldSetScrollPosition(fldP, FldGetTextLength(fldP));
    FldGetScrollValues (fldP, &scrollPos,
        &textHeight, &fieldHeight);
    SclSetScrollBar (sclP, scrollPos, 0,
        textHeight, fieldHeight);
    FldDrawField(fldP);
}
```

This function begins by getting a FieldPtr for the field and a ScrollBarPtr for the associated scroll bar. Then it sets the field handle for the field to NULL, which ensures that the Palm OS doesn't modify the handle while we're changing it. We lock the handle that the field uses (stored in a global variable named txtHandle) to get a pointer to the string, and compute the length of the string. If the current length plus the length of the new string to append is greater than the maximum size, we use the MemMove() Palm OS function to move the current string within the handle such that it frees up enough room for the new string at the end. Then we copy in the new text at the end, set the NULL terminator, and unlock the handle.

Now all we need to do is update the field and the scroll bar. Updating the field requires that we set the handle in the field, and set the field scroll position to the end of the string. Then we get the scroll values from the field and use them to update the scroll bar by calling the `SclSetScrollBar()` Palm OS function.

The last detail to attend to is to scroll the field when the user changes the scroll bar. We do this in the `sclExitEvent` Event `case` block of the `ChatFormHandleEvent()` function:

```
case sclExitEvent:
   fldP = GetObjectPtr(Chat_HostField);
   FldGetScrollValues (fldP, &scrollPos,
      &textHeight, &fieldHeight);
   if (scrollPos < eventP->data.sclExit.newValue)
      FldScrollField (fldP,
         eventP->data.sclExit.newValue - scrollPos, down);
   else
      FldScrollField (fldP,
         scrollPos - eventP->data.sclExit.newValue, up);
   FldDrawField(fldP);
   handled = true;
   break;
```

We get the scroll values from the field, and check the `scrollPos` of the field against the new scroll position indicated with the event. If the new scroll position is greater, we tell the field to scroll down the appropriate number of lines, and if it's less, we tell the Field to scroll up. The `FldScrollField()` Palm OS function tells the Field to scroll up or down a specific number of lines.

Label

The Label resource (`tLBL`) is a Catalog resource that displays one or more lines of non-editable text on a form, dialog box, or full screen. It is used to display text in order to label parts of the UI and to create text that appears to the left of a check box instead of its right.

Label's attributes

Labels have the following attributes:

- `Label ID`: ID of the label, assigned by Constructor.
- `Left Origin`: Form-relative position of the left side of the label.
- `Top Origin`: Form-relative position of the top of the label.
- `Usable`: When set, the label is usable and is displayed.

  ✔ Font: The font used to draw the label.

  ✔ Text: The actual text of the label.

Labeling an example

There are a pair of Form Palm OS functions that deal with labels. The FrmGetLabel() function takes a FormPtr and the ID of the label and returns a string pointer to the label's current text. The FormCopyLabel() function takes a FormPtr, the ID of the label, and a string pointer that points to the new label text, and changes the label to use this new text.

The FormCopyLabel() function isn't very smart, so you can't pass in a string for the new label that is longer than the original label text. If you do, very bad things happen. Also, the old label value isn't erased, so you have to do that yourself by calling the WinEraseRectangle() Palm OS function:

```
FormPtr frm = FrmGetActiveForm();
RectangleType r;
FrmGetObjectBounds(frm, FrmGetObjectIndex(frm,LabelId),&r);
WinEraseRectangle(&r, 0 );
FrmCopyLabel(frm, LabelId, "New Label" );
```

Labels aren't intended to change much in a form. If you want a label that changes and you don't know for sure how large the maximum text string will be, you must use a field. You can make the field non-editable when you define it, and then change its text as described in the previous section.

Scrollbar

The Scrollbar resource (tSCL) is a Catalog resource that aids developers in providing scrolling behavior for fields. This feature is available for Palm OS 2.0 (and later) devices. You can actually use a scroll bar any way you please, but fields provide several handy functions that simplify their use with a scroll bar.

Scrollbar's UI structure

The User Interface structure for scroll bars is ScrollBarType. You can find the type definition in the header file ScrollBar.h, in the PalmOS 3.0 Support\Incs\UI folder within the Metrowerks install folder, or the \Incs\UI folder within the GNU install folder.

When you get a pointer to a scroll bar, it's a ScrollBarPtr. This is just a typedef to a ScrollBarType*. There is also a ScrollBarAttrType that defines a struct containing the attributes of a scroll bar. Table 10-3 describes the fields of the ScrollBarType structure.

Table 10-3	Fields of `ScrollBarType` **structure**
Field	_Description_
`bounds`	The scroll bar's bounds as a structure containing: `Left Origin`, `Top Origin`, `Width`, and `Height`. These mean the same thing as they do for Controls.
`id`	The developer-specified ID of the scroll bar.
`attr`	Scroll bar attributes. The `attr` field is a bit field that contains: `usable` and `visible`. These attributes mean the same thing as they do for Controls.
`highlighted:`	When set, the scroll bar is highlighted.
`shown:`	Set when the scroll bar is visible and `maxValue` is greater than `minValue`.
`activeRegion:`	Indicates the active region of the scroll bar.
`value`	Current top value of the scroll bar's _scroll car_. The scroll car is the moveable piece that indicates where in the list, table, or page the current highlight is.
`minValue`	Position of the scroll car when the scroll bar is at the top. Default is 0.
`maxValue`	Position of the scroll car when the scroll bar is at the bottom. To compute this value use the following formula: Number of lines − Page size + Overlap.
`pageSize`	The number of lines to scroll when the user scrolls one page.

Scrolling along, singing a song example

We provide a detailed example of managing a scroll bar associated with a field in the field section of this chapter.

The `SclSetScrollBar()` Palm OS function sets a scroll bar's `value`, `minValue`, `maxValue`, and `pageSize`. The scroll bar generates `sclRepeatEvent` events as the user drags the pen inside it and one final `sclExitEvent` event when the user lifts the pen. If you want to update the field scroll position as the user changes the position, handle the `sclRepeatEvent` event and the `sclExitEvent` event; if you only want to update the field when the user is done, handle just the `sclExitEvent` event. In any case, you tell the field to scroll by calling the `FldScrollField()` Palm OS function. We do that in the Chat example of Bonus Chapter 1 (on the CD). This is done in the `sclExitEvent` event case block of the `ChatFormHandleEvent()` function:

```
// local variables
FieldPtr fldP;
Word scrollPos, textHeight, fieldHeight;
// only the sclExitEvent shown
case sclExitEvent:
    fldP = GetObjectPtr(Chat_HostField);
    FldGetScrollValues (fldP, &scrollPos, &textHeight,
            &fieldHeight);
    if (scrollPos < eventP->data.sclExit.newValue)
        FldScrollField (fldP,
            eventP->data.sclExit.newValue - scrollPos, down);
    else
        FldScrollField (fldP,
            scrollPos - eventP->data.sclExit.newValue, up);
    FldDrawField(fldP);
    handled = true;
    break;
```

We get the field's current scroll values by calling the `FldGetScrollValues()` Palm OS function. Then the program compares the current position with the new position of the scroll bar reported with the event. If the field scroll position is smaller, the program scrolls down, computing the difference (in lines) between the field and the scroll bar. If it's greater, the program scrolls up. Once the program has scrolled, it redraws the field by calling the `FldDrawField()` Palm OS function.

Making Lists and Checking Them Twice

The List resource (`tLST`) is a Catalog resource that provides a box with a vertical list of choices to the user.

Lists have a number of features, including the following:

- ✔ Lists have arrows for scrolling in the right margin (if necessary).
- ✔ The current selection in a list is displayed as inverted.
- ✔ If the list contains more choices than are visible, dragging the pen above/below the list causes scrolling.
- ✔ Scrolling through a list doesn't change the current selection.
- ✔ Lists can appear as popup lists when used with popup triggers.

Don't set a list's `usable` attribute if the list is linked to a Popup Trigger resource.

The List resource (tLST) and the Popup Trigger resource (tPUT) are used together to represent an active popup list. If a list becomes too large for the screen, the list becomes scrollable. If a list becomes too tall to fit below the popup trigger, it is displayed above the popup trigger.

Use a List to let users choose between items of data. Use a menu item, not a list item, to activate a command.

Lists' UI structure

The user interface structure for lists is ListType. You can find the type definition in the header file List.h, in the PalmOS 3.0 Support\Incs\UI folder within the Metrowerks install folder, or the Incs\UI folder within the GNU install folder.

When you get a pointer to a List, it's a ListPtr. This is just a typedef to a ListType.* There is also a ListAttrType that defines a struct containing the attributes of a list. Table 10-4 describes the fields of the ListType structure.

Table 10-4	Fields of ListType structure
Field	**Description**
id	The developer-specified ID of the List.
bounds	The coordinates of the outside bounds of the List, in window-relative terms. The structure contains Left Origin, Top Origin, and Width. These mean the same thing as they do for Controls.
attr	Field attributes. The attr field is a bit field that contains: usable, enabled, and visible: These attributes mean the same thing as they do for Controls.
	poppedUp: Set/cleared internally. When set, the choices are displayed in a popup window.
	hasScrollbar: When set, the list has a scroll bar.
	search: When set, incremental search is enabled.
itemsText	This attribute is a pointer to an array of pointers to the text of the choices.
numItems	Number of choices in the list.

(continued)

Table 10-4 *(continued)*

Field	Description
currentItem	Currently selected list choice. 0 is the first choice.
topItem	First choice displayed in the list.
font	ID of the font used to draw all list text strings.
popupWin	Handle of the window created when a list is displayed if the poppedUp attribute is set.
drawItem-Callback	Function used to draw an item in the list. If the attribute is NULL, the default drawing routine is used instead.

Errors may occur if the number of visible items (numItems) is set to a value that is greater than the actual number of items (array elements in itemsText) in the list.

Listing an example

The three common uses for a list are to:

- ✔ Display a scrolling list of records in an overview form
- ✔ Provide a popup list of choices when the user taps a trigger control
- ✔ Provide a list of categories for records in a database

The category popup list is a special case of the more general popup list. It requires using the Category Manager functions and not the usual list functions. We cover Categories in Chapter 13. The following sections look at how to do the other two types of lists.

Making an overview list

Chapters 9 and 13 include an example program that uses a list in an overview form. A list like this, that's always visible on a form, is pretty easy to deal with. You need to load data into the list when the form is displayed, and then respond to selections in the list.

To set up the list's choices, you call LstSetListChoices() and pass in an array of CharPtrs that point to the list item values to use. The problem with this function call is that it expects the array you pass in, as well as the strings the pointers in the array point to, to remain unchanged as long as the list is displayed. This means you must either declare global variables for the array of CharPtrs and the strings they point to, or you need to allocate handles and lock them to get pointers to memory to pass into the list.

TIP

Declare globals if you happen to know the exact number (or maximum number) of your list items, since it's a bit easier to deal with. Allocate handles if the number of items varies such as when using a list to display an overview of database records. The list described in Chapter 9 is fixed in size to a maximum of 10 items, so it uses globals. The list described in Chapter 13 displays a varying number of records from a database, so it allocates handles.

Because the actual details of initializing and using a list are the same in either case, we're going to show the handle method here. We sketch out how to use global memory with a list in Chapter 9.

In the example from Chapter 13, we allocate memory for the list and load the list items with the names of the Pin detail records in the currently displayed Category whenever the overview form is displayed. We also need to reload the list when the user selects a different category to display. In either case, we do this by calling our `InitOverviewFormList()` function. This function is rather long, so we're going to present it in several chunks. The first chunk declares all the local variables we need:

```
static void InitOverviewFormList() {
    ListPtr lstPtr;
    VoidHand overviewRecHandle;
    Err error;
    UInt recordNum;
    UInt numRecords;
    UIntPtr recIds;
    CharPtr choices;
    UInt choicesOffset = 0;
    UInt choicesBufSz = NAME_SIZE*5;
    UInt indexBufSz = 5;
    CharPtr storedName;
    UInt nameLen;
    UInt scrollPos = 0;
```

The function is going to create two blocks of memory. The block pointed to by choices is going to contain all the strings for the list, packed back to back. In other words, it ends up looking like this:

```
"First Choice\0Second Choice\0So on\0"
```

We need to keep track of the size of the `choices` buffer in the `choicesOffset` variable, as well as the size of the buffer in the `choicesBufSz` variable. The memory handle is stored in a global variable named `ChoicesHandle`.

In addition to this block of memory, we allocate another block of memory to hold an array of record IDs. These are the IDs of each record in the list. The `recIds` pointer points to the array we allocate. The handle for this array memory is kept in a global variable named `DbIdsHandle`.

The first thing we do is allocate the initial memory for these pointers:

```
lstPtr = (ListPtr)GetObjectPtr(Overview_PinList);
LstSetSelection(lstPtr, -1);
recordNum = 0;
overviewRecHandle = DmQueryNextInCategory (PinDB,
    &recordNum, prefs.categoryView);
ChoicesHandle = MemHandleNew(choicesBufSz *
    sizeof(Char));
DbIdsHandle = MemHandleNew(indexBufSz * sizeof(UInt));
recIds = (UIntPtr) MemHandleLock(DbIdsHandle);
choices = (CharPtr) MemHandleLock(ChoicesHandle);
*choices = 0;
```

We get a pointer to the list and then clear the current list selection. Then we begin the query for records in the current Category. Then we allocate a handle to hold the strings for the list. We allocate a large chunk of memory, and then keep track of how much of it is used. When we fill the chunk, we reallocate the handle to a larger size. We use the same technique to allocate the handle for the IDs, and then we lock both handles to get pointers to the memory. Finally, we set the beginning of the choices memory block to '\0' so that it holds an empty string.

We talk about databases and memory allocation in more detail in Chapter 13, so see that chapter for more information on database and memory functions.

We're all set up to build the list's array of strings and IDs from the database:

```
for (numRecords = 0; ;numRecords++) {
    if (!overviewRecHandle)
        break;
    if ((numRecords + 1) > indexBufSz) {
        indexBufSz += 5;
        MemHandleUnlock(DbIdsHandle);
        error = MemHandleResize(DbIdsHandle,
            indexBufSz * sizeof(UInt));
        recIds = MemHandleLock(DbIdsHandle);
    }
    recIds[numRecords] = recordNum;
    if (recordNum <= prefs.scrollPos)
        scrollPos = numRecords;
    storedName  = (CharPtr)
        MemHandleLock(overviewRecHandle);
    nameLen = StrLen(storedName)+1;
    if ((choicesOffset+nameLen) > choicesBufSz) {
        MemHandleUnlock(ChoicesHandle);
        error = MemHandleResize(ChoicesHandle,
            choicesBufSz * sizeof(Char));
        choices = MemHandleLock(ChoicesHandle);
    }
```

```
        StrCopy(choices+choicesOffset, storedName);
        choicesOffset += nameLen;
        MemHandleUnlock(overviewRecHandle);
        ++recordNum;
        overviewRecHandle = DmQueryNextInCategory (PinDB,
            &recordNum, prefs.categoryView);
    }
```

The code here looks more complex than it really is. What we're doing is visiting each record in the Category and then storing its record index in the recIds array. We also append the name from the record into the choices memory block. Before we do either action, we check to make sure that there is enough room allocated to hold these values. If there isn't, we reallocate the memory, asking for another large chunk. We then add the index and string to the two memory blocks and keep track of the additional memory used.

When we've visited all records, we're ready to set up the list:

```
    if (numRecords) {
        MemHandleUnlock(DbIdsHandle);
        MemHandleResize(DbIdsHandle, numRecords *
            sizeof(UInt));
        MemHandleResize(ChoicesHandle, choicesOffset);
        ChoicesPtrsHandle = SysFormPointerArrayToStrings(
            choices, numRecords);
        LstSetListChoices(lstPtr,
            MemHandleLock(ChoicesPtrsHandle), numRecords);
        if (prefs.scrollPos == 0)
            scrollPos = 0;
        LstSetTopItem (lstPtr, scrollPos);
        LstDrawList (lstPtr);
    }
    else {
        LstSetListChoices(lstPtr, 0, 0);
        MemHandleFree(ChoicesHandle);
        ChoicesHandle = 0;
        MemHandleFree(DbIdsHandle);
    }
}
```

If we actually found one or more records, we resize the two memory blocks so that they're exactly as big as needed. Because we always ask for more memory than we need, this frees up some memory, which is always a good idea. Then we use the SysFormPointerArrayToStrings() Palm OS function to allocate a Handle containing an array of CharPtrs from our choices-packed string block. This does all the work for us of allocating a handle of the correct size and then filling the handle with pointers to each string in choices. We call LstSetListChoices() and pass in the pointer to the memory of the new handle, as well as the number of items in the list. Then we set the initial scroll position of the list by calling the LstSetTopItem() Palm OS function, and finally draw the list.

If no record is found, we use LstSetListChoices() to indicate that there are no items in the list and free the Handles we allocated for the choice strings and record IDs.

You can initialize the contents of a list in another way that uses a callback function. When you use a callback function to initialize the list items, you define a function that matches this prototype:

```
ListDrawDataFunc(UInt itemNum, RectanglePtr bounds,
    CharPtr *itemsText)
```

Then you associate this callback with the list:

```
LstSetDrawFunction(1stPtr, ListDrawDataFunc)
```

In this code fragment, 1stPtr is a ListPtr to the desired list. When the Palm OS draws the list, this callback function is called for each visible item in the list. It's up to you to use the Window drawing functions to draw the list items.

Use a callback if you don't want to pre-load a very large list with strings, or if you want to display bitmaps or more complex list items; otherwise, just stick with the non-callback approach.

If you do use a callback function, and you're using the GNU tools, you'll need to use the CALLBACK_PROLOGUE and CALLBACK_EPILOGUE macros inside the callback function.

Setting the Table

Tables (tTBL) allow developers to organize a collection of several types of User Interface resources. Tables directly support a number of editable and read-only Field and Control types.

According to the Palm OS documentation, you can scroll tables vertically but not horizontally. What the documentation doesn't say is that you are responsible for adding a scroll bar or a pair of buttons to perform the scrolling, and then you must change the contents of the rows of the table within your program when you want to scroll.

Generally speaking, every row in a table contains the same kind of information, so you end up with columns of the same type. For example, you may have a table with three columns: The first is editable text, the second is a non-editable numeric value, and the last is a check box. The number of rows and the number of columns must be specified for each Table resource.

Table's UI structure

The User Interface structure for tables is `TableType`. You can find the type definition in the header file Table.h, in the PalmOS 3.0 Support\Incs\UI folder within the metrowerks install folder, or the Incs\UI folder within the GNU install folder.

When you get a pointer to a table, it's a `TablePtr`. This is just a `typedef` to a `TableType.*` There is also a `TableAttrType` that defines a `struct` containing the attributes of a table, a `TableRowAttrType` and a `TableColumnAttrType` that define the attributes of a table row and column, and a `TableItemType` that defines a `struct` containing information individual items in a table. The fields of the `TableType` structure are described in Table 10-5.

Table 10-5	**Fields of `TableType` structure**
Field	*Description*
`id`	The developer-specified ID of the table.
`bounds`	The position and size of the Table resource. The structure contains:
	`Left Origin`: Form-relative position of the left side of the table. Valid values are: 0–159.
	`Top Origin`: Form-relative position of the top of the Table. Valid values are: 0–159.
	`Width`: Width of the table in pixels. Valid values are: 0–160.
	`Height`: Height of the table in pixels. Valid values are: 1–160.
`attr`	Field attributes. The `attr` field is a bit field that contains:
	`visible`: This attribute is set/cleared internally when the table is drawn/erased.
	`editable`: When set, the user can modify the table.
	`editing`: When set, the table is in edit mode.
	`selected`: When set, the current item is selected.
	`hasScrollbar`: This attribute is only set programmatically. When `hasScrollbar` is set, the table has a scroll bar.

(continued)

Table 10-5 *(continued)*

Field	Description
numColumns	Number of columns in the table.
numRows	Number of rows in the table.
currentRow	Row of the table set to current.
currentColumn	Column of the table set to current.
topRow	First row in the table.
columnAttrs	Column attributes, such as its width, whether or not it is usable, and how the column draws itself.
rowAttrs	Row's attributes, such as its ID, height, and whether or not it is usable, selectable, or invalid.
items	Item attributes, such as the itemType, fontID, intValue, and a character ptr.
dcurrentField	The field that the user is currently editing.

Tabling an example

Like lists, tables are often pressed into service in overview forms. That's what they're used for with the built-in applications, including the To Do List, Memo List, Address List, and Calendar. They're also useful for detail forms, as you can see in the Address List application.

We've made an application that includes a table. The example displays a form with a table in it. The table has 10 rows with 4 columns and is the beginnings of a shopping list application. The full source code to the example is on the CD-ROM that accompanies this book in the Examples\Chap10\Table folder. If you're using CodeWarrior, just open the project file named table.mcp. If you're using GCC, the Src subdirectory contains all the necessary files, along with a makefile. In either case, all the program code is in the table.c file.

To use a table, you add a table to a form in Constructor (or use the TABLE element in pilrc for GNU) and specify the number of rows and column widths you need. Then you initialize and populate the table when the form is displayed.

Initializing a table

To initialize a table, you must enable every row and every column. Rows and columns that aren't enabled don't display on the device! You've also got to tell the table the type of information that every cell is displaying. You do this by calling TblSetItemStyle() for every row/column index and passing in a specific style value. Table 10-6 describes the values and their behavior.

Table 10-6	Table Style Values	
Style	*UI Element*	*Editable*
CheckboxTableItem	Check Box	Yes
DateTableItem	Date	No
LabelTableItem	Label	No
NumericTableItem	Non-editable Field displaying a Number	No
PopupTriggerTableItem	Trigger	Yes
TextTableItem	Field	Yes
TextWithNoteTableItem	Field with special Bitmap at end	Yes
TimeTableItem	Do Not Use	No
NarrowTextTableItem	Field using the Narrow Font	Yes
CustomTableItem	The program draw the contents	No

The table we created has 10 rows and 4 columns. The first column is a check box, the second is a popup list, the third is a non-editable field, and the fourth is an editable field that shows the Note icon when the contents are bigger than the column width. We initialize all the elements of the table when the form is first displayed, in the case block that processes the frmOpenEvent event in our MainFormHandleEvent() function:

```
// global variable
CharPtr shoppingList[] = {"Bread", "Milk", "Eggs", "Tofu",
    "Carrots", "Apples", "Grapes", "Orange Juice",
    "Cookies","Potatoes"};

static Boolean MainFormHandleEvent(EventPtr event) {
    Boolean handled = false;
    FormPtr frm;
    TablePtr table;
    ListPtr list;
    Word row, i;
    Word rowsInTable;
#ifdef __GNUC__
CALLBACK_PROLOGUE
#endif
    switch (event->eType) {
    case frmOpenEvent:
        frm = FrmGetActiveForm();
        FrmDrawForm(frm);
        LstNewList(&frm, 1099, 1, 1, 72, 0,
            boldFont, 0, 1001);
        list = FrmGetObjectPtr(frm,
```

(continued)

(continued)

```
        FrmGetObjectIndex(frm, 1099));
    LstSetListChoices(list, shoppingList, 10);
    LstSetHeight(list,10);
    table = FrmGetObjectPtr (frm,
        FrmGetObjectIndex(frm, Main_Table_Table));
    rowsInTable = TblGetNumberOfRows(table);
    for (row = 0; row < rowsInTable; row++) {
        TblSetItemStyle(table, row, 0, checkboxTableItem);
        TblSetItemStyle(table, row, 1,
            popupTriggerTableItem);
        TblSetItemInt(table, row, 1, row);
        TblSetItemPtr(table, row, 1, list);
        TblSetItemStyle(table, row, 2, textTableItem);
        TblSetItemStyle(table, row, 3, textTableItem);
    }
    for (i = 0; i < 4; i++)
        TblSetColumnUsable(table, i, true);
    TblSetLoadDataProcedure(table, 2, PriceBlock);
    TblSetLoadDataProcedure(table, 3, DescriptionBlock);
    TblSetSaveDataProcedure(table, 3, SaveDescription);
    FrmDrawForm(frm);
    handled = true;
    break;
// Other cases omitted
```

We need to set the style for every column in every row of the table. Before we do this, we need to create a list to use with the trigger cell, so we draw the form and then create a new list by calling the LstNewList() Palm OS function. Then we get a pointer to the new list, set it to a global variable containing an array of string pointers, and set its height to 10. Now we're ready to initialize the cells of the table.

We retrieve the TablePtr for the table and get the number of rows by calling the TblGetNumberOfRows() Palm OS function. Then we execute a loop that visits each row in the table and sets the style of every column in the row.

For each column, we set the style by calling the TblSetItemStyle() Palm OS function. The first column's style is checkboxTableItem, the second column's style is popupTriggerTableItem, and the third and fourth columns' style is textTableItem. For the popup trigger, we use the TblSetItemInt() Palm OS function to select the desired item in the list as the trigger value. We use the TblSetItemPtr() Palm OS function to place the ListPtr of the list into the cell.

Next we make all four columns usable by calling the TblSetColumnUsable() Palm OS function for each column.

Finally, we need to set callbacks for the text cells. The third column contains prices, so we will load them in our `PriceBlock()` function. The fourth column contains a description. We load the description in our `DescriptionBlock()` function, and process user edits in our `SaveDescription()` function.

Finally, we redraw the form, which will call our callbacks to load the text cells.

Initializing non-editable table text cells

Whenever a table that has `Load Data` callbacks is drawn, the callback function is called for each cell. Our third column uses a `Load Data` callback function to set up the prices cells. The callback is responsible for two actions:

- ✔ Configuring the field
- ✔ Allocating and returning a handle for the field data

We do both of these in our `PriceBlock()` function:

```
// global variables
CharPtr prices[] = {"1.99", "2.29", "2.45", "3.45", "1.20",
   "4.50", "2.34", "3.43", "2.98", "5.99"};
VoidHand PriceHandles = 0;

static Err PriceBlock (VoidPtr table,
      Word row, Word column, Boolean editable,
      VoidHand *dataH, WordPtr dataOffset,
      WordPtr dataSize, FieldPtr fld) {
   FieldAttrType attr;
   CharPtr p;
   VoidHand *handles;
#ifdef __GNUC__
CALLBACK_PROLOGUE
#endif
   FldGetAttributes(fld, &attr);
   attr.editable = 0;
   attr.underlined = 0;
   attr.justification = rightAlign;
   FldSetAttributes(fld, &attr);
   if (!PriceHandles) {
      ULong numBytes = TblGetNumberOfRows(table) *
         sizeof(Handle);
      PriceHandles = MemHandleNew(numBytes);
      handles = MemHandleLock(PriceHandles);
      MemSet(handles, numBytes, 0);
      MemHandleUnlock(PriceHandles);
   }
   handles = MemHandleLock(PriceHandles);
   if (!handles[row]) {
      handles[row] = MemHandleNew(StrLen(prices[row])+1);
      p = MemHandleLock(handles[row]);
      StrCopy(p, prices[row]);
```

(continued)

(continued)

```
                                MemHandleUnlock(handles[row]);
    }
  *dataH = handles[row];
  *dataSize = MemHandleSize(*dataH);
  *dataOffset = 0;
  MemHandleUnlock(PriceHandles);
#ifdef __GNUC__
CALLBACK_EPILOGUE
#endif
    return 0;
}
```

The function begins by setting the attributes of the field so that it is non-editable, not underlined, and right justified. That completes the field configuration, now we need to allocate the handle to hold the value.

We use a global named `PriceHandles` to hold an array of allocated handles for the rows of the table. The function begins by allocating a handle for this array if it hasn't been allocated yet. Next it allocates a handle for the actual row value and copies the value we have in a global array into the allocated memory. The function ends by setting the return values of the cell handle, its size, and the offset with it for this cell.

Use a `Data Load` callback to load data from a database record into the cell of a table. Just allocate a handle, copy the data from the record, and return the handle.

Initializing editable table text cells

The other Data Load procedure we have is for the description column. Our `DescriptionBlock()` function looks a lot like the function covered in the preceding section:

```
// global variable
VoidHand DescriptionHandles = 0;

static Err DescriptionBlock (VoidPtr table,
      Word row, Word column, Boolean editable,
      VoidHand *dataH, WordPtr dataOffset,
      WordPtr dataSize, FieldPtr fld) {
   FieldAttrType attr;
   VoidHand *handles;
   CharPtr p;
#ifdef __GNUC__
CALLBACK_PROLOGUE
#endif
   FldGetAttributes (fld, &attr);
   attr.dynamicSize = 0;
   FldSetAttributes(fld, &attr);
```

```
    if (!DescriptionHandles) {
        ULong numBytes = TblGetNumberOfRows(table) *
            sizeof(Handle);
        DescriptionHandles = MemHandleNew(numBytes);
        handles = MemHandleLock(DescriptionHandles);
        MemSet(handles, numBytes, 0);
        MemHandleUnlock(DescriptionHandles);
    }
    handles = MemHandleLock(DescriptionHandles);
    if (!handles[row]) {
        handles[row] = MemHandleNew(10);
        p = MemHandleLock(handles[row]);
        *p = '\0';
        MemHandleUnlock(handles[row]);
    }
    *dataH = handles[row];
    *dataSize = MemHandleSize(*dataH);
    *dataOffset = 0;
    MemHandleUnlock(DescriptionHandles);
#ifdef __GNUC__
CALLBACK_EPILOGUE
#endif
    return 0;
}
```

This time, the only field configuration we need to make is to set the field so that it does not resize dynamically. Fields in a table can expand when the user enters more text than the column width. You can see this behavior in the Address List built-in application. We don't want that behavior, so we turn it off.

Next, we allocate the handles much as we did for the price column. The only difference here is that we create the handle for cell with a size of 10. This might look small, but since the field is editable, the Palm OS will resize the handle as needed. We also initialize the memory to hold an empty string, since we want the user to be able to enter text in this field.

That's all the initialization. When the application is launched, a table with 10 rows and 4 columns is displayed, as shown in Figure 10-2.

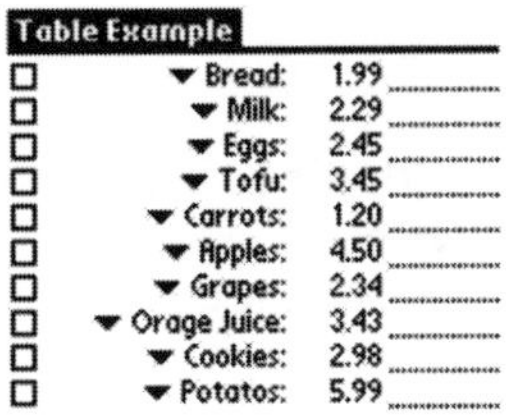

Figure 10-2:
A table
application.

Table Example		
▼ Bread:	1.99	
▼ Milk:	2.29	
▼ Eggs:	2.45	
▼ Tofu:	3.45	
▼ Carrots:	1.20	
▼ Apples:	4.50	
▼ Grapes:	2.34	
▼ Orage Juice:	3.43	
▼ Cookies:	2.98	
▼ Potatos:	5.99	

Tapping on any of the check boxes checks and unchecks them. Tapping any of the triggers pops up the list of choices, and selecting from the list changes the trigger label. Tapping any of the prices just selects the row, since the price cells are not editable. Tapping any of the description cells puts the cursor in the cell. You can now enter text into the cell, as much as you want. The cell scrolls if you run out of room. This is all standard table behavior that is done by the Palm OS after you initialize the table.

When you tap some other cell after entering a lot of text in a description cell, the cell changes to show a Note icon. Tapping the Note icon opens a modal form containing a single field, where you can see and edit the description. The following section discusses how these two behaviors are implemented.

Post-processing editable table text cells

Whenever a cell that has a Save Data callback function loses the focus, the callback function is called. Our description column has such a callback, so that callback is called after you enter description text and then tap another cell in the table:

```
static Boolean SaveDescription(VoidPtr table,
    Word row, Word column) {
   VoidHand *handles;
   CharPtr p;
#ifdef __GNUC__
CALLBACK_PROLOGUE
#endif
   handles = MemHandleLock(DescriptionHandles);
   p = MemHandleLock(handles[row]);
   if (FntLineWidth(p, StrLen(p)) >
         TblGetColumnWidth(table, column))
      TblSetItemStyle(table, row, 3,
         textWithNoteTableItem);
   else
         TblSetItemStyle(table, row, 3, textTableItem);
   MemHandleUnlock(handles[row]);
   MemHandleUnlock(DescriptionHandles);
   TblMarkRowInvalid(table, row);
#ifdef __GNUC__
CALLBACK_EPILOGUE
#endif
   return true;
}
```

The function retrieves the handle associated with the row and then gets a pointer to the text string in the handle. Next, we call the FntLineWidth() Palm OS function to determine the width, in pixels, that the text uses when displayed. If that width is greater than the width of the column, we set the style of the cell to textWithNoteTableItem. If it's not, we set the style to textTableItem. Finally, we mark the row invalid by calling the TblMarkRowInvalid() Palm OS function, which forces the Palm OS to redraw the row. The result is that when the text exceeds the width of the Field, a Note icon is displayed.

In addition to the kinds of things we did in this callback, you can also do other post processing tasks. These including validating the data entered, or even saving the data back into a database record.

Processing Table selections

When a cell is tapped, the application receives a `tblSelectEvent` event. We handle that event in the `case` block that processes the `tblSelectEvent` event in the `MainFormHandleEvent()` function:

```
// local variables
Boolean handled = false;
FormPtr frm;
TablePtr table;
Word row;
// other cases omitted
case tblSelectEvent:
   frm = FrmGetActiveForm();
   row = event->data.tblSelect.row;
   table = FrmGetObjectPtr(frm,
      FrmGetObjectIndex(frm, Main_Table_Table));
   if (event->data.tblSelect.column == 3 &&
         !TblEditing(table)) {
      FormPtr note;
      FieldPtr fieldPtr, noteText;
      VoidHand *handles;
      TblUnhighlightSelection(table);
      note = FrmInitForm (Note_Form);
      noteText = FrmGetObjectPtr (note,
         FrmGetObjectIndex (note, Note_Note_Field));
      handles = MemHandleLock(DescriptionHandles);
      FldSetTextHandle(noteText,handles[row]);
      MemHandleUnlock(DescriptionHandles);
      FrmDoDialog (note);
      FldSetTextHandle(noteText,NULL);
      FrmDeleteForm (note);
      TblMarkRowInvalid(table, row);
      TblRedrawTable(table);
      FrmSetFocus(frm,
         FrmGetObjectIndex(frm, Main_Table_Table));
      TblGrabFocus(table, row, 3);
      fieldPtr = TblGetCurrentField(table);
      FldSetInsPtPosition(fieldPtr, 0);
   }
   handled = true;
```

First, we figure out whether the user tapped a Note icon. The column the user tapped in is passed in with the event data in `event->data.tblSelect.column`, so we check to see if that is 3 (columns are numbered from 0). Unfortunately, this is true even when the user taps in the field, not just when they tap the Note icon. So we also call the `TblEditing()` Palm OS function, which is only `true` when the user taps in the Field. If that function returns `false`, and the selection is in the fourth column, we know the user tapped the Note icon.

We unhighlight the selected row next by calling the `TblUnhighlightSelection()` Palm OS function. Then we initialize our modal form, retrieve the handle for the description text, and set the field in the modal form to use this handle. We call `FrmDoDialog()` to display the modal form. The user can now edit the text of the description in this form and tap OK when done. When the call to `FrmDoDialog()` returns, we set the handle of the field in the modal form to `NULL`. If we didn't do that, the handle would be freed when we deleted the modal form, which we really don't want at all. We delete the modal form, mark the row of the table invalid, and redraw the table. That updates the cell text to reflect the edits the user made via the modal form.

All we need to do to wrap things up is set the focus to the cell. We accomplish that by calling the `FrmSetFocus()` Palm OS function to give the Table the focus. Then we use the `TblGrabFocus()` Palm OS function to set the focus to the specific cell in the Table. Finally we get the `FieldPtr` for the Field that represents the cell by calling the `TblGetCurrentField()` Palm OS function, and then use that `FieldPtr` to set the insertion point within the cell.

Making a Meal with Leftovers

In addition to the Catalog resources we've talked about so far, two more exist that we would like you to know about. These are the Gadget and the Graffiti Shift Indicator. The following sections take a look at each of these.

Gadget goes to Hawaii

The Gadget (`tGDT`) resource lets developers implement a custom User Interface element. The Gadget resource is essentially a rectangle. When a pen tap event is received, it is up to you, the application developer, to do something with it.

You can use gadgets in games, or place them on top of form bitmaps to create "hot spots" in images on Forms. You can also use the Window Drawing Palm OS functions to draw graphics and text within a gadget.

Gadget's Attributes

Gadgets have the following attributes:

- ✔ `Gadget ID`: ID of the gadget, assigned by Constructor.
- ✔ `Left Origin`: Form-relative position of the left side of the gadget. Valid values are: 0 – 159.

✔ Top Origin: **Form-relative position of the top of the gadget. Valid values are: 0 – 159.**

✔ Width: **Width of the gadget in pixels. Valid values are: 0 – 160.**

✔ Height: **Height of the gadget in pixels. Valid values are: 1 – 160.**

✔ Usable: **When this attribute is set, the gadget is usable and can be displayed. A nonusable gadget is not drawn. Nonusable resources can be programmatically set to usable.**

Gadget example

We've made an application that includes a gadget. The full source code to the example is on the CD-ROM that accompanies this book in the Examples\ Chap10\Gadget folder. If you're using CodeWarrior, just open the project file named gadget.mcp. If you're using GCC, the Src subdirectory contains all the necessary files, along with a makefile. In either case, all the program code is in the gadget.c file.

The following code fragment draws what looks like a Windows-style radio button within a gadget. It's called in the frmOpenEvent event case block of the MainFormHandleEvent() function:

```
// Local variables
Boolean handled = false;
FormPtr frm;
SWord x, y;
Word objIndex;
VoidHand bitmapRez, checkedRez;
BitmapPtr theBitmap, checkedBitmap;
DWord buttonSet;
switch (event->eType) {
case frmOpenEvent:
    frm = FrmGetActiveForm();
    FrmDrawForm(frm);
    objIndex = FrmGetObjectIndex(frm, Main_FakeRB_Gadget);
    FrmGetObjectPosition(frm, objIndex, &x, &y);
    bitmapRez = DmGetResource ('Tbmp', RBUnSet_Bitmap);
    theBitmap = (BitmapPtr) MemHandleLock(bitmapRez);
    WinDrawBitmap(theBitmap, x, y);
    WinDrawChars("Tap me!", 7, x+theBitmap->width+4, y+2);
    DmReleaseResource(bitmapRez);
    buttonSet = 0;
    FrmSetGadgetData (frm, objIndex, (VoidPtr)0);
    handled = true;
    break;
// Other cases omitted
```

This code begins by getting the index to the gadget. It uses this index to retrieve the gadget's X and Y location in the form. Then it loads a Bitmap resource from the application, and draws it into the gadget's window location. It also draws a label into the gadget. Finally, it sets the gadget's data to 0, indicating that it is not set.

When the user puts the pen down inside the gadget, the
MainFormHandleEvent() function receives a penDownEvent event. The
case block of the MainFormHandleEvent() function that handles that event
is shown below:

```
case penDownEvent:
    frm = FrmGetActiveForm();
    objIndex = FrmGetObjectIndex(frm, Main_FakeRB_Gadget);
    FrmGetObjectBounds (frm, objIndex, &gadgetRect);
    if (RctPtInRectangle(event->screenX,
        event->screenY,&gadgetRect)) {
        Boolean penDown;
        BitmapPtr lastDraw, thisDraw,
            drawInBounds, drawOutBounds;
        buttonSet = (DWord)FrmGetGadgetData (frm, objIndex);
        bitmapRez = DmGetResource ('Tbmp', RBUnSet_Bitmap);
        theBitmap = (BitmapPtr) MemHandleLock(bitmapRez);
        checkedRez = DmGetResource ('Tbmp', RBSet_Bitmap);
        checkedBitmap = (BitmapPtr)MemHandleLock(checkedRez);
        if (buttonSet == 0) {
            drawInBounds = checkedBitmap;
            drawOutBounds = theBitmap;
        }
        else {
            drawInBounds = theBitmap;
            drawOutBounds = checkedBitmap;
        }
        lastDraw = drawOutBounds;
        do {
            EvtGetPen (&x, &y,&penDown);
            if (RctPtInRectangle(x, y, &gadgetRect))
                thisDraw = drawInBounds;
            else
                thisDraw = drawOutBounds;
            if (lastDraw != thisDraw) {
                WinDrawBitmap(thisDraw,
                    gadgetRect.topLeft.x,
                    gadgetRect.topLeft.y);
                lastDraw = thisDraw;
            }
            SysTaskDelay (SysTicksPerSecond()/10);
        } while (penDown);
        if (lastDraw == drawInBounds) {
            buttonSet = (buttonSet == 0) ? 1 : 0;
            FrmSetGadgetData (frm, objIndex,
                (VoidPtr)buttonSet);
        }
        DmReleaseResource(bitmapRez);
        DmReleaseResource(checkedRez);
        handled = true;
    }
    break;
```

This is a lot of code! It should make you appreciate all the work the built-in controls do for you. When the penDownEvent event is received, we check to see if the initial X and Y pen coordinates are within the rectangle of the gadget. If they are, we begin tracking the pen until it's lifted. We retrieve the two bitmaps that represent the checked and unchecked display for the gadget, and then enter a loop. Within the loop, we get the current pen state, which includes the pen X and Y location and a Boolean that indicates if the pen is down. We check to see if the X and Y position is inside the bounds of the gadget, and if they are we draw the appropriate bitmap. We use the SysTaskDelay() Palm OS function to let the CPU rest for a tenth of a second each time through the loop, so we don't overtax the batteries.

Once the user lifts the pen, the gadget's data reflects the new state — if the pen is lifted within the bounds of the gadget. If it's not, we don't change the value.

Graffiti Shift Indicator

The Graffiti Shift Indicator resource (tGSI) specifies the window-relative or form-relative position of the Graffiti Shift Indicator. The different shift states are punctuation, symbol, uppercase lock, and uppercase shift. These indicators appear at the position of the Graffiti Shift resource.

Graffiti Shift Indicator's Attributes

The Graffiti Shift Indicator has the following attributes:

- ✔ Object ID: ID of the Graffiti Shift Indicator, assigned by Constructor.
- ✔ Left Origin: Form-relative position of the left side Indicator.
- ✔ Top Origin: Form-relative position of the top of the Indicator.

Graffiti Shift Indicator example

Chapter 17 includes an example that uses a Graffiti Shift Indicator. All you need to do to use one is put it somewhere on your form, and the Palm OS takes care of the rest! The usual location for the Graffiti Shift Indicator is in the lower-right side of the form.

Chapter 11

Manager's Corner

● ●

In This Chapter

▶ Featuring alarming errors

▶ The sound of file strings

▶ Timing system stuff

● ●

*T*he Palm OS consists of a single library of functions. This library is grouped into several managers. Each manager is a collection of functions that work together to implement a particular functionality. Some of the managers have a large collection of APIs (application program interfaces), and others, like the Alarm manager, have just a few.

To make things a bit easier to recognize, the folks at Palm made each function begin with a three letter prefix unique to the manager. For example, the two functions that are associated with the Alarm manager both begin with the three letters `Alm`: `AlmGetAlarm()` and `AlmSetAlarm()`.

Throughout this book we talk about many managers and their associated functions. Here is a list of the managers and the chapters in which they can be found:

✔ System Event manager — Chapter 8

✔ UI managers — Chapter 9

✔ Memory and Data managers — Chapter 13

✔ Serial manager — Bonus Chapter 1

✔ Exchange manager — Bonus Chapter 2

✔ Error manager — Chapter 16

We aren't going to duplicate manager information in this chapter. Instead, we are going to describe the managers that we haven't discussed. These also happen to be the managers that are not responsible for memory or interface management.

Featuring Alarms

This section discusses the Feature and Alarm managers. The *Feature manager* is the way your program finds out what Palm OS features are supported on the actual Palm device. The *Alarm manager* is the way your program can receive a notification event at a specific time in the future.

Finding features

Use the Feature manager to get information about the system software version, the optional system features, third party extensions, and an application's data.

A *feature* is a 32-bit value that is published by the system or by applications. Each feature has a feature creator and a feature number. The *feature creator* is the database creator type of the application publishing the feature. The *feature number* is a 16-bit value that is unique to the differing features of a particular creator. Once a feature is published, it exists until it is explicitly deleted.

The system version is an example of a feature. Table 11-1 lists the systems, software versions, and their feature numbers.

Table 11-1	Software System Feature Numbers	
System	*Software Version*	*Feature Number*
Pilot 1000 and Pilot 5000	Palm OS 1.0	0x01003001
PalmPilot and PalmPilot Professional	Palm OS 2.0	0x02003000
Palm III Connected Organizer	Palm OS 3.0	0x03003000

An application can test for the presence or absence of a system capability so that it can refine its behavior accordingly. An application can also publish a feature of its own.

The functions associated with the Feature manager are:

- FtrGet(): Gets a feature.
- FtrGetByIndex(): Gets a feature by using an index. Shell commands usually use this, not applications.

- ✔ FtrSet(): Sets a feature.

- ✔ FtrUnregister(): This function is used to unregister a feature.

The most common use of the Feature manager is to verify that the OS version is current enough to support the functions used in an application. For example, an application that uses dynamic forms can only run on Palm devices that use version 3.0 or later of the Palm OS. The application checks the version by using the Feature manager:

```
FtrGet(sysFtrCreator, sysFtrNumROMVersion, &romVersion);
if (romVersion < requiredVersion) {
    // let user know we cannot run on this device
}
```

Alarming developments

You use the Alarm manager to get and set real-time alarms, perform a periodic activity, or display a reminder.

There is an alarm queue that holds all the alarm requests. When an alarm requests' time is met, it is triggered and the Alarm manager notifies the appropriate applications via the sysAppLaunchCmdAlarmTriggered launch code. The application can now process this code by doing any one, or all, of the following three things: It can play a short sound, set the next alarm, or perform some maintenance activity. After an application processes the launch code, it receives the sysAppLaunchCmdDisplayAlarm launch code so that it can display a dialog or some other type of reminder.

The Alarm manager has two functions:

- ✔ AlmSetAlarm(): Sets and/or clears an alarm.

- ✔ AlmGetAlarm(): Used to discover the current alarm setting, expressed as the number of seconds elapsed since 1/1/1904. The value is 0 if no active alarms are set.

An application can set only one alarm at a time. If it sets an alarm and it already has an alarm set, the old alarm is discarded.

You can clear an alarm before it is triggered by setting an alarm with an alarm time of 0.

We've created a simple alarm example that lets you set an alarm for a time that is later in the day. The full source code to the example is on the CD-ROM that accompanies this book in the Examples\Chap11\Alarm folder. If you're using CodeWarrior, just open the project file named alarm.mcp. If you're using GCC, the Src subdirectory contains all the necessary files, along with a makefile. In either case, all the program code is in the alarm.c file.

The example application contains a lot of code, but the relevant portions are when the alarm is set, and handling the launch codes when they are triggered. The SetAlarmTime() function sets an alarm based on the user's selection:

```
static Boolean SetAlarmTime() {
    Char alarmTime[timeStringLength];
    TimeType start, end;
    DateTimeType fullTime;
    Boolean timeSet;

    TimSecondsToDateTime( TimGetSeconds()+(60*2),
        &fullTime);
    start.hours = fullTime.hour;
    start.minutes = fullTime.minute;
    end = start;
    timeSet = SelectTime ( &start, &end, false,
        "Select time for daily alarm", start.hours);
    if (start.hours != 255) {
        fullTime.hour = start.hours;
        fullTime.minute = start.minutes;
        fullTime.second = 0;
        prefs.alarmTime = TimDateTimeToSeconds(&fullTime);
        AlmSetAlarm(cardNo, appID, 0, prefs.alarmTime, 0);
        TimeToAscii( start.hours, start.minutes,
            tfColonAMPM, alarmTime);
        CtlSetLabel ((ControlPtr)GetObjectPtr(
            Overview_Time_SelTrigger), alarmTime);
        return true;
    }
    else
        return false;

}
```

This function uses the SelectTime() Palm OS function to let the user choose a time for the alarm. It saves the alarm time in the application Preferences and then sets an alarm by calling the AlmSetAlarm() Palm OS function. That function uses the card number and application resource database ID to uniquely identify the alarm for the application. We set the two global variables cardNo and appID to the correct values when the application first runs by calling the following function:

```
SysCurAppDatabase(&cardNo, &appID);
```

The `PilotMain()` function handles the three launch codes associated
with alarms:

```
case sysAppLaunchCmdAlarmTriggered:
   SndPlaySystemSound(sndAlarm);
   break;
case sysAppLaunchCmdDisplayAlarm:
   launched = launchFlags & sysAppLaunchFlagSubCall;
   if (!launched) {
      Word prefsSize;
      AlarmPreferenceType thePrefs;
      prefsSize = sizeof(AlarmPreferenceType);
      PrefGetAppPreferences(appFileCreator,
            appPrefID, &thePrefs, &prefsSize, true);
      thePrefs.alarmTime = DoAlert(thePrefs.message,
         false);
      PrefSetAppPreferences (appFileCreator, appPrefID,
         appPrefVersionNum, &thePrefs,
         sizeof(AlarmPreferenceType), true);
   }
   else {
#ifdef __GNUC__
CALLBACK_PROLOGUE
#endif
      prefs.alarmTime = DoAlert(prefs.message, true);

#ifdef __GNUC__
CALLBACK_EPILOGUE
#endif
   }
   break;
case sysAppLaunchCmdSystemReset:
   {
      Word prefsSize;
      UInt cardNo =0;
      LocalID appID =0;
      AlarmPreferenceType thePrefs;
      prefsSize = sizeof(AlarmPreferenceType);
      PrefGetAppPreferences(appFileCreator,
         appPrefID, &thePrefs, &prefsSize, true);
      if (thePrefs.alarmTime > 0)
         if (thePrefs.alarmTime > TimGetSeconds ()) {
            SysCurAppDatabase(&cardNo, &appID);
            AlmSetAlarm(cardNo, appID, 0,
               thePrefs.alarmTime, 0);
         }
         else {
            thePrefs.alarmTime = 0;
            PrefSetAppPreferences (appFileCreator,
               appPrefID, appPrefVersionNum, &thePrefs,
               sizeof(AlarmPreferenceType), true);
         }
   }
```

When the alarm is triggered, your application receives two launch codes. First, it receives the `sysAppLaunchCmdAlarmTriggered` launch code. You should perform any quick actions here, such as playing an alarm sound (as we do by calling the `SndPlaySystemSound()` Palm OS function). Next, your application receives the `sysAppLaunchCmdDisplayAlarm` launch code. This is the place you can perform slower actions, such as displaying an alert. That's what we do in the `DoAlert()` function. We'll look at that function in just a moment.

When the Palm device is reset, any set alarms are lost. You can detect the reset by handling the `sysAppLaunchCmdSystemReset` launch code, as we do in the alarm example, and then set the alarm again. For this to work, you need to know if your application needs to set an alarm. We keep the pending alarm time in the application Preferences, which are saved in a database and survive a device reset. When we receive the `sysAppLaunchCmdSystemReset` launch code, we check the application Preferences, and if the alarm time is set and has not passed, we set an alarm again. If the alarm time has passed, we just clear the alarm time in the application Preferences and save them.

The `DoAlert()` function displays an alert showing the text for the alarm and allows the user to tap a Snooze button and reschedule the alarm for one minute in the future:

```
static ULong DoAlert(CharPtr msg, Boolean loaded)  {
    ULong newAlarm = 0;
    if (FrmCustomAlert(Alarm_Alert, msg, "", "") == 1) {
        UInt cardNo =0;
        LocalID appID =0;
        newAlarm = TimGetSeconds() + 60;
        SysCurAppDatabase(&cardNo, &appID);
        AlmSetAlarm(cardNo, appID, 0, newAlarm, 0);
        if (loaded) {
            DateTimeType fullTime;
            Char alarmTimeStr[timeStringLength];
            TimSecondsToDateTime(newAlarm, &fullTime);
            TimeToAscii( fullTime.hour, fullTime.minute,
                tfColonAMPM, alarmTimeStr);
            CtlSetLabel ((ControlPtr)GetObjectPtr(
                Overview_Time_SelTrigger), alarmTimeStr);
        }
    }
    else if (loaded) {
        CtlSetLabel ((ControlPtr)GetObjectPtr(
            Overview_Time_SelTrigger), "Please set!");
        CtlSetValue((ControlPtr)GetObjectPtr(
            Overview_Enabled_Checkbox), 0);
    }
    return newAlarm;
}
```

This function displays a custom alert, showing the message associated with the alarm. If the user taps the Snooze button, a new alarm is set 60 seconds from the current time. The application also updates the controls on the display if the application was the running application when the alarm went off.

The Sound of File Strings

This section discusses the Sound manager, File Stream manager, and String manager. This motley crew of managers lets you play sounds, read and write files, and manipulate strings.

Sounding off

The Sound manager provides an extendible API for playing custom sounds, for playing system sounds, and for controlling default sound settings. This API currently supports only a single sound channel. The sound hardware plays only one simple tone at a time. End users control the volume of alarm, game, and system sounds by using the Preferences application.

Palm OS 3.0 supports standard MIDI files (called SMFs.) You can get the SMF format specification from www.midi.org. The Palm OS 3.0 does not support sampled sounds or multiple voices. All SMF records in the System MIDI Sounds database are available for use and can be added to.

Palm OS versions earlier than 3.0 don't support SMFs or asynchronous notes so if your application supports these, you must check the system's version number and change your application appropriately.

The Sound manager functions are:

- ✔ SndCreateMidiList(): Generates a list of MIDI records that have a specified creator. Use this function to display lists of sounds that are on a Palm device in the form of MIDI records.

- ✔ SndDoCmd(): Sends a Sound manager command to a specified channel. Currently the value of the chanP parameter must be NULL. This causes the command to be sent to the shared channel. Use this function to play simple sounds for user feedback. With this function, you can specify the frequency, duration, amplitude, and pitch of a note to be played. You can also stop the current note from playing.

- ✔ SndGetDefaultVolume(): Returns the default sound volume levels cached by the Sound manager.

- ✔ SndPlaySMF(): **Either synchronously plays the specified standard MIDI file (SMF) or it returns the duration of the entire SMF, expressed in milliseconds.**

- ✔ SndPlaySystemSound(): **Plays a standard system sound.**

Filing information

The File Streaming Application Program Interface (API) is based on the C programming language's stdio.h interface. If you are familiar with this, then you already know a lot about file streaming. The File Streaming API lets you work with arbitrarily large blocks of data. These blocks can exceed the 64K maximum size limit of the memory manager for allocated objects. In Palm OS 3.0, file streams are implemented as databases. Therefore, you can read, write, seek, and do other tasks that you would expect to do with a desktop file. There is no HotSync support for file streams. There are numerous File Streaming functions. The most commonly used ones are:

- ✔ FileControl(): **Changes the file stream to destructive read mode. This frees the memory that is ordinarily used to store the data as it is read. You change to destructive read mode by sending the value of** fileOpDestructiveReadMode **in the** op **parameter of this function.**

- ✔ FileDmRead(): **Reads data from a file stream directly into a record, a Database manager chunk, or resource, for immediate inclusion into a database.**

- ✔ FileOpen(): **Opens an existing file stream or creates an open file stream for input or output in the mode specified by the** openMode **parameter. These modes are read only; read/write, discarding previous version of stream; read/write, preserving previous version of stream; read/write, appending to end of stream.**

- ✔ FileRead(): **Reads data from a stream into a buffer.**

- ✔ FileWrite(): **Writes data to a stream. You cannot write to files that do not have write access or to those that are in the destructive read state.**

The fileOpDestructiveReadMode is designed to let you use a streaming file to store temporary memory used in a program. It's one way to get around the limits of the dynamic memory of the Palm device, as outlined in Chapter 13. You can write a lot of information into the streaming file and then read that information back into your program to perform some operation or calculation. After you read in the information, it's deleted from the streaming file for you.

Stringing along

The String Manager API consists of a set of string manipulation functions. To make things a bit easier to understand, this API is very similar to the standard C string manipulation functions (for example, `strcpy()`). If you are familiar with those functions, then you pretty much know what we are about to tell you concerning the String manager.

Use the String manager functions instead of the standard C functions. Doing this makes your applications smaller. Also, most standard C functions aren't supported.

The String manager functions are:

- ✔ `StrAToI()`: Converts a string to an integer. Returns an integer.

- ✔ `StrCaselessCompare()`: Compares two strings and returns 0 if they match, non-zero if they don't match. Use this function to find strings, such as when searching for matches to a Find request, but not to sort strings since it is insensitive to case and accent.

- ✔ `StrCat()`: Concatenates two strings and returns a pointer to the destination string.

- ✔ `StrChr()`: Finds a specified character within a specified string. Returns the first occurrence of the character.

- ✔ `StrCompare()`: Compares two strings and returns 0 if they match; returns a positive number if string1 > string2; returns a negative number if string1 < string2. Use this function to sort strings but not to find them.

- ✔ `StrCopy()`: Copies one string to another and returns a pointer to the destination string.

- ✔ `StrDelocalizeNumber()`: Converts a number from a localized notation to the US notation of a decimal point and thousandth comma.

- ✔ `StrIToA()`: Converts an integer to ASCII. Returns a pointer.

- ✔ `StrIToH()`: Converts an integer to a hexadecimal ASCII. Returns a string pointer.

- ✔ `StrLen()`: Determines the length of a string.

- ✔ `StrLocalizeNumber()`: Converts a number that is passed in as a string to a localized format, using a specified thousand separator and a decimal separator.

- ✔ `StrNCaselessCompare()`: Compares two strings out to N characters. Insensitive to case and accent. Returns 0 if they match, non-zero if they don't match; returns a positive number if string1 > string2; returns a negative number if string1 < string2.

✔ StrNCat(): Concatenates two strings while ensuring that the destination string is a maximum of N characters, including NULL at the end. Returns a pointer to the destination string.

✔ StrNCompare(): Compares two strings out to N characters while being case and accent sensitive. Returns 0 if they match, non-zero if they don't match; returns a positive number if string1 > string2; returns a negative number if string1 < string2.

✔ StrNCopy(): Copies up to N characters from a source string to a destination string. Returns a pointer to the destination string.

✔ StrPrintF():Implements the %d, %i, %u, %x, and %s format codes of the ANSI C sprintf() function. Returns the number of characters that are written to the destination string.

✔ StrStr(): Finds a specified substring within a specified string. Returns a pointer to the first occurrence of the substring or NULL if not found.

✔ StrToLower(): Converts all the characters in a string to lowercase except for accented characters. Returns a pointer to the destination string.

✔ StrVPrintF():Implements the %d, %i, %u, %x, and %s format codes of the ANSI C vsprintf() function. Returns the number of characters that are written to the destination string.

Timing System Stuff

This section discusses the Time manager and the System manager. The Time manager is where your programs find out and change the system date and time, as well as how they perform date conversions. The System manager is where your program can get some control over the Palm device itself.

Doing time

The Time manager (also called the Date and Time manager) supports the setting and getting of the real time clock and the getting of the current system ticks value. This manager doesn't support setting the system ticks value.

The real time clock is also called the *1 second timer*. It keeps track of the date and time even when the Palm device is in sleep mode. Real time is measured in seconds from midnight January 1, 1904.

The system tick value is kept by the 0.01-second timer. This timer is not updated when the Palm device is in sleep mode. The 0.01-second timer is reset when the Palm device resets. The tick increments 100 times/second when running on the Palm device.

The Time manager functions are:

- ✔ `DateAdjust()`: Returns a new date plus or minus the days adjustment (given in days).
- ✔ `DateDaysToDate()`: Given the days since 1/1/1904, this function stores the date in a `DateType` structure.
- ✔ `DateSecondsToDate()`: Given the seconds since 1/1/1904, this function stores the date in a `DateType` structure.
- ✔ `DateToAscii()`: Converts the specified date to an ASCII string. Handles short and long formats.
- ✔ `DateToDays()`: Returns the date in days since 1/1/1904.
- ✔ `DateToDOWDMFormatf()`: Converts the specified date to an ASCII string.
- ✔ `DayOfMonth()`: Returns the day of the month on which a specified date occurs.
- ✔ `DayOfWeek()`: Returns the day of the week on which a specified date occurs.
- ✔ `DaysInMonth()`: Returns the number of days in a specified month.
- ✔ `TimAdjust()`: Returns a new date plus or minus a time adjustment (given in seconds).
- ✔ `TimDateTimeToSeconds()`: Returns the date and time in seconds since 1/1/1904.
- ✔ `TimGetSeconds()`: Returns the seconds since 1/1/1904.
- ✔ `TimGetTicks()`: Returns the tick count since the last reset. The tick count doesn't accumulate while the device is in sleep mode.
- ✔ `TimSecondsToDateTime()`: Returns the date and time, given in seconds.
- ✔ `TimSetSeconds()`: Sets seconds since 1/1/1904.
- ✔ `TimeToAscii()`: Converts the specified time to an ASCII string.

We use several of these functions in various example programs throughout the book. The alarm example in this chapter uses several Time manager functions when setting an alarm and displaying the alarm time in a form. Refer to the section titled Alarming developments earlier in this chapter to see them in action.

Controlling system stuff

The System manager's API supports:

- ✔ System boot and reset.
- ✔ Power management of the three power modes.

✔ The Microkernel which provides basic task management.

✔ Application event processing and inter-application communication.

System boot and reset

The System Manager provides support for the system boot and reset. The Palm device is just like a toddler — it never really stops. Power is constantly supplied to the memory system, real time clock, and interrupt generation circuitry. The on/off key merely disables the LCD and reduces the device to low power mode. Booting only occurs when the user presses the reset switch on the Palm device.

Your program can handle the sysAppLaunchCmdSystemReset launch code to find out when the system has been reset and perform any necessary work. We do this in the alarm example presented earlier in this chapter.

Power management

The System manager provides support for three power modes: sleeping, dozing, and running. The System manager controls transitions between the modes.

When the Palm device appears to be off it is actually in *sleep mode*. In this mode, all peripherals such as the LCD and serial port are in low power mode. A hard key press or real time clock interrupt can wake the system up. The Palm device spends most of its "on" time in *doze mode*. In doze mode the processor is halted but the peripherals are powered up. The device only goes into *running mode* for short periods of time to process interrupts or to respond to user input. The system is considered to be in running mode when it is actually executing instructions. All peripherals are powered up in running mode. Here's a piece of trivia you can use at your next cocktail party: According to the Palm's documentation, most applications put the system into running mode only 5 percent of the time.

Use EvtGetEvent() to get the next system event since doing so causes power management to be done automatically.

Use SysTaskDelay() to perform delays because doing so conserves as much power as possible. Do not make a delay loop of your own.

The Microkernel

The Microkernel is a pre-emptive multi-tasking kernel providing basic task management. The functionality provided by the Microkernel is used primarily by the system, not directly by applications.

Most of the System manager's tasks are transparent to applications. Therefore, applications need not be concerned with this API.

Application support

Application support is provided by the System manager for application launching and cleanup, event processing, and inter-application communication. Applications are launched via three mechanisms: user presses button, user selects application icon, another application launches an application. Cleanup is performed by the System manager; however, your application should also perform cleanup tasks. Event processing is supported by the System manager. The System manager provides the infrastructure for event generation and handling. Inter-application communication is supported by the System manager via the capability of one application to send a launch code to another application.

The System manager functions are:

- SysAppLaunch(): Launches an application as a subroutine of the caller. Opens an application from a given database and card.
- SysAppLauncherDialog(): Displays the launcher popup, receives the input, sends request to system to launch, cleans up, and quits.
- SysBatteryInfo(): Retrieves the battery's settings.
- SysBatteryInfoV20(): Retrieves the battery's settings.
- SysBinarySearch(): Searches elements in an ascending sorted array for the specified data according to a specified comparison function.
- SysBroadcastActionCode(): Sends the given launch code and parameter block to every UI application.
- SysCopyStringResource(): Copies a resource string to a passed string.
- SysCreateDataBaseList(): Generates a list of databases which match a specific type that are found on the memory cards.
- SysCreatePanelList(): Generates a list of panels that are found on the memory cards.
- SysCurAppDatabase(): Returns the card number and database ID of the current application's resource database.
- SysErrString(): Looks up the textual description of a system error number and creates a string that can be used to display the error.
- SysFatalAlert(): Displays a fatal alert.
- SysFormPointerArrayToStrings(): Forms an array of pointers to strings in a block.
- SysGetOSVersionString(): Returns the version number of the Palm device's operating system.

- ✔ `SysGetRomToken()`: Returns the value of a specified token from ROM.
- ✔ `SysGetStackInfo()`: Returns the start and end of the current thread's stack.
- ✔ `SysGraffitiReferenceDialog()`: Displays the Graffiti Reference dialog.
- ✔ `SysGremlins()`: Accepts parameters for a function, performs the function call, and returns the result.
- ✔ `SysHandleEvent()`: Handles defaults for system events.
- ✔ `SysInsertionSort()`: Sorts elements in an array according to a comparison function.
- ✔ `SysInstall()`: Entry point for the System code resource 'CODE' #0 in the System resource file.
- ✔ `SysKeyboardDialog()`: Displays the system keyboard if there is a field object with the focus.
- ✔ `SysKeyboardDualogV10()`: Displays the system keyboard if there is a field object with the focus.
- ✔ `SysLibFind()`: Given a name, this function returns the reference number for an already loaded library.
- ✔ `SysLibLoad()`: Given a database creator and type this function loads a library.
- ✔ `SysQSort()`: Sorts elements in an array according to a comparison function. This sort scrambles the ordering of the records.
- ✔ `SysRandom()`: Returns a random number.
- ✔ `SysReset()`: Performs a soft reset and reinitializes the dynamic memory heap and globals.
- ✔ `SysSetAutoOffTime()`: Sets the time out value (in seconds) for auto-power off.
- ✔ `SysStringByIndex()`: Using an index this function copies a string out of a string list resource.
- ✔ `SysTaskDelay()`: Puts the processor into doze mode for a specified number of ticks.
- ✔ `SysTicksPerSecond()`: Returns the number of ticks per second.
- ✔ `SysUIAppSwitch()`: Quits the current UI application and starts another UI application that is specified by database ID and card number.

We use several of these functions in various example programs throughout the book.

Many example programs, such as the Chat example from Bonus Chapter 1, need to break out of the EvtGetEvent() Palm OS function if no event is received within a specific period of time. Rather than hard-coding the number of ticks to use in this call, we use the SysTicksPerSecond() System manager function, like this:

```
EvtGetEvent(&event, SysTicksPerSecond() / 5);
```

This lets us specify a 1/5th of a second timeout, without needing to know (or care!) how many ticks that is on any given Palm device.

The SysLibFind() function is used in the examples of Chapters 14 and 15 to locate and load the Serial and Network libraries. You'll need to use this function in these cases.

The SysKeyboardDialog() and SysGraffitiReferenceDialog functions are used by any program that fully implements an Edit menu. Two standard Menu items of the Edit menu are Keyboard and Graffiti Help. When the user selects either Menu item, you call the corresponding System manager function. We do this in the Simple Pin example of Chapter 9:

```
case Edit_GraffitiHelp:
    SysGraffitiReferenceDialog(referenceDefault);
    break;
  case Edit_Keyboard:
    SysKeyboardDialog(kbdDefault);
    break;
```

When you want to prevent the Palm device from powering off, the SysSetAutoOffTime() function is tempting. You might think that you can set the power off time so high that the unit will never power off. Resist the urge, and instead call the EvtResetAutoOffTimer() Palm OS function every so often. As its name implies, this function resets the auto off timer. Suppose that you're checking for some serial input every ⅕ of a second, as we do in the Chat example of Bonus Chapter 1. If you call EvtResetAutoOffTimer() every time you check for input, the device will never power off. When you stop checking for input (and resetting the auto off timer), the device will power off normally after the user-selected idle time has expired.

Part III
Targeted Applications

The 5th Wave   By Rich Tennant

"Well, here's what happened—I forgot to put it on my 'To Do' List."

In this part . . .

Part III concentrates on doing things with your applications. You will see how to do important things like save and retrieve information, communicate with other computers, and synchronize information with the desktop. We give you plenty of examples and lots of useful stuff to get you going with databases, inter-application communication, and conduits.

After you are through with this part, all your applications will become first class Palm citizens: They'll give the built-in applications a run for their money!

Chapter 12

Out to Launch

L aunch codes are the key to integrating your application into the family of applications installed on a Palm device. This chapter talks about launch codes, what they are and the details you need to know in order to effectively use them. But before we can do that, we need to tell you why launch codes exist.

Understanding Launch Codes

Suppose that you're the Palm OS, and you need to communicate to an application that is currently active. No big deal, other than the fact that you now have to live in a tiny little device. You just send an event to the application, to be processed on the event queue. But what do you do if you want to communicate with an application that isn't active? Do you make it active, "talk" to it, and then quit? Hardly. This would be a disaster. For example, suppose that you needed to get information from every application loaded on the Palm device. Imagine activating each and every application, one after the other, getting the desired information, and then quitting each application. No, don't do it. We changed our minds. If you do imagine this, you might get a big headache. So what's a developer to do?

The answer is launch codes. A *launch code* is the way that the Palm OS specifies to an application the reason for launching it, and what the application is to do. Many launch codes have a parameter block associated with them. A *parameter block* is a pointer to a structure that contains parameters that hold information required to handle the launch code. An application's `PilotMain()` function receives the launch code and its parameters.

Some scenarios require launch codes. These are:

- ✔ Doing a Find causes the Palm OS to request that each installed application search for any records that match the Find request.
- ✔ After data is synchronized by using HotSync, each application is notified.
- ✔ Resetting the Palm device causes each application to be notified that a reset has occurred.
- ✔ Powering up causes applications to be notified.
- ✔ Changing the country or the system date and time causes each application to be notified.
- ✔ Beaming data causes the Palm OS to tell the application that is registered to receive the data to actually receive the data.
- ✔ When it is necessary for the system to tell an application to save data. This often happens just before a Find is performed.

More scenarios exist, but the preceding list should give you a good idea of when launch codes are sent to your application.

Launch codes have various *launch flags* associated with them. These launch flags specify information about how the application is to handle the launch codes. Two examples of launch flags are the indications that the application:

- ✔ Is the active application
- ✔ Needs to create new global variables

Some things you should know about launch codes are:

- ✔ Launch codes allow direct communication between an application and the Palm OS, and between two applications.
- ✔ The direct communication involving launch codes takes priority over Events in an application's queue.
- ✔ The Palm OS uses launch codes to request information from an application, or to request that an application do something. This may involve interrupting other activities if necessary.
- ✔ Launch codes can be sent from the system's top level as well as from another application.
- ✔ When a launch code is sent from an application to another application, the launch flag should be set to zero.
- ✔ An application can ignore the launch flag even if it chooses to handle a particular launch code. There are some situations where you can get into trouble doing this, so we tell you when you must examine the launch flag.

Preparing for Launch

In this section, we provide a good background from which you can explore the wonderful world of launch codes. As you might expect, all this action happens within the `PilotMain()` function of your program.

You can find much more information about launch codes in the documentation provided by Palm. This documentation is available as Ref1.pdf, installed as part of CodeWarrior in the Third Party Bools\Palm folder, or as part of the Palm 3.0 SDK in the Docs directory. (You can download Palm 3.0 SDK from `www.palm.com/devzone/tools/sdk.html`.) To read this information, you need Adobe Acrobat, which can be found in the Tools\Acrobat folder on the CD-ROM.

The Web is also a great place to get more information. See `www.palm.com/developer`.

The general steps involved in preparing an application to accept launch codes are:

1. **Determine which launch codes you need to handle.**

2. **In your `PilotMain()` function, create a `case` block for each launch code you need to handle.**

3. **In each `case` block, check the launch flags to see if the launch flags indicate that this is a callback, or if your program needs to allocate global variables.**

4. **Call functions that perform the desired actions, based on the launch code.**

5. **Code the functions correctly, so they do or do not access global memory as appropriate.**

The first step is to figure out which launch codes you need to handle. Obviously, all programs need to handle the normal launch code. But what about the other 16 codes? It really does depend on what your application does. The best way to begin is to get a better understanding of all the launch codes.

Cracking the Codes

This section gets down to the nitty-gritty of the codes themselves. It provides each code and briefly describes the request that it is making.

Listing the codes

So that no code's feelings were hurt, we listed them alphabetically:

- ✔ `sysAppLaunchCmdAlarmTriggered`: Sent so that an application can perform fast, non-blocking, actions such as scheduling the next alarm or playing an alarm sound.

- ✔ `sysAppLaunchCmdCountryChange`: Sent so that an application can respond to a change in country. An application receiving this code should change the display of numbers.

- ✔ `sysAppLaunchCmdDisplayAlarm`: Sent so that an application can perform lengthy, possible blocking, actions to handle alarm-related actions. Notification dialogs are commonly displayed when this launch code is used.

- ✔ `sysAppLaunchCmdExgAskUser`: Exchange manager sends this launch code to an application when data needs to be given to the application. The launch code allows the application to choose whether or not to display a dialog asking users whether they want to receive information.

- ✔ `sysAppLaunchCmdExgReceiveData`: Notifies an application that it will be receiving incoming data by way of the exchange manager.

- ✔ `sysAppLaunchCmdFind`: This launch command is used to perform the global Find. It requests that an application find a particular text string.

- ✔ `sysAppLaunchCmdGoto`: Requests that an application go to a particular record, display it, and optionally select the specified text. This launch code is sent in conjunction with `sysAppLaunchCmdFind` to allow a user to inspect the record returned from a global Find. Or this launch code is sent in conjunction with `sysAppLaunchCmdExgReceiveData` to allow a user to inspect the data received from the exchange manager.

- ✔ `sysAppLaunchCmdInitDatabase`: This launch code is sent by the Desktop Link Server to an application whose creator ID matches the requested database. The system creates the database and passes it to the application for initialization. The application initializes the database and then passes the unclosed database back.

- ✔ `sysAppLaunchCmdLookup`: This launch code is used to perform a search in an application. It is different from the global Find in that it is not a straightforward "look this up" kind of thing. For example, an address that is associated with a specific telephone number is searched for. This involves looking up information related to other information, whereas a global Find is just "look this up as it is."

- ✔ `sysAppLaunchCmdNormalLaunch`: Tells an application to launch normally.

- ✔ `sysAppLaunchCmdPanelCalledFromApp`: This launch code allows an application to let users change preferences without switching to the Preferences application. Tells the Preference Panel that it was invoked via an application and not through the Preferences application.

✔ `sysAppLaunchCmdReturnFromPanel`: Notifies an application that it is restarting after the Preferences Panel has been called. Used in conjunction with `sysAppLaunchCmdPanelCalledFromApp`.

✔ `sysAppLaunchCmdSaveData`: Tells an application to save all data. Often performed just before a global Find.

✔ `sysAppLaunchCmdSyncNotify`: Notifies an application that a HotSync has been completed.

✔ `sysAppLaunchCmdSystemLock`: Tells the system's internal security application to lock the device.

✔ `sysAppLaunchCmdSystemReset`: Notifies an application that the system had a soft or hard reset. Upon receiving this launch code an application can perform initializing, indexing, and other setup activities. No user interface is allowed during the processing of this launch code.

✔ `sysAppLaunchCmdTimeChange`: Tells an application to respond to a time change that was initiated by a user.

Well that's the list. Not bad at all. But before we get on with the chapter, we need to also provide you with a short list of launch flags.

Flagging the details

Launch flags are extra bits of information that are supplied with a launch code. When your application gets a launch code, it may also have one or more of these launch flags set. Don't forget that when an application is launched with any launch command, it is also passed a set of launch flags. Here are the launch flags:

✔ `sysAppLaunchFlagNewGlobals`: Create a new globals world for the application. This really means your application should do whatever it normally does at startup.

✔ `sysAppLaunchFlagNewStack`: This launch flag creates a separate stack for the application.

✔ `sysAppLaunchFlagNewThread`: This launch flag creates a new thread for the application.

✔ `sysAppLaunchFlagUIApp`: Notifies launch function that this is a UI application that is being launched.

✔ `sysAppLaunchFlagSubCall`: Notifies an application it should treat the launch code as a subroutine call. The application can access global variables normally.

Switching the codes

The simplest approach to dealing with launch codes is to have a `switch` statement in your `PilotMain()` function. This is Step 2 in the step-by-step process. This is a basic `PilotMain()` function:

```
DWord PilotMain(Word cmd, Ptr cmdPBP, Word launchFlags) {
   Boolean launched = false;

   switch (cmd) {
   case sysAppLaunchCmdNormalLaunch:
      // Normal launch stuff here
      break;
   case sysAppLaunchCmdSaveData:
      {
#ifdef __GNUC__
      CALLBACK_PROLOGUE
#endif
      // Save Data stuff here
#ifdef __GNUC__
      CALLBACK_EPILOGUE
#endif
      }
      break;
   case sysAppLaunchCmdGoTo:
      launched = launchFlags & sysAppLaunchFlagSubCall;
      if (!launched) {
      // Do same stuff you would do in a normal launch
      // Then go to the selected record/Form
      }
      else {
#ifdef __GNUC__
      CALLBACK_PROLOGUE
#endif
      // Just go to the selected record/Form
#ifdef __GNUC__
      CALLBACK_EPILOGUE
#endif
      }
      break;
   // Other cases for other launch codes
   }
   return error;
}
```

This is not a complete, working `PilotMain()` function; it's just intended to give you an idea of what to do.

You see here a simple `switch` statement, followed by `case` blocks for a couple of launch codes.

Notice that for the `sysAppLaunchCmdSaveData` launch code, we use the `CALLBACK_PROLOGUE` and `CALLBACK_EPILOGUE` macros inside of a new set of curly braces, around whatever we do to handle the launch code. That's because we can be sure that this launch code is only sent as a subroutine call, without even checking the launch flags.

The `sysAppLaunchCmdGoTo` launch code case block does check the launch flags to see if they contain `sysAppLaunchFlagSubCall`. If they don't, then we know we need to perform all the normal application initialization as we did for the normal launch code. If they did contain this flag, then we don't need to do the initialization, but we do need to wrap our code with the macros, because this is a subroutine call.

You've seen Step 3 in the step-by-step process in action here. We check the launch flags (when we have to) to figure out if this is a callback, or subroutine call as it is also called.

The fourth step, calling functions to do the work associated with handling the launch codes, isn't shown in this example. You just put function calls in each `case` block to functions you write to handle the codes as needed.

The fifth and final step needs a bit more explaining.

Avoiding globals like the plague

Coding the functions you call when processing launch codes takes a little care. There are only two scenarios possible for these functions:

- ✔ They are called from a launch code with the `sysAppLaunchFlagSubCall` launch flag set.
- ✔ They are called from a launch code without the `sysAppLaunchFlagSubCall` launch flag set.

When that launch flag is set, then it's just as if you were calling the function from your own program. You can access globals, and they'll have whatever value you put in them before the call. When that launch flag is not set, you cannot access your global variables at all. Doing so will generate a nasty run-time error, and your application will crash. This is obviously a bad thing.

The solution is simple: avoid accessing global variables when you're writing functions that you know might be called without the `sysAppLaunchFlagSubCall` launch flag set. It turns out that this only happens for a few launch codes, so it's not that big a deal.

The only global variable you may be tempted to use is the one holding your application preferences anyway. It's a common practice to read the application preferences into a global when the application starts, and then write them back when the application ends. The solution is to read in the preferences into a local variable when coding a function that needs access to them.

A typical scenario is dealing with Find. When doing a Find, the system sends the sysAppLaunchCmdFind launch code to all applications. That means there will be times when your application is not running and it gets this launch code, and other times that it is running. Rather than write two versions of your function that perform a Find, you should just have one version that doesn't access any globals.

Here's the Search() function from the example in Chapter 8. It finds all matches in our preferences data based on the user's search criteria:

```
static void Search(FindParamsPtr findParams,
      Boolean launched) {
   Word pos, i;
   UInt fieldNum;
   RectangleType r;
   Boolean match;
   SimplePinPreferenceType loadPrefs;
   Word prefsSize;

   findParams->more = false;
   prefsSize = sizeof(SimplePinPreferenceType);
   if (PrefGetAppPreferences(appFileCreator, appPrefID,
         &loadPrefs, &prefsSize, true) ==
         noPreferenceFound) return;
   if (FindDrawHeader(findParams, "PIMs")) {
      findParams->more = true;
      return;
   }
   for (i = findParams->recordNum; i < 10; i++) {
      if (loadPrefs.PinDetail[i].Used) {
      if ((match =
            FindStrInStr(loadPrefs.PinDetail[i].Name,
            findParams->strToFind. &pos)) == true)
               fieldNum = Detail_PIN_NameField;
      else if ((match =
            FindStrInStr(loadPrefs.PinDetail[i].PIN,
            findParams->strToFind, &pos)) == true)
               fieldNum = Detail_PINField;
      if (match) {
         CharPtr matchStr = loadPrefs.PinDetail[i].Name;
         findParams->recordNum = i;
         if (FindSaveMatch(findParams, i, pos,
               fieldNum, 0, 0, 0)) {
            findParams->more = true;
            return;
         }
         FindGetLineBounds(findParams, &r);
         WinDrawChars (matchStr, StrLen(matchStr),
               r.topLeft.x, r.topLeft.y);
         findParams->lineNumber++;
      }
   }
  }
 }
}
```

The first thing you'll notice is that we read in the preferences into a local variable, right at the top of this function. In this program, those preferences are usually stored in a global variable. However, we can't be sure we have access to the globals in all cases, so we play it safe and read the preferences into a local variable in this function.

The rest of the function does what you always need to do when you handle Find. There are six steps to doing Find right:

1. **Access the data you're searching.**

   This might be stored in your application preferences, as it is here, or it may be in a database.

2. **Display the header for your results by calling the** `FindDrawHeader()` **Palm function.**

   This function returns `true` if the Find dialog is out of space. In that case, you need to exit your function, setting the `findParams->more` value to `true` first.

3. **Iterate over your data, starting at position** `findParams->recordNum.`

4. **Test every text field of your data against the search string, using the** `FindStrInStr()` **Palm function.**

5. **When you find a match, stop testing the current record, and display it as a match. This is a four-step process in itself:**

   a. **Set** `findParams->recordNum` **to the matching record number.**

   b. **Call the** `FindSaveMatch()` **Palm function, passing in the** `findParams`**, record number, position in the field where the match occurs, the field number of the match, and other information you need to locate and display the match if the user chooses it from the results.**

   This function also returns `true` if there is no more room to display matches. If that happens, set `findParams->more` to `true` and exit your function.

   c. **Determine where to draw the matching string by calling the** `FindGetLineBounds()` **Palm function.**

   d. **Draw the matching text string by calling the** `WinDrawChars()` **Palm function and using the correct** x **and** y **positions determined in the preceding step.**

6. **Continue the search at the next record number.**

Dealing with Common Codes

Seventeen launch codes sure sounds daunting, but fortunately, they travel in packs, much like wild dogs do. Like any good pack, groups of launch codes have a leader, or at least a central theme that binds them together.

The following sections examine the most common activities and their associated launch codes.

Handling alarms

If you set an alarm, you'll receive the `sysAppLaunchCmdAlarmTriggered` launch code first, followed shortly by `sysAppLaunchCmdDisplayAlarm`. You must check the launch flags when handling these alarms, since it's very possible that the user has left your application well before any alarm you set has gone off.

Handling Find

If your application stores textual data (either in a database or in the application preferences) it really should handle the Find Events. If your application is the application running when the user taps Find, it gets a `sysAppLaunchCmdSaveData` launch code. It can only get this if the application is running, so you can safely assume it is a subroutine call. If you want to be paranoid, you can check the launch flag to see if it is `sysAppLaunchFlagSubCall`, but it always is. This is your application's notification that it needs to save any changes the user has made right away. Save the data in the current Form, if appropriate, and also save the application preferences, if they might be used to do the search.

Next, your application receives the `sysAppLaunchCmdFind` launch code. Check the launch flags to determine if your application has access to global variables, or code your search function such that it doesn't use any global variables. Your application returns any matches and then returns.

If the user selects one of the matches from your application, it receives the `sysAppLaunchCmdGoto` launch code. You must check the launch flags to see if your application is already running (`sysAppLaunchFlagSubCall`) and if not, you need to do all the same things your application normally does when it's launched. Then you display the match and enter a normal event loop, just as if the program was launched normally.

If your application was already running, you just display the match in the appropriate form.

See Chapter 9 for an example of handling the `sysAppLaunchCmdGoto` launch code.

Handling exchanges

The Exchange manager hides a lot of the messy details of exchanging data between two Palm devices (or a Palm device and some other IR-enabled device) via infrared. We talk more about the Exchange manager in Chapter 11.

If your application supports beaming, it will need to deal with these launch codes. The first code your application receives is often not handled at all, since the default behavior is the most desirable. This is the `sysAppLaunchCmdExgAskUser` launch code. If you choose to handle it, your application can decide to always accept or always reject exchanges. If you don't handle it, the user will be prompted to choose to accept or reject an exchange.

If your program or the user accepts an exchange, the `sysAppLaunchCmdExgReceiveData` launch code is sent to the application, and it uses the information supplied to receive the data. Since your application may have to update its display if it is the running application, it should check the launch flags to determine whether it is running.

Working with Preferences

It's possible to integrate your application into the built-in Preferences application. Your application may want to open Preferences to a particular panel on behalf of the user. When you want this to happen, your application sends the `sysAppLaunchCmdPanelCalledFromApp` launch code to the preferences application by using the `SysUIAppSwitch()` Palm function.

When Preferences closes after it was opened in this way, your application receives the `sysAppLaunchCmdReturnFromPanel` launch code. By using this technique, you can give the user access to a preference panel such as the Network, Modem, or Formats preferences, directly from your application. When the user is done, they're returned to your application.

An example of this is the HotSync application. Tap the Menu button, tap Options, and then tap Modem Setup, and you see the Preferences application opened to the Modem preferences. When you tap the Done button, you're returned to the HotSync application. It's not done with smoke and mirrors; it's done with these launch codes!

Handling HotSync

HotSyncs happen, as the saying goes. When HotSyncs happen, your application might just find itself with a whole lot of new or changed information in its associated databases. Your application might what to have a look at that new information as soon as it arrives, so there's a launch code named `sysAppLaunchCmdSyncNotify` that's sent to all applications after a HotSync is completed.

Since HotSync must be launched to do a synchronization, your application will never be the current application when it receives this launch code. It doesn't need to check the launch flags, you can just assume that it does not have access to global variables when it handles this launch code.

The other HotSync launch code has to do with restoring databases. It's `sysAppLaunchCmdInitDatabase`, and your application should create the database and return it, still open and ready for use by HotSync. Like the other HotSync launch code, just assume that you do not have access to global variables when handling this launch code.

Handling other big changes in the Palm device

The remaining launch codes don't really belong in a pack — they're the lone wolves of the launch code world. About the closest thing they have to each other is that they all indicate something fundamental has changed in the Palm device.

Resetting the device

We're not sure why, but the `sysAppLaunchCmdSystemReset` launch code is sent to every application after a system reset. Since no applications are running after a reset, you can bet your application isn't the running application! It's also not a good idea to display any sort of forms, alerts, or dialogs when handling this launch code.

Changing the time

Since time is relative, and precious, your application gets the `sysAppLaunchCmdTimeChange` launch code when the user changes the time. Although you might think this could never happen while your application is running, since you must enter Preferences to change the time, it's possible to change the time via a Palm OS call within your own application. For this reason, you might need to check the launch flags to discover if your application is already running when you get this launch code.

Taking a trip

If your user crosses an international border, they're going to change country codes. Hence the `sysAppLaunchCmdCountryChange` launch code is your application's cue to display its numbers, times, currency, and whatnot as appropriate for the new location.

Making Codes For Fun and Profit

You're probably asking yourself, how can I get in on all this fun and make my own codes? Okay, you're probably not asking yourself that, but we're telling you how anyway.

There is actually a good reason to make your own launch codes, since they allow two or more applications to talk to each other, and in fact control each other, without the user really knowing about it. This lets you do lots of nifty stuff, like create shared libraries of code that gets called by lots of different applications. Or you can create truly massive applications that are actually made up of several smaller applications, flipping back and forth via launch codes.

The only hard rule with making your own launch codes is that they must be numbered in the range 32768–65535. That's right! You only have 32,000 or so free numbers to use. We bet you'll be able to squeeze your codes in there.

Defining a launch code is a simple as picking a number in that range and then making sure both the sender and receiver agree on it. The sender simply uses it in one of two Palm function calls:

- ✔ `SysUIAppSwitch()`: To close the current application and start the new application with a user interface.
- ✔ `SysAppLaunch()`: To call the new application as a subroutine.

The called application simply has a `case` block in their `PilotMain()` switch statement with the appropriate numeric value, and presto, the two are communicating via launch codes.

Chapter 13

Storing Information

· ·

· ·

*I*f events are the engine that drives an application, and the user interface is the steering wheel, then databases are the gas tank. You may never need to put a tiger in your application's tank, but you will need to put information into it. When you're ready to keep track of information in your applications, it's time to understand how to use databases.

Databases in the Palm OS are not quite like anything you may have already seen in the computer world. That's because they're tuned to the unique characteristics of the Palm device. Those characteristics are:

- ✔ No floppy, hard, or even slipped disk

- ✔ Limited memory

- ✔ Relatively slow CPU

- ✔ A user expectation for instant responses to every action

These characteristics have lead to some interesting design choices by the folks at Palm. For the Palm OS, a *database* is:

- ✔ Just a bunch of chunks of protected memory

- ✔ A collection of variably sized records

- ✔ Usually kept sorted in a specific order

- ✔ Without multiple indexes

- ✔ A do-it-yourself proposition

Although you may have heard of some of the terms in that list already, we'd like to make sure that we're all talking about the same thing:

- ✔ A *chunk* is a contiguous segment of memory of a specific length. It is *protected* from access from your (and all other) programs, except via specific Palm OS functions. That means that you can't just set a pointer to random memory locations and write data.

- ✔ A *record* is the smallest directly accessible chunk of information in a database. It contains all the relevant information for one item. A Palm OS record is simply a chunk of memory. It's up to your application to decide how to interpret the memory. A record has a local ID that uniquely identifies its memory chunk, and an index that identifies its sort position in the database.

- ✔ A *database* is a collection of records. A Palm OS database has a bit of information about the database itself (the application creator code, some flags, and some application specific information such as the categories used) and then has a list of all the records in the database. The list keeps the local ID, category, and other flags for each record, in whatever order you put it in.

- ✔ A database maintains a single list of records, which acts as the sole *index*. If you maintain the index in a sorted order, you can access the records in sorted order, or quickly locate a specific record. Fortunately, there are a couple of Palm OS functions for sorting databases that work very quickly.

- ✔ For everything to work correctly, you've got to *do a lot of work yourself*. This includes inserting new records into the proper position for the desired sort order, resorting the list when you edit a record, and moving deleted records to the end of the database.

You have to attend to a great deal of little details when you're working with databases, but we're going to get you through it all. One thing that helps is to have a good understanding of how the Palm OS deals with memory.

Improving Your Memory

The Palm OS manages all of the memory in the Palm device. The memory is divided into two categories:

- ✔ Dynamic memory
- ✔ Storage memory

These two types of memory coexist within the RAM of the Palm device. To help manage memory, the Palm OS groups it into large blocks, called *heaps*. The total dynamic memory is contained in a single heap, while the storage memory contains one or more heaps.

Getting a dynamic memory

The dynamic memory is where your programs get memory when they execute. It's a lot like the RAM in your desktop PC, in that it only holds information while a program is running. When you reset a Palm device, this memory is cleared. Dynamic memory is further carved up into five categories:

- ✔ **System globals:** Includes the screen buffer, user interface globals, database references, and other operating system data.
- ✔ **TCP/IP stack:** Used for network communications, which we cover in Chapter 16.
- ✔ **System dynamic allocation:** Allocated by the system during a Find, Beam, and other tasks.
- ✔ **Stack for the currently running application:** All the local variables are stored here.
- ✔ **Free space:** The currently running application's global variables, static variables, and allocated memory are stored here.

The amount of memory available in each category varies based on the Palm device. Table 13-1 summarizes the available memory in each category for each OS version/memory configuration.

Table 13-1	**Available Memory By OS**			
Category (512KB)	*OS 3.1 (4MB)*	*OS 3.0 (>1MB)*	*OS 2.0 (1MB)*	*OS 2.0/1.0*
Total dynamic memory	128KB	96KB	64KB	32KB
System globals	about 2.5KB	about 2.5KB	about 2.5KB	about 2.5KB
TCP/IP Stack	32KB	32KB	32KB	0KB (not available)
System dynamic allocation	more than 15KB (varies)	more than 15KB (varies)	about 15KB	about 15KB
Application stack	8KB	4KB	2.5KB	2.5KB
Free space	60KB or less	36KB or less	12KB or less	12KB or less

It's pretty obvious that we're not talking about a lot of memory here. When writing your application, you must be mindful of these very tight memory constraints. If you write a function that has a 3KB array as a local variable, it won't run correctly on a machine with less than 2MB of memory.

Although 3KB sounds like a lot, this simple declaration uses that much memory:

```
DWord myLocalArray[770];
```

This statement allocates an array of 4 byte entries. Multiplying that by 770 entries puts the total allocation at 3080 bytes, which is a shade more than 3KB.

It's even worse than you might think, since the application stack is just that, a stack of memory. When you call a function from within a function, the local variables from both functions (along with some other stuff) have to fit on the stack at the same time.

Does this mean the Palm OS is hopelessly inadequate for all but the simplest of applications? No, it just means you need to do a bit of work managing memory yourself.

Follow these rules for using dynamic memory:

- ✔ Create only small local variables. If a variable needs to be larger than 100 bytes, it probably shouldn't be a local variable.

- ✔ For larger local variables, a simple solution is to declare them `static`. This moves them into the much larger Free space area while keeping them usable only in the function they are declared in. The Free space area is still limited to 12–36KB.

- ✔ Use globals for small to medium sized variables that you need to access throughout your program.

- ✔ Use allocated memory for larger, variable sized data.

- ✔ Use databases for truly large data, 5KB or more in size.

We're going to hold off on discussing databases for a little longer and find out more about allocating dynamic memory in the Palm OS.

Using dynamic memory

If you've done any C programming, you've already learned the dreaded `malloc()` and `free()` functions for allocating and freeing memory. If you haven't learned these functions, rejoice: You won't have to unlearn them now. The Palm OS doesn't allocate memory this way, even when you write your programs in C.

Instead, large blocks of memory are carved up into heaps. Heaps are further broken up into chunks. A *chunk* is a block of memory anywhere from 1 byte to 64KB in size. When you want some dynamic memory, you ask for a chunk of a specific size, by using the following Palm OS function:

```
VoidHand MemHandleNew (ULong size)
```

This allocates memory from the Free space, which is between 12 and 36KB in size. Don't expect to allocate huge amounts of memory this way! That's what databases are for.

The MemhandleNew() Palm function allocates a new chunk and returns to you a handle to that chunk. A *handle* is a reference to the memory stored in the chunk, not a pointer. You can't use the memory in the chunk until you lock it. When you *lock* a handle, you get an actual pointer that you can use to access the allocated memory.

Locking the handle tells the Palm OS to leave the chunk where it is in memory; otherwise, when the OS needs to allocate a new chunk, it can move the chunk around to make more room. Since programs contain only handles that reference the chunks of memory, the Palm OS can move all the unlocked chunks as needed. To pull this off, the Palm OS maintains an internal table that maps a handle to a particular chunk's current address. When the chunk moves, this table is updated. The next time your program locks the handle, it gets the new, updated pointer back. When the handle is locked, the OS knows the chunk is in use and cannot be moved.

There are the two reasons to allocate dynamic memory:

- ✔ When you need a local variable larger than will fit on the stack
- ✔ When you need a large global variable that varies in size as the program runs

The following sections look at each case in detail.

Locally dynamic memory

Follow these steps when allocating memory to store a large local value:

1. **Obtain a handle by calling** MemHandleNew(), **store it in a local variable.**

2. **Lock the chunk and get a pointer by calling** MemHandleLock(), **and then store the pointer in a local variable.**

3. **Use the allocated memory in your function, via the pointer.**

4. **Free the chunk by calling** MemHandleFree(), **which also unlocks it.**

You cannot use the pointer obtained in Step 2 after you've freed the chunk. The pointer won't point to valid information, and your program will crash. It's a bad thing.

This small block of code allocates a chunk of memory, locks it, and then frees it:

```
{
    CharPtr memPtr;
    VoidHand memchunk;
    memchunk = MemHandleNew(1024); // allocate 1kb chunk
    memPtr = (CharPtr) MemHandleLock(memchunk); ·
    // do something wonderful with memPtr!
    MemHandleFree(memchunk);
}
```

This style of programming is so common that there are a pair of functions available to do it. Instead of creating a new chunk and then locking it, you can use MemPtrNew() and pass in the desired size. This allocates a chunk, locks it, and returns a pointer all in one call. When you're done, just call MemPtrFree() and pass in the pointer. This unlocks and frees the chunk. We prefer to stick with one set of functions, but you can use these if you like.

The memory pointer returned from MemHandleLock() is a VoidPtr. This type is a general pointer type. It's good programming style to typecast this pointer to the actual type you need. That's why we use (CharPtr) in front of our call.

Global dynamic memory

Follow these steps when allocating memory to store a large global variable that varies in size:

1. **Obtain a handle by calling** MemHandleNew(), **and then store it in a global variable.**

2. **Resize the chunk as needed, by calling** MemHandleResize(). **The Palm OS may need to move the chunk to find a larger free block of memory, so you should unlock it first.**

3. **When you need to access the allocated memory, lock the chunk and get a pointer by calling** MemHandleLock(), **and then store the pointer in a local variable.**

4. **Use the allocated memory as desired, via the pointer.**

5. **Unlock the chunk when you're finished accessing it, by calling** MemHandleUnlock().

6. **When you're done with the allocated memory, free the chunk by calling** MemHandleFree().

You cannot use the pointer obtained in Step 3 after you've unlocked or freed the chunk. You should free the chunk when you're done with it, so your application can allocate it again as needed. The Palm OS frees all handles your application allocated but forgot to free when it exits.

This program fragment illustrates the steps for allocating global dynamic memory:

```
static VoidHand LongString = 0;

static void CreateLongString() {
   CharPtr memPtr;
   LongString = MemHandleNew(sizeof(Char));
   memPtr = (CharPtr) MemHandleLock(LongString);
   *memPtr = '\0';
   MemHandleUnlock(LongString):
}
static void AppendString(CharPtr str) {
   CharPtr memPtr;
   ULong chunkSize;
   chunkSize = MemHandleSize(Memchunk);
   MemHandleResize(chunkSize + StrLen(str) + 1);
   memPtr = (CharPtr) MemHandleLock(LongString);
   StrCat(memPtr, str);
   MemHandleUnlock(LongString):
}
static void FreeLongString() {
   if (LongString) {
      MemHandleFree(LongString);
      LongString = 0;
   }
}
```

This fragment declares a global variable named LongString to hold the handle of the chunk. The CreateLongString() function allocates an initial chunk holding 1 byte and initializes this chunk to hold a zero.

The AppendString() function appends the string pointed to by str to the chunk. It does this by determining the current size of the chunk via the MemHandleSize() Palm function. That function returns the current size of the chunk. This size is increased by the length of the string to add, plus one for the NULL terminator. This new size is used to resize the chunk by calling the MemHandleResize() Palm function. Note that this is called before locking the chunk. To append the string, the chunk is locked to get a pointer to the memory. This is used in the StrCat() Palm function to append the string, and then the chunk is unlocked.

The FreeLongString() function frees the chunk by calling the MemHandleFree() Palm function.

It's not a good idea to free a chunk twice, or to free a chunk that was never allocated, so set the global holding the handle to 0 whenever it does not have an allocated chunk in it. That way, you can test the global to make sure it has an allocated handle in it, before you free it.

Knowing when to lock

In the previous examples, we show a basic pattern of accessing dynamic memory:

1. **Lock the chunk.**
2. **Access the memory.**
3. **Unlock the chunk.**

In general, accessing dynamic memory in this way is a good idea, because a locked chunk can't be moved around by the Palm OS to make room for other memory allocation requests. However, this isn't always going to work for your application. Why, you ask? Some Palm OS function calls take pointers to memory as parameters and then use the pointed-to memory even after the function returns. It's quite handy to use dynamic memory for these pointers, but in this case you must leave the chunk locked. If you unlock the chunk, the pointer you supplied to the Palm function ceases to be valid. You can get some truly befuddling application crashes this way!

You say you want an example? When you have a List on a Form, your program tells the list to display a particular set of values by calling the LstSetListChoices() Palm function. That function takes an array of CharPtr as one of its parameters. This array represents the items to display in the list. If there were ever a candidate for dynamic memory, this is it! The snag is that the list keeps the array you pass in for its own uses. If you do use one or more chunks for this call, they've all got to remain unlocked as long as the list is using them.

Knowing what to unlock

You have two choices when you decide to unlock a chunk. You can use one of the following:

- MemHandleUnlock() and pass in the handle you locked
- MemPtrUnlock() and pass in the pointer you received when you locked the handle

The option you choose is really a matter of convenience. Try to use MemHandleUnlock(), since it's easier to identify the place in the code where you forgot to unlock a chunk that you previously locked.

Now you know the basics of dynamic memory allocation. But what about those times when you need to save the data in memory, even when your application isn't running? That's when it's time to use a database.

Making Memories That Last

The Palm OS clears the dynamic memory heap whenever the Palm device is reset, but it doesn't clear the heaps assigned to storage memory. Storage heaps are where databases live. Recall that a database is just another form of memory allocation, but in this case, the memory is protected from writing via pointers. Instead, you must use special Palm functions to update the values in memory.

To use a database, follow these steps:

1. **Open the database to obtain a** `dbOpenRef` **database reference. This reference is used by all the other database functions.**

2. **If the open fails, create the database and then initialize the database and open it.**

3. **Add a new record to the database and insert it into the proper position to maintain the sort order.**

4. **Locate a specific record in the database quickly.**

5. **Edit an existing record in the database and then resort the database to maintain the sort order.**

6. **Access the records in the database in sorted order.**

7. **Delete, archive, or remove an existing record from the database.**

   Removing a record simply gets rid of it entirely, and deleting and archiving records allows them to also be handled correctly when the data is synchronized with the desktop via a HotSync.

8. **Close the database.**

9. **Delete the database in special cases.**

The following sections examine each step in detail. We're going to need an actual example project to explain how databases work.

The example we've created is a reworking of the Simple Pin example described in Chapter 9. It is a simple application that stores PIN numbers for you. This time, we store the Name and PIN number as records in a database, so that you can have unlimited PINs. We support Categories for organizing the PINs. We also support making a PIN as private, even though it's not shown when the user selects Hide private records in the Security application.

The Simple Pin application is not meant for actual use, it's just an example program, we don't intend for you to rely on it in your real life. Don't use it. Just learn from it.

There is actually a lot of code in Simple Pin that we don't discuss in this chapter. The full source code to the example is on the CD-ROM that accompanies this book in the Examples\Chap13 folder. If you're using CodeWarrior, simply open the project file named simplepindb.mcp. If you're using GCC, the Src subfolder contains all the necessary files, along with a makefile. In either case, all the program code is in the SimplePinDB.c file.

Opening a database

Step 1 in the step-by-step process is opening the database. To open a database, you've got to understand how the Palm OS organizes databases. Each database has a number of fields. These are the most useful:

- ✔ name: This is a string containing whatever you want, up to 31 characters in length. Make sure the database name is unique on the device. A simple way to do this is to add the application creator code to the end of the name, like "SimplePinDB-PDBe." This ensures that the name of every database is unique, which is required by the Palm OS.

- ✔ creator: This is the creator code you've registered for the application to which this database belongs. Recall that the creator code is a four-character code that uniquely identifies your application, such as 'PFDe'.

- ✔ type: This is another code you can use to differentiate multiple databases for the same application.

- ✔ attributes: This is a bunch of flags. They include a flag that indicates that the database should be backed up to the desktop during a HotSync.

- ✔ version: This is the version number used to create the database. If your application changes in the future and the changes involve the internal structure of records, you can detect whether the version of the database matches the version expected by the application by using this field.

When you open a database, you use the creator and type values to locate it, not the name. For example:

```
UInt mode = dmModeReadWrite;
DmOpenRef PinDB;
PinDB = DmOpenDatabaseByTypeCreator('Pins', 'PDBe', mode);
```

The DmOpenDatabaseByTypeCreator() Palm function attempts to locate the database based on your supplied type (in this case 'Pins') and creator code ('PDBe'). If it finds the database, it tries to open it using the supplied mode parameter. The mode can be any combination of these values:

- ✔ dmModeReadWrite: Open for reading and writing

- ✔ dmModeRead: Open just for reading

- ✔ dmModeWrite: Open just for writing

- ✔ dmModeShowSecret: Allow access to secret records

- ✔ dmModeLeaveOpen: Don't close the database when application ends

- ✔ dmModeExclusive: Don't let others open the database at the same time

You can use the DmFindDatabase() function to locate a database by name. Supply a card number (always 0) and the string name as parameters. This function returns a local ID (explained later in this chapter) which you then pass to DmOpenDatabase() Palm function, along with the card number and mode. Here's the same example using this technique:

```
LocalID dbId;
UInt mode = dmModeReadWrite;
DmOpenRef PinDB;
UInt CardNo = 0;
dbId = DmFindDatabase(CardNo, "SimplepinDB-PDBe");
if (dbId)
   PinDB = DmOpenDatabase(CardNo, dbId, mode);
```

As you can see, this is a lot more work than just using the creator and typing codes!

Staying secret

The built-in security application lets the user decide whether the Palm device shows or hides private records. All this does is set a flag in the system's preferences. It's up to your application to do the right thing with it. Since secret records are very nice for the user, and relatively easy to implement, we suggest that you honor the preference setting when using databases. All you need to do is change your open database call to something like this:

```
UInt mode = dmModeReadWrite;
DmOpenRef PinDB;
SystemPreferencesType sysPrefs;

PrefGetPreferences(&sysPrefs);
if ((ShowSecret = !sysPrefs.hideSecretRecords) == true)
   mode |= dmModeShowSecret;
PinDB = DmOpenDatabaseByTypeCreator('Pins', 'PDBe', mode);
```

The PrefGetPreferences() Palm function returns the system preferences. That structure contains a field named hideSecretRecords, which is true when the user selects the Hide option of the Security application. If this is false, then we want to show the records. We just add the dmModeShowSecret flag to our mode in this case, and then open the database as usual.

Creating a database

Step 2 in our step-by-step process is creating and initializing the database. To create a database, you first use the `DmCreateDatabase()` Palm function:

```
Err err
UInt CardNo = 0;
err = DmCreateDatabase(CardNo, "SimplepinDB-PDBe", 'PDBe',
    'Pins', false);
```

The first parameter specifies the card on which to begin the creation of the database. Currently, all Palm devices always have a single card, numbered 0, so just use that. The next parameter is the name of the database, followed by its creator and type codes. The last parameter is always `false` for databases containing data.

If for some reason the create fails, `err` will be the error code. The most common errors are:

- `dmErrAlreadyExists`: The name is not unique.
- `dmErrInvalidDatabaseName`: The name is not valid.
- `dmErrMemError`: You're probably out of memory.
- `dmErrWashOverFlow`: Your washing machine is overflowing.

Opening the SimplePin database

The `StartApplication()` function is the perfect place to open the databases you need to use in your application. That's where we open (or create and then open) our database:

```
static Err StartApplication(void)
{
    Word prefsSize;
    Err err = 0;
    UInt mode = dmModeReadWrite;
    SystemPreferencesType sysPrefs;

    CardNo = 0;
    prefsSize = sizeof(SimplepinDBPreferenceType);
    if (PrefGetAppPreferences(appFileCreator,
            appPrefID, &prefs, &prefsSize, true) ==
                noPreferenceFound)
        CreateDefaultPrefs();
    PrefGetPreferences(&sysPrefs);
    if ((ShowSecret = !sysPrefs.hideSecretRecords) == true)
        mode |= dmModeShowSecret;
    PinDB = DmOpenDatabaseByTypeCreator('Pins', 'PDBe', mode);
    if (! PinDB) {
```

```
        err = DmCreateDatabase(CardNo, "SimplepinDB-PDBe",
            'PDBe', 'Pims', false);
    if (err) return err;
    PinDB = DmOpenDatabaseByTypeCreator('Pins', 'PDBe',
            mode);
    if (!PinDB) return DmGetLastErr();
    err = AppInfoInit(PinDB);
    }
    return err;
}
```

This function begins by reading in your application preferences by using the
`PrefGetAppPreferences()` Palm function. If there are none stored yet, it
calls your `CreateDefaultPrefs()` function to establish default preferences.
Next it checks the system preferences to see if private records should be
shown or not. The global variable `ShowSecret` is set to `true` if we're showing
secret records.

The database is opened. If the open succeeds, the function is done. If the
open fails then the database is created and then opened. Assuming that all
went well, the next step is to initialize the newly created database. This is
where you set the flags to enable backing up the database via HotSync and
where you initialize the category information.

Supporting categories, part 1

Every database has one special record in it called the *application information
record*. This record can contain whatever you want — it's a lot like the application preferences, but it's just for your database. One thing that's very
common to put in this record is the categories currently in use.

The Palm OS supports up to 15 categories. If you use them, the first part of
your application information record must be an `AppInfo` structure. If you're
using CodeWarrior, you must also create an app info resource containing the
initial categories for the application. The first category must be `"Untitled"`.
You've also got to create exactly 16 entries for the categories in Constructor.
After you've done this, it's pretty easy to set up categories in a database.

We initialize our database to use categories in Simple Pin by calling our
`AppInfoInit()` function and passing it in the open database reference:

```
static Err AppInfoInit(DmOpenRef theDB)
{
    UInt CardNo;
    AppInfoPtr appInfoPtr;
    UInt theAttributes;
    VoidHand h = NULL;
    LocalID appInfoID, dbID;
```

(continued)

(continued)

```
    if (DmOpenDatabaseInfo(theDB. &dbID. NULL. NULL.
        &CardNo, NULL))
      return dmErrInvalidParam:
    if (DmDatabaseInfo(CardNo, dbID, NULL, &theAttributes,
        NULL, NULL, NULL, NULL,
        &appInfoID, NULL, NULL, NULL))
      return dmErrInvalidParam;
    if (appInfoID == NULL) {
      h = DmNewhandle(theDB, sizeof (AppInfoType));
      if (! h) return dmErrMemError;
      theAttributes |= dmHdrAttrBackup;
      appInfoID = MemHandleToLocalID(h);
      DmSetDatabaseInfo(CardNo, dbID, NULL, &theAttributes,
          NULL, NULL, NULL, NULL, NULL,
          &appInfoID, NULL, NULL, NULL);
    }
    appInfoPtr = MemLocalIDToLockedPtr(appInfoID, CardNo);
    DmSet (appInfoPtr, 0, sizeof(AppInfoType), 0);
#ifdef __GNUC__
    GNU_CategoryInitialize(appInfoPtr,
    Categories_AppInfoStr);
#else
    CategoryInitialize (appInfoPtr, Categories_AppInfoStr);
#endif
    MemPtrUnlock(appInfoPtr);
    return 0;
}
```

This looks like a lot of code, but it's pretty straightforward. The function gets the database information by using a pair of Palm functions. First it calls `DmOpenDatabaseInfo()` and passes in the `DmOpenRef` of the opened database, and pointers to variables that receive the database ID and card number for the open database. It then uses those two values in a call to `DmDatabaseInfo()` to retrieve the attributes of the database, and the ID of the existing `AppInfo` record. If that ID is `NULL`, then no `AppInfo` record has been created yet, so it allocates a new database record. This is a lot like allocating a new dynamic memory chunk, except `DmNewhandle()` allocates the chunk in a storage memory heap. Next, the attributes flag for the database has its `dmHdrAttrBackup` bit set, so the database will be backed up during HotSyncs. Finally, the `MemHandleToLocalID()` function takes the handle of the `AppInfo` record and returns a local ID to it. The attributes flag and the `AppInfo` record local ID are then written into the database by using the `DmSetDatabaseInfo()` Palm function.

A *local ID* is a lot like a handle, except that it's card independent. This is one of those things that will make more sense when there is ever a Palm device with more than one memory card. All you really need to know is that you must use a local ID for the `AppInfo` record.

You want to know more? Assuming that a Palm device has more than one memory card, all the memory from all the cards is to be arranged sequentially. Suppose that there's a Palm device that supports three cards. If your database is created on the second card, all the chunks that contain its records exist within a range of memory addresses assigned to that card. Now suppose that the user removes the card, puts in a different card, and then puts the card with the database in the third slot. Now all the chunk addresses in the database aren't correct, since the memory addresses for the card have changed. Local IDs to the rescue! A *local ID* is a memory address that is card relative, meaning it is the offset to the chunk, relative to the beginning of the card. Because the Palm OS knows where each card starts in memory, it can convert a local ID to a handle with ease. So internally, a database keeps track of all its records via local IDs. A side effect of this scheme is that all records in a database are allocated on the same card.

After the `AppInfo` record is written to the database, all that's left to do is initialize it with the initial categories for the database. Because every record is just a chunk, you still have to lock the handle before you can access the `AppInfo` record. Because we already have a local ID for the record, we use `MemLocalIDToLockedPtr()` and pass in both the local ID and the card.

Next we want to initialize all the bytes for the `AppInfo` record to 0. Normally, we'd use the `MemSet()` Palm function to do this, but we can't in this case. Because the pointer returned is a pointer to protected memory in the database, we can't just write directly to it. Instead, we must use `DmSet()` to set all the bytes of the record to 0.

The `CategoryInitialize()` Palm function reads the 16 strings in the app info resource (`'tAIS'`) specified by the resource ID you pass in and initializes the `AppInfo` record correctly. If you're using the GNU tools, you'll find there is no way to create this type of resource by using pilrc. See the sidebar titled "GNU and categories" for an explanation of the `GNU_CategoryInitialize()` function, which does the initialization for GNU.

GNU and categories

Normally, using the GNU tools is just like using CodeWarrior, at least as far as the program code is concerned. When you use categories, you can't use the `CategoryInitialize()` Palm function because pilrc doesn't support the `'tAIS'` resource type. Rather than feel left out, or avoid categories, all you need to do is write a function that populates the `AppInfo` structure just like `CategoryInitialize ()` does. That's just what we did. In a burst of creativity, we called it `GNU_CategoryInitialize()`. You can see the code for this function in the `SimplePinDB.c` source file on the CD-ROM. This function accepts a resource ID for a single string resource, and uses it to initialize a single category.

We have one last detail to attend to, and the opening phase is complete. You may be wondering why we bother to make the `AppInfoInit()` function a separate function at all. The answer is not "because we felt like it!"

Always code your database application information initialization as a separate function, because you'll want to call it when you create your database, and when your application receives the `sysAppLaunchCmdInitDatabase` launch code.

This launch code is sent by HotSync when the user restores our database. HotSync creates the database, and then sends this launch code to the application so it can initialize it correctly. The case block in `PilotMain()` that handles this launch code is simple:

```
case sysAppLaunchCmdInitDatabase:
#ifdef __GNUC__
{
CALLBACK_PROLOGUE
#endif
    AppLaunchCmdDatabaseInit
        (((SysAppLaunchCmdInitDatabaseType*)cmdPBP)->dbP);
#ifdef __GNUC__
CALLBACK_EPILOGUE
}
#endif
    break;
```

And our `AppLaunchCmdDatabaseInit()` function is:

```
static Boolean AppLaunchCmdDatabaseInit(DmOpenRef dbP) {
    Err err;
    if (!dbP) return false;
    err = AppInfoInit (dbP);
    if (err) return false;
    return true;
}
```

All this code does is call our `AppInfoInit()` function and pass in the `DmOpenRef` open database reference that HotSync supplies.

Dealing with records

The database is finally open. You're probably ready to see some records added and updated. Anyway, you look ready to us.

Adding records

Step 3 in the step-by-step process is adding records to the database. Fortunately, this is pretty simple. You add a record in one of three ways:

- ✔ At the beginning or end of the database via the DmNewRecord() Palm function.
- ✔ At a specific location via the DmNewRecord() Palm function.
- ✔ Unattached via the DmNewhandle() Palm function, and then insert it at a specific location via the DmAttachRecord() Palm function.

To add a record 100 bytes in size at the beginning of an open database, use code like this:

```
VoidHand newRechandle;
UInt location = 0;
newRechandle = DmNewRecord( dbRef, &location, 100);
```

The record is created at index 0, and all other existing records are shifted down by 1. The call returns a handle to a new record. The record is marked as busy and dirty. This either means that it's a three-year-old, or that the Palm OS won't let anyone else access the record until you say you're done with it by using the DmReleaseRecord() Palm function. The dirty thing means you've changed the record. This dirty flag is used by conduits to decide which records to synchronize. We cover conduits in Chapter 14.

To add a 100-byte-long record to the end of an open database, use this code:

```
VoidHand newRechandle;
UInt location = DmNumRecords(dbRef);
newRechandle = DmNewRecord (dbRef, &location, 100);
```

The record is created at the end because the number of records in a database is always 1 greater than the index of the last record. That's a nice side-effect of starting the indexes off with 0!

You've probably guessed that you can add records anywhere you want by specifying the desired index for the record. That's cool, because it means you can insert records into the correct position in a database that's already sorted, and maintain the sorted order. All you need to do is figure out where to insert the record. That's where the third case comes in:

```
VoidHand newRecordhandle;
VoidPtr newRecord;
UInt newRecordIndex;

newRecordhandle = DmNewhandle (dbRef, sizeof(RecordData));
newRecord = MemHandleLock(newRecordhandle);
DmWrite(newRecord, 0, RecordData, sizeof(RecordData);
```

(continued)

(continued)

```
newRecordIndex = DmFindSortPosition(dbRef, newRecord, 0,
    (DmComparF *) CompareRecordFunc, 0);
DmAttachRecord (dbRef, & newRecordIndex,
    (handle) newRecordhandle, NULL);
MemHandleUnlock(newRecordhandle);
```

This block of code begins by allocating a new record by using the
DmNewhandle() Palm function. This is a record that's not currently assigned a
record index; it's just a chunk of storage memory. Next the handle is locked to
get a pointer to the record memory. The record's data is filled in by using the
DmWrite() Palm function, because the memory is protected from regular
pointer-based writes. Now we're ready to figure out where this new record goes.

Palm provides a general purpose search function called
DmFindSortPosition() that takes a memory handle and a pointer to a function in your program. That function has a specific job: It gets pointers to two
records in the database, and it returns a negative value if the first record is
less than the second, 0 if they are equal, and a positive value if the first is
greater than the second. DmFindSortPosition() quickly searches the current sorted records in the database to figure out exactly where the new
record should be inserted, by calling your function.

It's up to you to code the compare function to create the sorted order you
desire for your application. It can compare just one field of each record,
many fields, or all fields. Let's say your records contain a first name and a last
name field, and you want the database sorted by name. You'd compare the
last names, and if they were equal you'd compare the first names.

Once you have the correct index for the new record, you use
DmAttachRecord() to insert the new record's handle in the appropriate
place, and then you unlock the handle.

Finding records quickly

Step 4 in the step-by-step process is locating a specific record in the database
quickly. In case you haven't guessed, you can use DmFindSortPosition() to
do to just that, if you have the specific values you're looking for. All you need
to do is build a record in dynamic memory containing the desired record's
key information (for example, the first and last name) and then call
DmFindSortPosition(). It will return the index of the record that matches
(or is closest to) this information, or a value 1 greater than the number of
records in the database if none matched.

The DmFindSortPosition() Palm function assumes that all deleted records
are at the end of the database. If you delete or archive a record rather than
remove it, you must move it to the end of the database.

Editing and resorting records in the database

Step 5 in the step-by-step process is editing an existing record in the database and then resorting the database to maintain the sort order. This isn't as hard as you might expect.

To edit a record and then resort the database, you need to:

1. **Find a record you want to edit.**
2. **Use** `DmGetRecord()` **to lock the record and get a handle.**
3. **Lock the handle to get a pointer to the record.**
4. **Do something to edit the record.**
5. **Load the changed information back into the record by using** `DmWrite()`.
6. **If you're supporting categories and/or private records, update the record information Word by using** `DmSetRecordInfo()`.
7. **If necessary, move the record to its new sorted position in the database.**
8. **Use** `DmReleaseRecord()` **to unlock the record and mark it dirty.**

Finding a record is either accomplished by using `DmFindSortPosition()`, or by having the user select an existing record from a list or table. In the latter case, you keep the record indexes associated with each record in an array and use that array to find the record index based on the selection from the list or table.

Of all the steps in the editing and resorting process, the middle ones are the trickiest. Suppose that you've found a record to edit, and you have its index. Steps 2 and 3 are simple:

```
Rechandle = DmGetRecord (dbRef, recordIndex);
recordPtr = (RecordPtr) MemHandleLock (Rechandle);
```

Now you have a pointer to some memory, but what is in that memory? You have two choices when it comes to database records:

✔ C `struct` records, often called *unpacked records*

✔ Packed records

The simple way to make records, even those with string fields, is to use *unpacked records*, represented by a C `struct`. You declare the `struct`, fix the maximum size of every string field, and you're all set. You know how many bytes to read, and exactly where in each record to find every field. In the Simple Pin DB example, this is how we do it using a C `struct`:

```
#define NAME_SIZE 17
#define PIN_SIZE 17
 typedef struct {
   Char Name[NAME_SIZE];
   Char PIN[PIN_SIZE];
} UnpackedRecord;
typedef UnpackedRecord* UnpackedRecordPtr;
static void InitDetailForm() {
   // Other stuff not shown...
   Rechandle = DmGetRecord (PinDB, prefs.editPinNo);
   editRecordPtr =
     (UnpackedRecordPtr)MemHandleLock(Rechandle);
```

This is great, because it means we can just use expressions like
editRecordPtr->Name and editRecordPtr->PIN to get the name and PIN
from the record.

That's exactly what we do in InitDetailForm():

```
SetFieldText(Detail_PIN_NameField, editRecordPtr->Name);
SetFieldText(Detail_PINField, editRecordPtr->PIN);
```

Unfortunately, using unpacked records carries a huge cost in wasted space. It
will always be the case that a good number of the records won't use the full
size for these fixed size strings, and all that extra blank space represents
wasted storage memory. We suggest that you don't use unpacked records to
hold strings that will vary greatly in size.

So, what's a conscientious person to do? Why, they pack the heck out of
every record, squeezing out wasted space. To do this, you need to take a different tack to creating, reading, and updating records.

Now we look at the same portion of InitDetailForm(), but this time we'll
use a *packed record*. That's a record where we don't store any unused
memory in the record. This means that there are no fixed length strings!

```
typedef CharPtr PackedRecordPtr;
#define PACKED_NAME(packRec) ((CharPtr)(packRec))
#define PACKED_PIN(packRec)
   ((CharPtr)(packRec+StrLen(packRec)+1))
static void InitDetailForm() {
   // Other stuff not shown...
   Rechandle = DmGetRecord (PinDB, prefs.editPinNo);
   packedPinRecPtr =
     (PackedRecordPtr)MemHandleLock(Rechandle);
   SetFieldText(Detail_PIN_NameField,
     PACKED_NAME(packedPinRecPtr));
   SetFieldText(Detail_PINField,
     PACKED_PIN(packedPinRecPtr));
```

Designing and updating records

It's recommended that you edit your database records in place to conserve precious memory. That's doubly important if you're considering using local variables to hold a record, because you have very little stack memory available. If you're using a C `struct` to represent an unpacked record, you can read a specific field simply by using the `struct` member variable name, such as `editRecord->PIN`. To write this field back to the database, you must know the offset of the particular `struct` member variable within the structure. You can use the `offsetof()` macro to do this, however that macro is not usually included in the normal Palm OS include files. This is the definition of `offsetof()`, which you can simply place at the top of your source file:

```
#ifndef offsetof
#define offsetof(s,m)
    (size_t)&(((s *)0)->m)
#endif
```

Even if you want to use packed records, your record might contain a mix of variable and fixed size elements. If it contains simple types such as `Int`, `Boolean`, and so on, you can still use a C `struct` to represent the fixed-size portion of the record. Just end the `struct` with a `Char` array of size 1, where you'll actually write the packed strings into the record. For example, a record with two `Int` values followed by three packed strings can use this `stuct`:

```
typedef struct {
    Int height;
    Int weight;
    Char packedNameAddr[1];
} MyRecord;
```

Then when you read this record, use the `struct` member variable names to get the fixed values and to find the start of the packed strings. To write the record, use `offsetof()` to update the fixed values, and to begin writing the packed strings. Use `sizeof(MyRecord)-1` to compute the size of the fixed portion, and add the `StrLen()+1` of each packed string to compute the total size of the packed record.

Notice that we `#define` a pair of macros for accessing the fields of the packed record. The `PACKED_NAME()` macro just returns whatever it has passed, typecast as a `CharPtr`. That's because we always store the name first. The PIN follows the name, right after the `'\0'` byte. The `PACKED_PIN()` macro just computes the length of the Name field, adds one, and returns a pointer to this memory location.

When you create a new packed record, you need to compute the size needed to hold the packed record. This means you need to use the `StrLen()` Palm function (adding one for the `NULL` byte!) for each string you're going to store into the record. When you have the total bytes needed, create the new record.

The Simple Pin DB program does exactly this, when saving a new or edited record from within the PIN Detail Form. That Form contains two Fields that hold the Name and PIN being created or edited. When it's time to save the changes, our SaveDetailForm() function creates a new record or edits an existing one. First, we get pointers to the Name and PIN Field text, and compute the packed record length:

```
CharPtr namePtr, pinPtr;
VoidHand newRecordhandle;
UInt recordSize;
namePtr = FldGetTextPtr((FieldPtr)GetObjectPtr(
    Detail_PIN_NameField));
pinPtr  = FldGetTextPtr((FieldPtr)GetObjectPtr(
    Detail_PINField)):
if (!namePtr) namePtr = "";
if (!pinPtr) pinPtr = "";
nameLen = StrLen(namePtr) + 1;
pinLen = StrLen(pinPtr) + 1;
recordSize = nameLen + pinLen;
```

This is the relevant part of the function when creating a new record:

```
newRecordhandle = DmNewhandle (PinDB, recordSize);
newPinRecord = MemHandleLock(newRecordhandle);
DmWrite(newPinRecord, 0, namePtr, nameLen);
DmWrite(newPinRecord, nameLen, pinPtr, pinLen);
```

The last tricky bit with packed records comes when it's time to update an existing record. When you're using C struct records, an existing record can never change size. Not so with packed records! Suppose that an existing PIN record had a Name of "Bank" and a PIN of "1234". If the user edits this PIN, and changes the Name to "Bank of RainTown", then the packed record size jumps from 10 bytes to 22 bytes. We're going to need to resize the record before we write it! Our SaveDetailForm() function resizes the edited record when it saves it. This is the relevant part of the function:

```
PackedRecordPtr editPackedPinRecord;
Rechandle = DmResizeRecord (PinDB, prefs.editPinNo,
    recordSize);
editPackedPinRecord = (PackedRecordPtr)
    MemHandleLock(Rechandle);
DmWrite(editPackedPinRecord, 0, namePtr, nameLen);
DmWrite(editPackedPinRecord, nameLen, pinPtr, pinLen);
```

We simply resize the record by using the DmResizeRecord() Palm function, then lock the handle. Once we have the pointer to the resized record, we use DmWrite() to write the name and PIN into the appropriate areas of the record.

After the edited record has been written, we need to update the record attributes to reflect the private setting, and the new category of the record. This is accomplished by using the DmSetRecordInfo() Palm function.

Finally, if we edited a record, we need to resort the database. You've got two choices here. The easy way out is to simply resort the database whenever a record changes. This approach is easy on you but hard on the Palm device, because it's often a lot more work than necessary. The harder, but better, way is to test to see if the record needs to be moved at all, and if so to just find its new sort position and move it.

The fastest way to sort a nearly sorted database is by using the
DmInsertionSort() Palm function:

```
DmReleaseRecord(PinDB, prefs.editPinNo, true);
DmInsertionSort (PinDB,
    (DmComparF *)ComparePackedPinFunc, 0);
```

The compare function we pass in is just like the one we use for
DmFindSortPosition(). In fact, it can be the exact same function.

If you want to do things the more battery-friendly way, you need to do a bit more work. First, you need to test to see whether the user changed the bit of the record that determines the sort position of the record. If he did, then you need to figure out the new sort position for the record, and move it there. That's accomplished by creating a dummy record in dynamic memory, that just contains the portion of the edited record needed for sorting. Then call DmFindSortPosition(), passing in the dummy record, to find the index where the record really belongs. Then move the edited record to the new location by calling DmMoveRecord(), passing in the old and new indexes. It seems like a lot of work, but your batteries will thank you.

Always release a record once you're done with it. You do this by using the DmReleaseRecord() Palm function. If you don't want the record marked as dirty, pass false as the last parameter.

Sequentially accessing records

Step 6 in the step-by-step process is accessing the records in the database in sorted order. It's devilishly simple. All you need to do is call the DmQueryNextInCategory() Palm function, passing in an open database DmOpenRef, a pointer to the record number to begin at, and the category to return or dmAllCategories to get all records. This code fragment visits every non-deleted record in a database:

```
UInt recordIndex;
handle searchRechandle;
recordIndex = 0;
for (;;) {
    searchRechandle = DmQueryNextInCategory (dbRef,
        &recordIndex, dmAllCategories);
    if (searchRechandle == NULL) break;
    // do something with the record
    recordIndex+++;
}
```

Getting rid of records

Step 7 in the step-by-step process is deleting, archiving, or removing an existing record. Actually doing any of these things is a matter of a Palm function call, deciding which one to use is the key.

If you're not ever going to write a conduit for the application, just remove the record. That's accomplished by using the DmRemoveRecord() Palm function:

```
DmRemoveRecord (dbRef, recordIndex);
```

If you are going to have a conduit, your desktop database will surely want to know that a record was deleted. The only way to pull that off is to not really remove the record, but rather to mark it as deleted and leave the final removal up to the conduit. When you delete a record, the record chunk is freed but the record information entry is retained and marked as deleted. When you archive a record, the entire record is retained but marked as deleted.

In these cases, it's quite typical to have a delete confirmation dialog appear. The dialog contains a checkbox where the user indicates if they want the record to be archived on the desktop. The Simple Pin DB example application includes this dialog. The code that handles the archive or delete based on the user choice is shown below:

```
DmReleaseRecord(PinDB, prefs.editPinNo, true);
if (doArchive)
    DmArchiveRecord (PinDB, prefs.editPinNo);
else
    DmDeleteRecord (PinDB, prefs.editPinNo);
DmMoveRecord (PinDB, prefs.editPinNo, DmNumRecords(PinDB));
```

This code begins by releasing the record, then it either archives or deletes the record. Then it moves the record to the end of the database, as required by the searching Palm functions.

Wrapping up database use

After you finish working with a database, you should close it. This frees some of that precious dynamic memory that your application can then use for other things. Once you're all done with the data in a database, you might want to delete it completely.

Closing up shop

The Palm OS will close any open databases for you when your program exits, but it's a better idea to close it yourself as soon as you're done with a database. This is very important if you have to access more than one database in a program. Closing an open database is as simple as calling DmCloseDatabase():

```
DmCloseDatabase(dbRef);
```

A great place to close your open databases is in your `StopApplication()` function.

Deleting a database

In rare instances, you need to delete databases. Most of the time, you let the Palm OS delete the databases with the same creator code when the user deletes the application. If you're creating a database just to hold very large data while your program runs, you need to delete the database from within your program. It's as simple as calling `DmDeleteDatabase()`:

```
LocalID dbId;
UInt CardNo = 0;
dbId = DmFindDatabase(CardNo, "SimplepinDB-PDBe");
if (dbId)
    DmDeleteDatabase (CardNo, dbID);
```

Knowing where to do what, and when

It's entirely up to you to know how you work with databases and records in your application. However, a few guidelines can help you get started. Unless you can think of a better reason, follow these rules when using databases in your application:

- ✔ Open the application database(s) in your `StartApplication()` function. You also need to open (and close) the database while processing the `sysAppLaunchCmdFind` launch code. We do this in a function named `Search()`. Be sure to check the system preferences for the show secret setting, and set the `mode` correspondingly. Also be sure to use `dmAllCategories` for the category.

- ✔ Create a separate function (we call ours `AppInfoInit()`) to initialize the application information record of the database. Call this function from within `StartApplication()` when you create a new database, and from the case block in `PilotMain()` which processes the `AppLaunchCmdDatabaseInit` launch code.

- ✔ Sequentially access all the records in a given category, or in all categories, when initializing the overview form of the application. This is usually done to create a list or table showing all the current records in the selected category so the user can select one to edit. We do this in our `InitOverviewForm()` function. You also need to sequentially access all the records in all categories while processing the `sysAppLaunchCmdFind` launch code. We do this in a function named `Search()`.

✔ When the user selects an existing record from the list or table in the overview form, find that record's index and place it in a global variable. If the user wants to create a new record, put the value `dmMaxRecordIndex` into this global variable. Then open the detail form.

✔ Read the selected record while initializing the detail form. Copy the values from the record directly into the fields and controls of the detail form, not into temporary variables. If the record index to edit is `dmMaxRecordIndex`, just initialize the fields and controls with default or blank values for the new record. We do this in our `InitDetailForm()` function.

✔ When the user is done with the detail form, or when your program receives the `sysAppLaunchCmdSaveData` launch code, save the current values in the detail form into the record. This means you either create a new record if the index is `dmMaxRecordIndex`, or you update the existing record if it is not. If the user decides to delete the current record, you need to delete, archive, or discard the current record. If it's a new record, you simply don't create the record at all. We do all this in our `SaveDetailForm()` function.

✔ When the application ends, close the database in your `StopApplication()` function.

Categorizing Records

You've already seen how to initialize a database that supports categories by using the `CategoryInitialize()` Palm function. But what do you do to actually use categories? We're glad you asked, because it leads right into this section's contents.

Grasping categories

If you haven't already done so, take a close look at the Address Palm application. Notice that in the initial overview form, there is a category picker in the upper-right corner. Tap this category picker, and a list of categories pops up, which includes All, Untitled, and Edit Categories choices. When you select a new category from this list, the overview is updated to show only those records in that category.

In the detail view of an address, a similar category picker is displayed in the upper-right corner. This picker lacks an All category, and when you pick a new category from this list, the record is moved into the selected category. So how do you make this work?

Initializing categories

The categories themselves are kept in the database application information record. We've already shown how this is done in the section titled "Supporting categories, part I". When you do this, you get your application ready to support categories. The rest of the work is done by a set of category functions that you use, along with a Trigger and List Form item on the overview and detail forms.

The Category functions maintain the database application information record for you. They handle adding, deleting, renaming, and merging categories in the Palm OS standard way, so they're worth using.

Handling categories in an overview form

You need to do four things to handle categories in your overview form:

✓ Add a trigger and a list to the form, when using CodeWarrior Constructor or editing the GNU tools pilrc resource definition file.

✓ Use the category index when sequentially accessing the records of the database to build the overview list or table, so it only shows records in the selected category.

✓ Set the trigger label to display the currently selected category.

✓ Handle pen taps on the category trigger.

Defining resources

We're not going to go into the details of Step 1 here since resource editing is explained elsewhere in the book. Refer to Chapter 3 if you're using CodeWarrior or Chapter 6 if you're using the GNU tools.

Setting up the categories and overview display

Steps 2 and 3 of the step-by-step process happen when you initialize the overview form. When you initialize your overview form, you add a couple of lines of code to set up the category list. The code in the Simple Pin DB example program is in the `InitOverviewForm()` function:

```
static void InitOverviewForm() {
    static Char overviewCatName[dmCategoryLength];
    prefs.inDetail = false;
    InitOverviewFormList();
    CategoryGetName(PinDB, prefs.categoryView,
        overviewCatName);
```

(continued)

(continued)

```
    CategorySetTriggerLabel(
      (ControlPtr)GetObjectPtr(
      Overview_CategoryPopTrigger), overviewCatName);
}
```

This code begins by declaring a `static` character array that holds the current category name displayed by the Trigger. The character buffer you use to set the Trigger name must not disappear, as it would if it were a local variable.

Next, we call the function to actually build the overview list. We're not going to show that here, but you can see how to do this by looking at the source code on the CD-ROM, or by reading Chapter 10 where we discuss controls and other form elements. You've already seen that the `DmQueryNextInCategory()` Palm function uses the desired category index as the third parameter, so you can guess that we just use the desired category index when we build our list contents.

In our application, we store the index of the currently selected category for the overview form in the application preferences. It's in a global variable named `prefs.categoryView`. We use this index to retrieve the category name by calling the `CategoryGetName()` Palm function, passing in the open database reference, category index, and category name buffer pointer. Then we call the `CategorySetTriggerLabel()` Palm function, passing in the pointer to the Trigger Control, and the buffer holding the category name.

Handling pen taps on the trigger

Step 4 of the step-by-step process happens when the user taps on the category trigger in the overview form. Contrary to what you might expect, you don't let the trigger handle the user pen tap to pop up the list of categories. Instead, you handle the `ctlSelectEvent` for the trigger control as a `case` block in your overview form event handler. This happens in the `OverviewFormhandleEvent()` function. The `case` block is shown in the following code:

```
// local variables declared in the function
Boolean handled = false;
Word selectedCat;
ListPtr lstPtr;
Boolean categoryEdited;
FormPtr frm;
Char overviewCatName[dmCategoryLength];

case ctlSelectEvent:
   switch (eventP->data.ctlEnter.controlID) {
   case Overview_CategoryPopTrigger:
      selectedCat = prefs.categoryView;
      CategoryGetName(PinDB, prefs.categoryView,
         overviewCatName);
      frm = FrmGetActiveForm();
```

```
        categoryEdited = CategorySelect (PinDB, frm,
                Overview CategoryPopTrigger,
                Overview CategoriesList.true.
                &selectedCat, overviewCatName, 1, 0);
        if (categoryEdited ||
                (selectedCat != prefs.categoryView)) {
            prefs.categoryView = selectedCat;
            prefs.scrollPos = 0;
            FreeListhandles();
            InitOverviewFormList();
        }
        handled = true;
        break;
    // other cases
    }
```

This block begins by getting the category name of the currently selected category, but this time we can use a local variable for the string buffer. Next, we
call the CategorySelect() Palm function, passing in the open database reference containing the categories, the form pointer, the resource ID of the trigger
and list that make up the category picker, a Boolean value of true to include
an "All" choice, a pointer to a UInt to receive the index of the selected category, the current category name, an integer representing the index of the first
editable category, and a 0 to use the default choice of "Edit Categories" at
the end of the list. This call pops up the list, handles the user's choice to edit
the list, updates the database as needed to reflect user edits, and returns true
if the user edited or deleted the current category. It also updates the UInt we
passed in a pointer to, so it contains the selected category.

Now we need to figure out what to do with the user's actions. If the current
category was edited, or the selected category is different than the one the
overview form is showing, we need to redo the overview list and update the
saved category; otherwise, we don't need to do anything.

Handling categories in a detail form

Handling categories in a detail form is almost identical to doing it in an
overview form. One difference is that you pass false into the
CategorySelect() Palm function, so you don't have an "All" choice. The
other difference is that you get (and set) the category in the record's attributes. Getting the current category for a record is as simple as:

```
Word RecAttr; // this is a global

Word recCategory;
DmRecordInfo (dbRef, recordIndex, &recAttr, NULL, NULL);
recCategory = recAttr & dmRecAttrCategoryMask;
```

This is exactly what we do in our `InitDetailForm()` function, when we're editing an existing record. If we're editing a new record, we just set `recCategory` to `dmUnfiledCategory`. We keep the record attribute in a global variable, so we can update it if the user changes the category in the detail form.

In your detail form event handler's `case` block that processes the user tapping the category trigger, you need to set the record attribute to reflect the category:

```
RecAttr &= ~dmRecAttrCategoryMask;
RecAttr |= selectedCat;
```

You also need to be sure to change the overview category if it was showing the same category that was renamed or deleted. The simplest thing to do is just switch the overview category to the selected category:

```
if (categoryEdited && (prefs.categoryView == recCategory))
    prefs.categoryView = selectedCat;
```

Finally, when it's time to save the record in the database, update the record's attributes as well:

```
DmSetRecordInfo (dbRef, recordIndex, &RecAttr, NULL);
```

We do this last step in our `SaveDetailForm()` function.

Chapter 14

Conduits to the Desktop

· ·

In This Chapter
▶ Understanding conduits
▶ Digging into a Java Conduit
▶ Modifying the Palm application
▶ Installing the Conduit
▶ A brief view of the other choices

· ·

*E*very Palm device comes with the capability to communicate with a desktop computer by using the HotSync application. You can support synchronization of the data in your application database with the desktop by writing a conduit.

The Big Picture of Conduits

When the HotSync application runs, it does a lot of interesting things. Before it does any work at all, it determines whether this synchronization (or *sync* for short) is the first time that the Palm device has ever been synced with the desktop computer. If it is the first time, or if it has synced with a different desktop computer before this one, then HotSync does what's called a *slow sync*.

A *slow sync* is really just a state of mind. It means that every conduit that runs must examine every record in the associated database it is syncing, since there is no way to be sure that a record might have been modified just by considering the modification flags of the record.

If the Palm device last synced with this same desktop computer, HotSync does what's know as a *fast sync*.

A *fast sync* just means that every conduit can really trust the flags in each record of the Palm database. It can only look at those records that have their modified flag set and deal with them.

Running the conduits

Once the choice of slow or fast sync has been determined, the HotSync application examines every database on the device. For each database, it checks to see whether there is a registered conduit. If there is, that conduit is executed, and it does the actual work of synchronizing the records in the Palm database with those on the desktop.

A *conduit* is simply a desktop program. It has access to several functions in the HotSync application, and it uses the data connection HotSync establishes with the Palm device to move data between a desktop database and the Palm database.

You can use whatever you want or need to use on the desktop to store the data. Anything from a simple tab-delimited text file to a third party application is possible. HotSync really doesn't care. To keep things simple, we use a tab delimited text file as our desktop "database" in our conduit example.

Three SDKs and a baby

Sometimes there are too many choices in life, and with conduits, this is triply true. Conduits are supported for multiple versions of the HotSync application, and on two different (Macintosh and Windows) hardware platforms. Just to make things even more complex, under Windows you may use either Java or C++ for your Conduit, and on the Mac, you can use only C++. Because you also need to use Microsoft's Visual C++ compiler for Windows Conduits, or the full Metrowerks C++ compiler for the Mac, you're looking at a pretty significant investment of time and money if you want to cover all the bases.

We're taking the simple route instead and using the Java SDK. You can use the free Sun JDK to develop your Conduit in Java. Sure, it only works with Windows, but it's enough to get you started. You can use any Java development system, although the Java Conduit SDK has only been tested with the Sun, Microsoft, and Symantec tools.

For a commercial application, you really should create both Macintosh and Windows versions of your conduit. You'll need to dig into the documentation provided with the SDKs to learn how to do that, but this chapter will give you a good understanding of the issues you need to deal with.

The conduits home page, where you can download the Mac, Windows, and Java Conduit SDKs for free is `www.palm.com/devzone/conduits.html`.

Making Conduits in Java

Using the Java version of the Conduit SDK is relatively painless. It's basically a four-step process:

1. **Figure out what kind of synchronization makes sense for your application and how you will store this information on the desktop.**

2. **Create a subclass of the provided** AbstractRecord **class. This class holds the specific information in one record of your Palm OS database.**

3. **Create a class that implements the interface of the provided** Conduit **class. This class actually does the work of synchronizing the Palm OS and desktop databases.**

4. **Install the conduit by using the provided tools in the SDK.**

Our example conduit for this chapter synchronizes the records from the Simple Pin DB application developed in Chapter 13 with a tab-delimited text file on a Windows PC.

The full source code to the example is on the CD-ROM that accompanies this book in the Examples\Chap14 directory. The updated Simple Pin DB application is in the SimplePin subfolder.

Planning the synchronization

Deciding what your conduit is going to do is probably harder than implementing it. You've got many choices, and you can get as fancy (or as simple) as you'd like.

You are trying to attain three goals with a Conduit. You want to provide:

- A secure backup for the data on the Palm device
- Access to the information on the Palm device from a desktop application
- A means for the user to enter or edit information on the desktop and then move that information to the Palm device

You can decide to support one or more of these activities. It may make sense for your application to simply provide a text dump of the data in the Palm device (second bullet), or a simple backup (first bullet) or full synchronization with a desktop application (third bullet).

You need to consider several issues when creating a conduit. These issues impact how the conduit is written. Consider the following before you begin to design your conduit:

- ✔ Will you synchronize the information in a central location, shared by more than one Palm device on a single desktop?
- ✔ Does each record on the desktop contain a unique identifier?
- ✔ Can your Conduit determine if a desktop record has been added, modified, or deleted just by examining flags in the desktop record?
- ✔ Does the desktop application support categories? Are they similar to the categories used by the Palm OS?

In order to provide a fairly complete example, we synchronize the Simple Pin records to a central text file. This file contains tab-delimited records (where each field in a record is separated by a tab character). Each record on the desktop has a unique identifier, as well as a set of Boolean values that indicate if its new, modified, deleted, or archived. Categories are synchronized also, as well as the private flag.

Because of these choices, we need to maintain a text file for each Palm device that maps the desktop identifier for each record to the corresponding Palm OS database record ID. This file is created in the synchronization folder of the specific user, within the HotSync folder.

Abstracting the Palm OS records

Step 1 is to create a new Java class that the conduit uses to store records it reads from the Palm device. This class needs to:

1. **Load the values of the record directly from the Palm device, or from a desktop text file.**
2. **Store the values to the Palm device or to a desktop text file.**
3. **Write the mapping text file that contains the desktop and Palm OS IDs.**
4. **Retrieve the various values of the record.**
5. **Test it against a different Simple Pin record.**

The `PinRecord.java` source file contains the `PinRecord` class. This class is fairly large, so we'll discuss it in several chunks. The first chunk declares the class and the variables it holds:

```
import palm.conduit.*;
import java.io.*;
public class PinRecord extends AbstractRecord {
    String name;
    String pin;
    int desktopId;
```

We import the required classes for the PinRecord class and then declare it as a subclass of the Palm-supplied AbstractRecord class. That class holds the category, as well as the private, new, modified, and deleted flags. It also holds the Palm OS ID for the record. To these variables, we add the two strings that each record contains (the name and pin) as well as the unique identifier of the record as it is stored on the desktop.

The next batch of methods implement get and set operations for the three class variables:

```
public String getName() {
    return name;
}
public String getPin() {
    return pin;
}
public int getDesktopId() {
    return desktopId;
}
public void setName(String name) {
    this.name = name;
}
public void setPin(String pin) {
    this.pin = pin;
}
public void setDesktopId(int desktopId) {
    this.desktopId = desktopId;
}
```

No surprises here! The get methods return the current values of the variables, and the set methods update those values.

Next, we implement a pair of methods that write and read the values of the name and pin via the conduit:

```
public void writeData(DataOutputStream out)
        throws IOException{
    if (name != null)
        writeCString(out, name);
    if (pin != null)
        writeCString(out, pin);
}
```

(continued)

(continued)

```
public void readData(DataInputStream in)
    throws IOException{
  this.name = readCString(in);
  this.pin = readCString(in);
}
```

The writeCString() and readCString() methods are provided in the AbstractRecord class. We use them to write (and read) the values via the DataStream provided by the conduit.

The Palm record is read and written exactly as it is stored on the Palm device. That means your conduit must read and write the various fields of the record in their internal Palm format. For the Simple Pin DB example application, the data record on the Palm device holds two strings, packed together. If we read or write two C strings, one after the other, then we correctly access the data via the conduit. The AbstractRecord class also includes the readDate() and writeDate() methods for accessing date (DateType type for Palm OS) values. For integer values, you can use the following methods of the DataInputStream and DataOutputStream:

- ✔ readByte() and writeByte() for 8 bit integers (Byte type for Palm OS)

- ✔ readShort() and writeShort() for 16 bit integers (Word type for Palm OS)

- ✔ readInt() and writeInt() for 32 bit integers (DWord type for Palm OS)

We need to be able to test the values of this record against another record, to see if they are equal. The next method implements this test:

```
public boolean isEqual(PinRecord other) {
  if (other == null) return false;
  if (getCategoryIndex() != other.getCategoryIndex())
    return false;
  if (!name.equals(other.name)) return false;
  if (!pin.equals(other.pin)) return false;
  return true;
}
```

The method returns true if the records are in the same Category, and both the name and pin values are exactly equal between this record and the passed-in record. If either differs, or the passed in record is null, it returns false.

Because we store a PinRecord as a tab delimited text record, we need to be able to write and read this type of record from the desktop text file. The next two methods implement writing and reading to a tab-delimited file:

```
      public void writeFile(FileOutputStream out)
          throws IOException{
     writeTabInteger(out, getDesktopId ());
     writeTabInteger(out, getCategoryIndex());
     writeTabBoolean(out, isPrivate());
     writeTabBoolean(out, isNew());
     writeTabBoolean(out, isModified());
     writeTabBoolean(out, isDeleted());
     writeTabBoolean(out, isArchived());
     writeTabString(out, name);
     out.write(pin.getBytes());
     out.write("\r\n".getBytes());
 }
public void readFile(FileInputStream in)
        throws IOException {
    setDesktopId(readTabInteger(in));
    setCategoryIndex(readTabInteger(in));
    setIsPrivate(readTabBoolean(in));
    setIsNew(readTabBoolean(in));
    setIsModified(readTabBoolean(in));
    setIsDeleted(readTabBoolean(in));
    setIsArchived(readTabBoolean(in));
    this.name = readTabString(in);
    this.pin = readTabString(in);
 }
```

When we write the record to the desktop file, we store the desktop ID, category, flags, name, and pin as strings, separated by tab characters. You'll see the various write methods a little later. When we read the record from the desktop file, we read each of the items back in using the same order.

If your desktop records are stored within a database, you need to use the appropriate database calls in your `readFile()` and `writeFile()` methods.

We also need to create a text file that contains a pair of IDs (desktop and Palm OS) for each record. This mapping file is stored in the specific HotSync folder for the user, so more than one Palm device can synchronize with the same desktop:

```
      public void writeIdFile(FileOutputStream out)
          throws IOException{
     writeTabInteger(out, getDesktopId());
     out.write((new Integer(getId()
        ).toString()).getBytes());
     out.write("\r\n".getBytes());
 }
```

This method just writes string versions of the desktop ID and Palm OS ID for this record, separated by a tab.

Several functions are available that are used to write string versions of different Java data types to a text file. Because they don't access any of the variables of the class, we declare them as `static`. This enables you to call them from other classes as well:

```
static public void writeTabString(FileOutputStream out,
        String s) throws IOException {
    out.write(s.getBytes());
    out.write('\t');
}
static public void writeTabInteger(FileOutputStream out,
        int i) throws IOException {
    out.write((new Integer(i).toString()).getBytes());
    out.write('\t');
}
static public void writeTabBoolean(FileOutputStream out,
        boolean b) throws IOException {
    out.write((new Boolean(b).toString()).getBytes());
    out.write('\t');
}
```

For each type, the value is converted to a string, and then the bytes of the string are written to the file.

We use several methods to read values of various types from a file. This method reads the next tab (or end of line) delimited string from the file, converts it to the appropriate Java type, and returns it. Because they don't access any of the variables of the class, we declare them as `static`. This enables you to call them from other classes, as well:

```
static public String readTabString(FileInputStream in)
        throws IOException {
    StringBuffer buf;
    int c;
    buf = new StringBuffer();
    for (c = in.read(); (c != '\t' && c != '\r');
        c = in.read())
            buf.append((char)c);
    if (c == '\r') c = in.read();
    return buf.toString();
}
static public int readTabInteger(FileInputStream in)
        throws IOException {
    return (new Integer(readTabString(in))).intValue();
}
static public boolean readTabBoolean(FileInputStream in)
        throws IOException {
    return (new
        Boolean(readTabString(in))).booleanValue();
}
}
```

Using the `PinRecord` class, we can now represent a Simple Pin record on the desktop. You're almost ready to write the conduit! Before you can, you must create another class that holds the records that map the desktop ID to the Palm OS ID.

Mapping desktop IDs to Palm OS IDs

If your desktop database is shared among more than one Palm device, you cannot store the Palm OS IDs for each record in the desktop record. That's because each Palm OS device may use a different unique identifier for the same desktop record. When HotSync runs a conduit, it passes in a path string that points to a subfolder within the HotSync folder that is unique for each Palm device that synchronizes with the desktop. It is in this subfolder that we create a file that maps each desktop ID to the corresponding Palm OS ID for each record in the database.

The PinIds.java source file contains the `PinIds` class. This class is similar to the `PinRecord` class, but it's a lot simpler:

```java
import palm.conduit.*;
import java.io.*;
import PinRecord;
public class PinIds {
    int desktopId;
    int palmId;
    boolean onPalm;

    boolean onDesktop;
    public int getDesktopId() {
        return desktopId;
    }
    public int getPalmId() {
        return palmId;
    }
    public boolean isOnPalm() {
        return onPalm;
    }
    public boolean isOnDesktop() {
        return onDesktop;
    }
    public void setDesktopId(int desktopId) {
        this.desktopId = desktopId;
    }
    public void setPalmId(int palmId) {
        this.palmId = palmId;
    }
```

(continued)

(continued)

```
    public void setIsOnPalm(boolean onPalm) {
        this.onPalm = onPalm;
    }
    public void setIsOnDesktop(boolean onDesktop) {
        this.onDesktop = onDesktop;
    }
    public void readFile(FileInputStream in)
            throws IOException {
        setDesktopId(PinRecord.readTabInteger(in));
        setPalmId(PinRecord.readTabInteger(in));
    }
}
```

The `desktopId` and `palmId` variables hold the IDs for the desktop and Palm device. These values have `get` and `set` methods. The `onPalm` and `onDesktop` Boolean values are `true` if the corresponding ID has actually been located on the Palm device and on the desktop. We use these values during the synchronization process to figure out if a record has been added or deleted from the desktop or Palm device when we can't trust the flags in the Palm or desktop records. They too have `get` and `set` methods. Finally, the `readFile()` method loads the IDs from a tab-delimited file. Recall that the `PinRecord` class has a method that writes the IDs to the file.

Synchronizing records via a conduit

The Conduit SDK includes an abstract class named `Conduit`. You create an implementation of that class that includes an `open()`, `name()`, and `configure()` method. When HotSync executes the Conduit, it calls the `open()` method to do the synchronization. The PinCond.java source file contains the `PinCond` class, which implements the `Conduit` class. It's quite long, so we present it in several chunks. The first chunk contains the required methods of the class:

```
import palm.conduit.*;
import PinRecord;
import PinIds;
import java.io.*;
import java.util.*;

public class PinCond implements Conduit {
    Hashtable currentRecs;
    Hashtable currentIds;
    Vector archivedRecs;
    Vector pendingChanges;
    int db;
    int nextId;
    boolean isSlow;
```

```
boolean isNewUser;
SyncProperties myProps;

public void open(SyncProperties props) {
    Log.startSync();
    myProps = props;
    InitializeDataStorage();
    isSlow = (myProps.syncType ==
        SyncProperties.SYNC_SLOW);
    isNewUser = false;
    LoadDesktopRecords();
    try {
        db = SyncManager.openDB(
            myProps.remoteNames[0], (short)0,
            (byte)(SyncManager.OPEN_READ |
                SyncManager.OPEN_WRITE |
                SyncManager.OPEN_EXCLUSIVE));
        if (currentRecs.isEmpty()) {
            copyPalmDb();
        }
        else if (isNewUser) {
            mergeSync();
        }
        else if (isSlow) {
            slowSync();
        }
        else {
            fastSync();
        }
        SyncManager.purgeDeletedRecs(db);
        SyncManager.resetSyncFlags(db);
        SyncManager.closeDB(db);
        SaveDesktopRecords();
        Log.AddEntry("OK Simple Pin", Log.TEXT, false);
        Log.endSync();
    } catch (Throwable t) {
        t.printStackTrace();
        Log.abortSync();
    }
}

 public String name() {
     return "PinCond";
 }

public int configure(ConfigureConduitInfo info) {
    return 0;
}
```

We begin by creating a class that implements the conduit interface. This
interface includes the three required methods:

✔ open(): To perform the actual synchronization

✔ name(): To return a string representing the conduit name

✔ configure(): To provide any configuration options supported by the conduit

The name() and configure() methods are trivial. You can display a Java window within the configure() method to allow the user to select options for your conduit if your need to.

The real meat of the conduit is in the open() method. Before we get to that, we need to explain the member variables we declare at the beginning of the class. The currentRecs hash table holds a PinRecord object for each desktop record. The key for the hash table is an Integer that is the unique desktop ID of the record. The currentIds hash table holds a PinIds object for each record that is on the desktop, Palm device, or both. The key for hash table is an Integer that is the unique Palm OS assigned ID of the record. These two hash tables allow us to quickly locate a desktop record, using either the desktop ID or Palm OS ID. The archivedRecs vector holds Palm OS records that are to be archived. The pendingChanges vector holds Desktop records that need to be modified or deleted on the Palm device. We add all pending modified or deleted records to this vector as we perform the synchronization, and then process them at the end. This way, we don't need to be concerned about possibly changing the Palm device database as we're looking for new or modified records on the device during synchronization.

The db variable holds the open Palm device database identifier. Other methods in the class use this to read and write to the Palm device database. The nextId variable holds the next unique desktop ID for new records. The isSlow Boolean is true if we need to do a slow sync, and the isNewUser Boolean is true if we detect that the desktop database exists, but the Palm device has never synchronized with it. Finally, the myProps variable holds a copy of the SyncProperties object passed into the open() method. Other methods in the class need access to this object during the synchronization process.

The open() method is where you code your synchronization. We provide a fairly detailed and complete example here, and most Conduits will follow this general form. However, depending on where and how your desktop records are stored, your own Conduit may be quite different.

The open() method follows these steps:

1. **The hash tables and vectors used to store the desktop and Palm device records during synchronization are allocated.**

2. **The** isSlow **and** isNewUser **Booleans are given initial default values.**

3. The existing desktop database records, ID mapping records, and archive records are read into the hash tables and vectors allocated in step 1.

4. The Palm device database is opened.

5. The appropriate synchronization is performed.

6. All deleted and archived records in the Palm device database are removed.

7. All new and modified flags in the Palm device database are set to `false`.

8. The desktop database, ID mapping file, and archived record file are written.

Most of these steps take the form of a method call. The following sections look at each step in detail.

Allocating memory to hold records

Step 1 in the step-by-step process is accomplished by calling the `InitializeDataStorage()` method. That method simply allocates the initial empty hash tables and vectors used in the conduit:

```
public void InitializeDataStorage() {
    currentRecs = new Hashtable(100);
    currentIds = new Hashtable(100);
    archivedRecs = new Vector(20,10);
    pendingChanges = new Vector(20,10);
}
```

We provide initial sizes that are reasonable for the typical Palm OS database.

Deciding how to synchronize

Step 2 in the step-by-step process is to assign `true` to the `isSlow` variable if the `SyncProperties` object's `syncType` variable is set to `SYNC_SLOW`. Recall that the HotSync application sets this variable to `SYNC_SLOW` if it determines that the Palm device has either never synced with this desktop machine, or last synced with a different desktop machine. We also initialize the `isNewUser` variable to `false`. Later, we may set this to `true` if we determine that this user hasn't synced with an existing desktop database, in the next section.

Reading in desktop records

Step 3 in the step-by-step process is accomplished by calling the `LoadDesktopRecords()` method. That method opens and reads several files, creating `PinRecord` and `PinIds` objects and inserting them into the hash tables and vectors we use during the synchronization:

```java
public void LoadDesktopRecords() {
    FileInputStream in;
    PinIds idRec;
    PinRecord desktopRec;
    nextId = 1;
    try {
        in = new FileInputStream("C:\\SimplePinDB.id");
        nextId = PinRecord.readTabInteger(in);
        in.close();
    } catch (IOException other) {
    }
    try {
        in = new FileInputStream("C:\\SimplePinDB.txt");
        for (;in.available() > 0;) {
            desktopRec = new PinRecord();
            desktopRec.readFile(in);
            if (desktopRec.isNew())
                desktopRec.setDesktopId(nextId++);
            currentRecs.put(new
                Integer(desktopRec.getDesktopId()),
                desktopRec);
        }
        in.close();
    } catch (IOException other) {
    }
    try {
        in = new FileInputStream(myProps.pathName +
            myProps.localName + ".ids");
        for (;in.available() > 0;) {
            idRec = new PinIds();
            idRec.readFile(in);
            idRec.setIsOnPalm(false);
            currentIds.put(new Integer(idRec.getPalmId()),
                idRec);
            desktopRec = (PinRecord)currentRecs.get(new
                Integer(idRec.getDesktopId()));
            if (desktopRec != null) {
                idRec.setIsOnDesktop(true);
                desktopRec.setId(idRec.getPalmId());
            }
            else
                idRec.setIsOnDesktop(false);
        }
        in.close();
    } catch (IOException other) {
        isSlow = true;
        isNewUser = true;
    }
    try {
        in = new FileInputStream(myProps.pathName +
            myProps.localName + ".sav");
        for (;in.available() > 0;) {
```

```
            desktopRec = new PinRecord();
            desktopRec.readFile(in);
            archivedRecs.addElement(desktopRec);
        }
        in.close();
    } catch (IOException other) {
    }
}
```

First, we open and read a file named "C:\SimplePinDB.id". This file contains the next unique identifier for new desktop records. We read the value into the nextId variable. If no such file exists, we set nextId to 1.

Next, we read in the desktop database. It's stored in a file named "C\SimplePinDB.txt". We allocate a new PinRecord object and then use its readFile() method to load each record in the desktop database. If a record has the new flag set, we assign the next unique desktop database to it, and increment nextId. Then we add the desktop record to the currentRecs hash table, using the desktop ID as the hash key.

Next we read in the ID mapping file for the particular Palm device that's performing the synchronization. We use the SyncProperties object's pathName and localName variables to create a filename. This name will include the full path to the HotSync folder for the Simple Pin DB conduit, within the current user's HotSync subdirectory. On our example machine, this path is "C:\Palm\SchettJ\SimplePin\PinCond.ids". See the section later in this chapter titled "Installing a Conduit during development" for the details on how these variables are set.

We allocate a new PinIds object and then use its readFile() method to load each record in the ID mapping file. We use the setIsOnPalm() method to indicate that we don't yet know if this record still exists on the Palm device. Then we add the mapping record to the currentIds hash table, using the Palm device record ID as the hash key.

We then try to locate the desktop record that the mapping record refers to by looking up the desktop ID in the currentRecs hash table. If the record is found, we use the setIsOnDesktop() method of the PinIds object to indicate that the record does exist on the desktop. We also set the desktop record's Palm device record ID by calling the setId() method of the PinRecord object. This establishes the link between the desktop and Palm device record. If no desktop record is found, we use the setIsOnDesktop() method of the PinIds object to indicate that the record is no longer on the desktop.

If the mapping file does not exist or cannot be read, then we set the isSlow and isNewUser Boolean variables to true. That indicates that this user has not synchronized with this desktop yet.

Finally, we read in the archived records file for the particular Palm device that's performing the synchronization. We use the SyncProperties object's pathName and localName variables to create a file name. On our example machine, this path is "C:\Palm\SchettJ\SimplePin\PinCond.sav". We allocate a new PinRecord object and then use its readFile() method to load each record in the archived records file, and save it in the archivedRecs vector.

This reads all the necessary desktop files and loads them into memory.

Opening a Palm device database

You accomplish Step 4 in the step-by-step process by calling the openDB() method of the SyncManager object. This opens a Palm device database. We use the remoteNames[0] variable as the database name and open the file for reading and writing. We also use the exclusive flag, which prevents any Palm programs from accessing the database while we update it.

Doing the right kind of synchronization

After the desktop files have been opened, we have everything we need to perform Step 5 in the step-by-step process. You accomplish this step by calling one of four methods:

- copyPalmDb(): To copy the Palm device database onto the desktop. This happens when there is no desktop database when the HotSync is performed.

- mergeSync(): To merge an existing desktop database with a Palm device database. This happens when there is already a desktop database and a Palm device that's never synchronized with this desktop performs a HotSync. In this case, both isNewUser and isSlow are true.

- slowSync(): To synchronize an existing database with a Palm device, when the Palm device last synchronized with a different desktop machine. In this case, the new, modified, and deleted flags of the desktop and Palm device database cannot be trusted, so we need to use other methods to detect new, modified, and deleted records on either.

- fastSync(): To synchronize an existing desktop and Palm device database, when the last synchronization by the Palm device was with this desktop. In this case we can trust the desktop and Palm device database flags, so the synchronization need not examine ever record in detail.

The following sections look at each of these methods in detail.

Loading the desktop database for the first time

The copyPalmDb() method simply copies all Palm device database records into the currentRecs hash table:

```
public void copyPalmDb() throws IOException {
    PinRecord rec;
    int count, i;

    count = SyncManager.getDBRecordCount(db);
    for (i = 0; i < count; i++) {
        rec = new PinRecord();
        rec.setIndex(i);
        SyncManager.readRecordByIndex(db, rec);
        if (rec.isArchived()) {
            archivedRecs.addElement(rec);
            rec = new PinRecord();
        }
        else if (!rec.isDeleted()) {
            rec.setIsNew(false);
            rec.setIsModified(false);
            rec.setDesktopId(nextId++);
            currentRecs.put(new
                Integer(rec.getDesktopId()), rec);
        }
    }
}
```

We call the getDBRecordCount() method of the SyncManager object to find out how many records are in the Palm device database. Then we enter a for loop, visiting each record in the Palm device database by index. We allocate a new PinRecord object and set its index to the next record index to read by calling the setIndex() method of the PinRecord object. Then we call the readRecordByIndex() method of the SyncManager object to read the record from the Palm device database. If the record has its archived flag set, we add it to the archivedRecs vector; otherwise, if the record does not have its deleted flag set, we clear its new and modified flags, assign it the next unique desktop ID, and then add it to the currentRecs hash table. We use the desktop ID as the hash key.

Merging desktop and Palm device databases

The mergeSync() method has the unenviable task of trying to merge two existing databases with no clue as to how they match up. We do our best to match existing records on each device, but if a record has been modified on either or both devices, then after the synchronization the record will be duplicated on both devices:

```
public void mergeSync() throws IOException {
    PinRecord rec;
    int count, i;

    count = SyncManager.getDBRecordCount(db);
    for (i = 0; i < count; i++) {
        rec = new PinRecord();
```

(continued)

(continued)

```
            rec.setIndex(i);
            SyncManager.readRecordByIndex(db, rec);
            findPalmRecord(rec);
        }
        syncDesktop();
        processPendingChanges();
    }
```

This method reads all the records from the Palm device database. For each record, it calls the findPalmRecord() method. This method attempts to find a matching desktop record for the passed in record. We'll show it in just a moment. After all Palm device records have been processed, we call the syncDesktop() method to detect added, deleted, and modified desktop records. These records are added to the pendingChanges vector. Finally, the processPendingChanges() method is called to update the Palm device database using the pendingChanges vector.

The findPalmRecord() method tries to find a Palm record within the currentRecs hash table. Because we're doing a merge synchronization, it means that no mapping file exists for this user. That also means all the PinRecord objects in the currentRecs hash table do not yet have valid Palm device IDs. That means that as long as this ID is 0, the desktop record has not been matched to a Palm device database record:

```
public boolean findPalmRecord(PinRecord rec) {
    PinRecord desktopRec;
    PinIds idRec;

    Enumeration allDesktopRecs = currentRecs.elements();
    while(allDesktopRecs.hasMoreElements()) {
        desktopRec = (PinRecord)
            allDesktopRecs.nextElement();
        if (desktopRec.getId() == 0) {
            if (desktopRec.isEqual(rec)) {
                desktopRec.setId(rec.getId());
                idRec = new PinIds();
                idRec.setDesktopId(
                    desktopRec.getDesktopId());
                idRec.setPalmId(rec.getId());
                idRec.setIsOnPalm(true);
                idRec.setIsOnDesktop(true);
                currentIds.put(new
                    Integer(idRec.getPalmId()), idRec);
                return true;
            }
        }
    }
    return false;
}
```

We use an enumeration to retrieve every record in the currentRecs hash table. If the desktop record has a 0 Palm device ID, we call the isEqual() method of the desktop record object to see if it is the same as the Palm record. Recall that the isEqual() method tests the name, pin, and Category for equality, and returns true if they are all equal.

If the two records are equal, we set the desktop record's Palm device ID to the ID of the Palm record. Then we allocate a new PinIds object, set its desktop and Palm device IDs, and set its onPalm and onDesktop flags to true. Then we add it to the currentIds hash table. This associates the Palm device record and desktop record.

The syncDesktop() method looks at the currentRecs hash table to figure out which desktop records have been added, deleted, or modified:

```
public void syncDesktop() {
    PinRecord desktopRec;
    PinIds idRec;

    Enumeration allDesktopRecs = currentRecs.elements();
    while(allDesktopRecs.hasMoreElements()) {
        desktopRec = (PinRecord)
            allDesktopRecs.nextElement();
        if (desktopRec.getId() == 0) {
            syncDesktopRecord(desktopRec, null);
        }
        else if (desktopRec.isNew()) {
            pendingChanges.addElement(desktopRec);
        }
        else if (isSlow) {
            Integer key = new Integer(desktopRec.getId());
            idRec = (PinIds)currentIds.get(key);
            if (idRec == null || !idRec.isOnPalm()) {
                desktopRec.setIsNew(true);
                pendingChanges.addElement(desktopRec);
            }
        }
        else
            syncDesktopRecord(desktopRec, null);
    }
}
```

As in the last method, we use an enumeration to visit each record in the currentRecs hash table. If a desktop record has a 0 Palm device ID, then we know it currently does not exist on the Palm device. We call the syncDesktopRecord() method to synchronize the desktop record with a null Palm record. This will add, delete, or archive this desktop record based on its flags. If the record has a Palm device ID, we see if its new flag is set. If it is, we add it to the pendingChanges vector so it will be added to the Palm device. If the new flag is not set and we're doing a slow sync, the desktop record is either new or deleted for the Palm device. We look up the record in the currentIds ID mapping hash table. If the record isn't in this hash table, or the onPalm flag of the mapping record is false, then we add the record to the Palm device. We set the new flag of the desktop record to true and add it to the pendingChanges vector.

If the record has a Palm device ID, and we're not doing a slow sync, then we call syncDesktopRecord() to synchronize the desktop record with a null Palm record. This will add, delete, or archive this desktop record based on its flags.

Next we look at the syncDesktopRecord() method. This method tries to figure out what to do given both a desktop and Palm device record:

```
public void syncDesktopRecord(PinRecord desktopRec,
      PinRecord palmRec) {
   Integer key = new Integer(desktopRec.getDesktopId());
   if (desktopRec.isDeleted() ||
         desktopRec.isArchived()) {
      currentRecs.remove(key);
      if (desktopRec.isArchived())
         archivedRecs.addElement(desktopRec);
      desktopRec.setIsDeleted(true);
      pendingChanges.addElement(desktopRec);
   }
   else if (isSlow) {
      if (!desktopRec.isEqual(palmRec)) {
         if (isNewUser || palmRec == null)
            desktopRec.setIsNew(true);
         else
            desktopRec.setIsModified(true);
         pendingChanges.addElement(desktopRec);
      }
   } else if (desktopRec.isModified()) {
      pendingChanges.addElement(desktopRec);
   } else if (palmRec != null && palmRec.isModified()) {
      currentRecs.remove(key);
      palmRec.setIsNew(false);
      palmRec.setIsModified(false);
      currentRecs.put(key, palmRec);
   }
}
```

If the desktop record has its deleted or archived flag set, we remove it from the currentRecs hash table. This effectively deletes it from the desktop database. If it has the archive flag set, we add it to the archivedRecs vector, so it will be saved in the archive file at the end of the synchronization. In either case we set the deleted flag of the desktop record to true, and add the record to the pendingChanges vector.

If the desktop record is not deleted or archived, and we're doing a slow sync, we call the isEqual() method to compare the desktop and Palm device record. This returns false if the two records are not equal, or if the Palm device record is null. If the records are not equal, and this is a new user or the Palm record is `null`, then this desktop record represents a new record for the Palm device. If they're not equal and there is a Palm device record, then the desktop record is flagged as modified and added to the `pendingChanges` vector.

If we're not doing a slow sync, then we check the desktop record's modified flag. If it is modified, then we add it to the `pendingChanges` vector so it will overwrite the Palm record. If the desktop record is not modified, and the Palm device database record is not `null` and is modified, then we remove the existing desktop record and replace it with the Palm device database record.

It's up to you to determine the rules of synchronization. You can even allow the user to indicate how they want records to be synchronized. This conduit does the following:

1. **If the desktop record is deleted, the Palm device database record is deleted.**

2. **Otherwise, if the desktop record exists and there is no Palm record during a slow sync, the desktop record is added to the Palm device.**

3. **Otherwise, if there is a Palm record, and the desktop record and Palm record don't match during a slow sync, the desktop record always overwrites the Palm record.**

4. **Otherwise, during a fast sync if the desktop record is modified, it always overwrites the Palm record.**

5. **Otherwise, if the Palm record is modified, it overwrites the desktop record.**

After the synchronization of the Palm and desktop records is completed, the `processPendingChanges()` method applies adds, modifies, and deletes to the Palm device database:

```
public void processPendingChanges() throws IOException {
    int numChanges = pendingChanges.size();
    int i;
    PinRecord desktopRec;

    for (i = 0; i < numChanges; i++) {
        desktopRec = (PinRecord)
            pendingChanges.elementAt(i);
        if (desktopRec.isNew()) {
            desktopRec.setId(0);
            desktopRec.setIsNew(false);
            desktopRec.setIsModified(false);
            SyncManager.writeRec(db, desktopRec);
        }
        else if (desktopRec.isModified()) {
            desktopRec.setIsModified(false);
```

(continued)

(continued)

```
            SyncManager.writeRec(db, desktopRec);
        }
        else
            SyncManager.deleteRecord(db, desktopRec);
    }
}
```

The `pendingChanges` vector contains `PinRecord` objects that have either
the new, modified, or deleted flag set. We examine each record in the vector,
and if its new flag is set we add it to the Palm device database. We set the
Palm device ID to 0, so that the Palm OS will assign a new, unique ID. We clear
the new and modified flags and then call the `writeRec()` method of the
`SyncManager` object to write the record to the Palm device database. Note that
this will update the record's Palm device ID to reflect the newly assigned ID.

If the modified flag is set, we clear the flag and write the record to the Palm
device database. Otherwise, we delete the Palm device database record by
calling the `deleteRecord()` method of the `SyncManager` object.

That sure is a lot of work! The good news is that most of these methods are
also used by the slow and fast synchronization methods.

Syncing slowly

The `slowSync()` method synchronizes desktop and Palm device database
records when you cannot trust the flags on either device:

```
public void slowSync() throws IOException {
    PinRecord rec, desktopRec;
    int count, i;
    PinIds idRec;

    count = SyncManager.getDBRecordCount(db);
    for (i = 0; i < count; i++) {
        rec = new PinRecord();
        rec.setIndex(i);
        SyncManager.readRecordByIndex(db, rec);
        idRec = (PinIds)currentIds.get(
            new Integer(rec.getId()));
        if (idRec == null) {
            idRec = new PinIds();
            if (!findPalmRecord(rec)) {
                idRec.setDesktopId(nextId);
                idRec.setPalmId(rec.getId());
                currentIds.put(new
                    Integer(idRec.getPalmId()), idRec);
            }
        }
        idRec.setIsOnPalm(true);
        SyncPalmRecord(rec);
```

```
        }
    syncDesktop();
    Enumeration allDesktopIds = currentIds.elements();
    while(allDesktopIds.hasMoreElements()) {
        idRec = (PinIds)allDesktopIds.nextElement();
        if (idRec.isOnPalm() && !idRec.isOnDesktop())
            desktopRec = new PinRecord();
            desktopRec.setId(idRec.getPalmId());
            desktopRec.setIsDeleted(true);
            pendingChanges.addElement(desktopRec);
        }
    }
    processPendingChanges();
}
```

The slowSync() method begins by accessing each record in the Palm device
database by index. We look up the Palm ID in the currentIds mapping hash
table. If the ID is not found, then we need to add the record to the desktop.
First, we create a new PinIds object and use it to associate the Palm device
ID to a new desktop unique ID. We then add the new PinIds object to the
currentIds hash table.

We set the onPalm flag of the PinIds object to true, since we just verified
that the record does exist on the Palm device. We next call the
SyncPalmRecord() method to synchronize the Palm and desktop record.
We'll look at that method in just a moment.

After all the Palm device database records have been examined, we call the
syncDesktop() method to synchronize the desktop records. The last step is
to scan the desktop records to find Palm device records that aren't on the
desktop. We do this by visiting every record in the currentIds hash table,
and checking the onPalm and onDesktop flags to see if the record is on the
Palm device but not on the desktop. When we find this situation, we assume
that this means the desktop record has been deleted on the Palm device. We
create a new desktop record, assign it the Palm device ID and set its deleted
flag. Then we add it to the pendingChanges vector. Because we're not interested in the record's contents, we don't bother loading them in from the
Palm record.

After this step, we process the pendingChanges vector by calling the
processPendingChanges() method.

The SyncPalmRecord() method is a lot like the SyncDesktopRecord()
method:

```
public void SyncPalmRecord(PinRecord rec) {
    PinRecord desktopRec = null;
    PinIds desktopIdRec;
    Integer key = new Integer(0);

    desktopIdRec = (PinIds)currentIds.get(
        new Integer(rec.getId()));
    if (desktopIdRec != null) {
        key = new Integer(desktopIdRec.getDesktopId());
        desktopRec = (PinRecord)currentRecs.get(key);
    }
    if (desktopRec != null) {
        if (rec.isDeleted() || rec.isArchived()) {
            currentRecs.remove(key);
            if (rec.isArchived())
                archivedRecs.addElement(rec);
        }
        else
            syncDesktopRecord(desktopRec, rec);
    }
    else {
        if (rec.isArchived())
            archivedRecs.addElement(rec);
        else if (!rec.isDeleted()) {
            rec.setIsNew(false);
            rec.setIsModified(false);
            rec.setDesktopId(nextId++);
            currentRecs.put(new Integer(rec.getId()), rec);
        }
    }
}
```

We begin by looking up the desktop record that corresponds to the Palm device database record. We find the mapping record in the currentIds hash table, and if it's found we check to see if the Palm device database record's delete or archive flag is set. If either is true, we remove the desktop record from the currentRecs hash table. If the archive flag is set, we add the desktop record to the archivedRecs vector. If neither flag is set, we call the syncDesktopRecord() method, passing in both the desktop and Palm device database record and the desktop record.

If no desktop record is found, we check the Palm device database record to see if it is archived. If it is, we add it to the archivedRecs vector. If it is not archived or deleted, then it must be a new record, so we add it to the currentRecs hash table. Before we add it, we clear the new and modified flags, and assign it a new unique desktop ID.

Syncing quickly

The fastSync() method synchronizes desktop and Palm device database records when you can trust the flags on both devices:

```
public void fastSync() throws IOException {
    PinRecord rec;
    int count, i;

    try {
        for (;;) {
            rec = new PinRecord();
            SyncManager.readNextModifiedRec(db, rec);
            SyncPalmRecord(rec);
        }
    }
    catch(SyncException e){
    }
    syncDesktop();
    processPendingChanges();
}
```

Unlike the other synchronization methods, this method examines only the
modified records in the Palm device database. We do this by calling the
readNextModifiedRec() method of the SyncManager object repeatedly,
until an exception is thrown. For each modified record, we call the
SyncPalmRecord() method to synchronize the Palm device database record
with the desktop database. Once all modified Palm device database records
have been processed, we call the syncDesktop() method to process added,
modified, and deleted desktop records. Then we call
processPendingChanges() to update the Palm device databases.

Cleaning up the Palm device database

After the desktop and Palm device database are in sync, we need to finish up
with the Palm device. That's steps 6 and 7 in the step-by-step synchronization
process. We call the purgeDeletedRecs() method of the SyncManager
object to remove all deleted and archived records from the Palm device database. Then we call the resetSyncFlags() method of the SyncManager
object to reset all the new and modified flags in the records of the Palm
device database. Finally, we close the Palm device database by calling the
closeDB() method of the SyncManager object.

Updating the desktop database files

Step 8 in the step-by-step process brings the synchronization to completion.
All we need to do is write out the updated desktop files in our
SaveDesktopRecords() method:

```
public void SaveDesktopRecords() throws IOException {
    FileOutputStream out;
    FileOutputStream ids;
    PinRecord desktopRec;

    out = new FileOutputStream("C:\\SimplePinDB.id");
```

(continued)

(continued)

```
    out.write((new
        Integer(nextId).toString()).getBytes());
    out.write("\r\n".getBytes());
    out.flush();
    out.close();
    out = new FileOutputStream("C:\\SimplePinDB.txt");
    ids = new FileOutputStream(myProps.pathName +
        myProps.localName + ".ids");
    Enumeration allDesktopRecs = currentRecs.elements();
    while(allDesktopRecs.hasMoreElements()) {
        desktopRec = (PinRecord)
            allDesktopRecs.nextElement();
        desktopRec.writeFile(out);
        desktopRec.writeIdFile(ids);
    }
    out.flush();
    out.close();
    ids.flush();
    ids.close();
    out = new FileOutputStream(myProps.pathName +
        myProps.localName + ".sav");
    int numArc = archivedRecs.size();
    int i;
    for (i = 0; i < numArc; i++) {
        desktopRec = (PinRecord)archivedRecs.elementAt(i);
        desktopRec.writeFile(out);
    }
    out.flush();
    out.close();
    }
}
```

This looks like a lot of code, but all it's doing is writing four files. First, the updated next unique identifier is written to "C:\SimplePinDB.id". Next, the desktop database file "C:\SimplePinDB.txt" and the ID mapping file in the conduit subdirectory of the HotSync folder (in our case, "C:\Palm\SchettJ\SimplePin\PinCond.ids") are written. Then the archived records are written to the Conduit subdirectory of the HotSync folder. In our case, this is written to the file named "C:\Palm\SchettJ\SimplePin\PinCond.sav".

That's almost all there is to the conduit! All we need to do is install it, and we're ready to use it.

Handling HotSync in Your Application

Your Palm OS application needs to support one additional Launch Code in order to correctly support HotSync. This new Launch Code tells your application that a HotSync has been completed, and it's your clue to resort the database. Why resort the database? Because new records might have been added, or existing records edited, such that your database is no longer in sorted order.

The full source code to the updated Simple Pin DB example is on the CD-ROM that accompanies this book in the Examples\Chap17\SimplePinDB folder. If you're using CodeWarrior, just open the project file named simplepindb.mcp. If you're using GCC, the Src subfolder contains all the necessary files, along with a makefile. In either case, all the program code is in the SimplePinDB.c file.

The `case` block in the `PilotMain()` function that handles the `sysAppLaunchCmdSyncNotify` launch code is as follows:

```
    case sysAppLaunchCmdSyncNotify:
        launched = !(launchFlags & sysAppLaunchFlagSubCall);
        if (launched) {
            DmOpenRef db;
            db = DmOpenDatabaseByTypeCreator('Pins',
                'PDBe', dmModeReadWrite);
            if (db) {
                Resort(db);
                DmCloseDatabase(db);
            }
        }
        else {
#ifdef __GNUC__
CALLBACK_PROLOGUE
#endif
            Resort(PinDB);
#ifdef __GNUC__
CALLBACK_EPILOGUE
#endif
        }
        break;
```

This `case` block just calls our `Resort()` function. Technically, it's impossible for the application to be running when it receives this launch code, but we coded it to handle that situation anyway. If the application is not running, we open the database for reading and writing and then close it after we call the `Resort()` function.

The `Resort()` function does exactly what its name implies; it resorts the database:

```
static void Resort(DmOpenRef db) {
#ifdef PACKED_RECORD
    DmQuickSort (db, (DmComparF *) ComparePackedPinFunc, 0);
#else
    DmQuickSort (db, (DmComparF *) ComparePinFunc, 0);
#endif
}
```

All we need to do is call the `DmQuickSort()` Palm OS function and pass it the pointer to the same compare function we used for inserting new Pin records. Refer to Chapter 13 for a description of the `ComparePinFunc()` and `ComparePackedPinFunc()` functions.

The only other change we need to make to the Simple Pin DB application is to the code that initially creates the database. Because we're going to have a conduit, we don't want HotSync to back up the database for us. The only change to that function that's needed is to delete the following statement from the `AppInfoInit()` function:

```
theAttributes |= dmHdrAttrBackup;
```

If this attribute is not set, then HotSync won't backup the database.

If you've already got the Simple Pin DB application from Chapter 13 installed, you need to remove it first before you install the version from this chapter; otherwise, the original Simple Pin database, with the backup bit set, will still be used, and the database will be backed up. Just remove the non-conduit version of Simple Pin DB before you install this version.

Getting Your Conduit Installed

You've got the coolest conduit on the planet, but unless you install it into the HotSync application, it's not going to be much use. There is a simple tool you can use to install a Java Conduit during development, but when it's time to send your conduit to general users, you'll have to write a Windows application to install and uninstall your conduit. We're not going to cover the installer in detail, as it's no different than any other C application you'd write. In fact, there are a number of "installer builder" applications that do a great job of building an install/uninstall application. We will show you what you need to do when it's time to write your installer.

Installing a conduit during development

You can develop Java Conduits under Windows 95, 98, and NT. First, you must have an installed and working HotSync application, version 2.0, 2.1, or 3.0. You also need to have a Java SDK installed (J++, Symantec, or the Sun JDK work well). When you install your Java SDK, it installs a Java VM on your machine. Finally, you need to install the Java Conduit SDK, which will add the appropriate DLLs and Java classes onto your system. At this point, you're ready to develop and ultimately install your Java Conduit.

Installing a Java Conduit during development is a matter of running the `CondCfg.exe` program that's in the `bin` directory of the Conduit SDK install directory. Before you run this utility, make sure that the HotSync application is not running. You can exit the HotSync application by right clicking on the HotSync icon in the System Tray, and select the Exit menu item.

When you run `CondCfg.exe` and click the Add button, the window shown in Figure 14-1 appears.

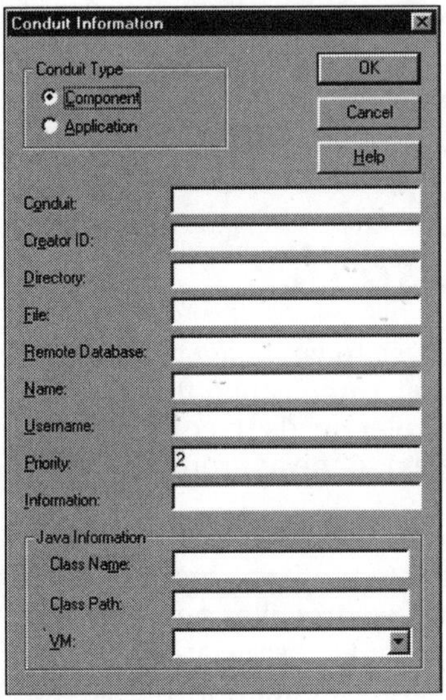

Figure 14-1:
Conduit
Configuration
utility.

Fill in the fields of this window as follows:

- ✔ **Conduit:** Enter **jsync.dll.**
- ✔ **Creator ID:** Enter your application Creator ID (`PFDe` for Simple Pin DB).
- ✔ **Directory:** Enter the name of the folder for the user files (`PinCond` for the example).
- ✔ **File:** Enter the filename for synced files (`PinCond` for the example).
- ✔ **Remote Database:** Enter the database name on the Palm device (SimplepinDB-PDBe for the example).
- ✔ **Name:** Enter the conduit name (Simple Pin for the example).
- ✔ **Username:** Leave blank.
- ✔ **Priority:** Leave as 2.
- ✔ **Information:** Leave blank.
- ✔ **Class Name:** The name of your Conduit class file (`PinCond` for the example).
- ✔ **Class Path:** The full path to your Conduit class file.

    ✔ **VM:** Select the VM (MS for Microsoft, SUN for Sun) to use to run the Conduit.

Click OK to close the window, and then click Exit to exit the CondCfg.exe application. Now you can start HotSync and test your Conduit.

If you make a change to your Conduit code and recompile the Java class files, you need to exit and then relaunch HotSync in order for the new classes to run.

You can remove an installed Conduit using the CondCfg.exe program as well. Simply select the Conduit in the main window and click the Delete button.

Making a conduit installer

When it's time to ship your masterpiece to your eager customers, you need to create a simple install (and uninstall) application that does all this without any user intervention. The same installer needs to copy the required support files (like jsync.dll and your class files) to the appropriate directory on the user's system.

The Conduit SDK includes an installer in the JSync Installer folder that installs the jsync.dll file and all other required files on a user's system. You only need install your own class files, and possibly a Java VM. After these files are copied, you need to register your Conduit with HotSync. The Java SDK includes a file named CondMgr.dll that you can use in your installer. This DLL has several functions that perform the same functions as the CondCfg.exe program you use when you're developing your Conduit.

Conduits in C++ for MacOS and Windows

Two other conduit SDKs are available to you. These SDKs allow you to create native applications in C++ that implement conduits. If you want to create a conduit for the MacOS, this is your only option. If you want to create a conduit for Windows and need to access a desktop database that doesn't have a Java interface, you're also stuck using C++.

The good news is that you still need to deal with exactly the same issues when creating your conduits in these other SDKs. In fact, the interfaces for things like the SyncManager are even similar. We don't want to sugarcoat things — you are in for quite a bit of work to create a conduit in C++ — but the information in this chapter should help somewhat.

Part IV
Flying On Instruments

"OKAY, SO MAYBE COMDEX WASN'T READY FOR OUR MICROWAVE SLOW-COOKER THIS YEAR, BUT I STILL THINK WE SHOULD GO AHEAD WITH THE TRACKBALL GARAGE DOOR OPENER."

In this part . . .

We wrap up our topics in Part IV. When you're ready to get a little jazzy and you want to do things on the fly, you can go beyond static interfaces and add dynamic behavior to your applications. This not only makes your applications more interesting, it gives the fly something to do, too. After you have completed your application, there's nothing like a boatload of testing to deflate your ego. We show you how to use the Debugger with the Palm device and with the emulator.

You can impress all your friends with the neat tips you get from this part. When you're done with these chapters, you'll be a Palm OS programming pro. Just try saying that three times fast!

Chapter 15

Dynamic Forms and Menus

● ●

In This Chapter

▶ Creating forms on the fly

▶ Adding, modifying, and deleting elements

▶ Being contextual with multiple menus

● ●

*S*ometimes, you just can't know exactly everything that belongs on a form. A powerful application also demands a powerful menu system. In addition to the "one form, one menu" approach used by most of your programs, you can add more power and flexibility by creating interface elements and switching menus when necessary.

Giving Form to an Idea

In the traditional approach to creating an application, you create all the forms you need by using Constructor in CodeWarrior, or by creating a pilrc file that describes the interface with the GNU tools. These predefined forms are then compiled into your application as resources that are loaded when a form is displayed. This approach is great for several reasons:

✔ Resource-based forms require less dynamic memory

✔ Resource-based forms require less program memory

✔ Resource-based forms are quicker to display

✔ Resource-based forms are more battery-friendly

With all these advantages, you may be thinking that there is never a reason to use anything else. However, to every ironclad set of rules, you can always find exceptions. When your form is pre-defined, it's obviously less flexible. If your interface is *data-driven*, a predefined form just isn't going to work as well.

A *data-driven* interface is one that changes based on the data it displays. An example of a data-driven Form is one that presents a multiple-choice questionnaire. This application might read a record in a database that describes a question and the list of answer choices.

Understanding the options

When using dynamic forms, you have two choices:

✔ Completely dynamic forms

✔ Predefined forms with some dynamic elements

To use completely dynamic forms, you create your forms and all the interface elements on each form completely dynamically. When you take this approach, your application won't contain any form resources at all.

To use predefined forms with some dynamic elements, you define the form resource with as many static interface elements as you want and then dynamically add interface elements as needed in your program.

Knowing the limitations

There are some limitations to what you can do dynamically. The biggest limitation is that your application will work only with Palm devices running Palm OS 3.0 or later. You also have the following limitations of what you can do dynamically:

✔ You cannot create tables.

✔ You cannot create repeating buttons.

✔ You cannot create help strings or menus.

✔ You cannot move an interface element after it's created.

Furthermore, you're responsible for assigning interface identifiers when you create forms or form elements. Since these IDs are used elsewhere in your application (to figure out which form or element generated the event) you may not be able to use `switch()` statements in your event handlers.

Making a form

Dynamic forms are no different in their behavior from predefined forms in all ways except their initial loading. Refer to Chapter 9 for a complete description of creating applications that use predefined forms. Recall from that chapter that you use the `FrmGotoForm()` Palm OS function, passing in the resource ID of the desired Form, to begin the process of loading a predefined form. When the form is fully loaded, your application receives and handles the `frmLoadEvent` event. In that handler, your application calls the `FrmInitForm()`, `FrmSetActiveForm()`, and finally `FrmSetEventHandler()` Palm OS functions for the loaded form.

For a dynamic form, you kick off the whole process by calling the FrmNewForm() Palm OS function to create the form, and then you call the FrmSetActiveForm(), and then the FrmSetEventHandler() Palm OS functions. After that, you create any desired interface elements, and then you draw the form by calling the FrmDrawForm() Palm OS function. From that point on, your program structure is identical to a predefined form.

Instead of drawing the form right after you create it, you can more closely mimic the behavior of the FrmGotoForm() Palm OS function instead by adding a frmOpenEvent event to the event queue once you're finished adding dynamic interface elements to the new form. Then your form event handler can initialize the form and draw it when the handler receives the frmOpenEvent event.

We've reworked the Hello World example from Chapter 8 to use a dynamic form. The full source code to the example is on the CD-ROM that accompanies this book in the Examples\Chap15\helloworld folder. If you're using CodeWarrior, just open the project file named helloworld.mcp. If you're using GCC, the Src subfolder contains all the necessary files, along with a makefile. In either case, all the program code is in the helloworld.c file.

The changes needed to use a dynamic form are first apparent in the PilotMain() function:

```
DWord PilotMain(Word launchCode, Ptr cmdPBP,
    Word launchFlags) {
  Err error;

  error = RomVersionCompatible (ourMinVersion,
    launchFlags);
  if (error) return (error);
  if (launchCode == sysAppLaunchCmdNormalLaunch) {
    if ((error = StartApplication()) == 0) {
      MakeMainForm();
      EventLoop();
      StopApplication();
    }
  }
  return error;
}
```

Because we're using dynamic forms, we must verify that the ROM version is 3.0 or later. Other than that, we add a call to our MakeMainForm() function, where we will create the form. Here's a look at that function:

```
static void MakeMainForm(void) {
   FormPtr newForm;
   EventType openEvent;

   newForm = FrmNewForm(Main_Form, "Hello World!",
      0, 0, 160, 160, false, 0, 0, Main_MenuBar);
   FrmSetActiveForm(newForm);
   FrmSetEventHandler(newForm, MainFormHandleEvent);
   FrmNewLabel (&newForm, Main_Form+1,
      "Hello there, world!", 20, 20, largeFont);
   openEvent.eType = frmOpenEvent;
   openEvent.data.frmOpen.formID = Main_Form;
   EvtAddEventToQueue (&openEvent);
}
```

First we create the main form by calling the FrmNewForm( ) Palm OS event.
We pass in an identifier for the form, its title string, dimensions, false to indicate it's not a modal form, zeros for the default button and help ID, and the
resource ID of the Form menu. Then we set it as the active form, and associate an event handler function with it. To complete the form, we add a label.
After the form is complete, we create a frmOpenEvent event and add it to the
event queue. That's about all the changes needed to the program to use
dynamic forms.

The only other change we make is to remove the call to our
ApplicationHandleEvent( ) function in the event loop. We also can remove
the function from the program. We don't need this function any more; its only
job was to handle the frmLoadEvent event. The new EventLoop( ) function
looks like this:

```
static void EventLoop(void) {
   EventType event;
   Word error;

   do {
      EvtGetEvent(&event, evtWaitForever);
      if (! SysHandleEvent(&event))
         if (! MenuHandleEvent(0, &event, &error))
            FrmDispatchEvent(&event);
   } while (event.eType != appStopEvent);
}
```

Getting Dynamic with Elements

You can do much more than hard coding adding elements to a form. After all,
this is hardly a data-driven approach! When you don't know ahead of time
just how many or what type of interface elements are on a form at any given
time, it makes handling form events a bit more complex.

Consider an application that creates a form based on data it reads from a database. This application needs to keep track of the elements it creates so that it can properly handle form events. It might also need to remove some of the elements and add new ones in response to user actions. One example of such an application is the Testing application. The Testing application reads a record from a database, and based on that record's contents, it creates the necessary form elements to allow the user to answer a question. It then records the answer and moves on to the next question.

To show you how this works, we create a Testing example program that implements a simple testing application. To keep things simple, we're not actually going to use a database to hold the data for the program. Instead, we just use a global variable to hold an array of structures with the data. This lets us focus on the dynamic form portion of the program. Refer to Chapter 13 to see how to create an application that uses Palm OS databases.

The full source code to the example is on the CD-ROM that accompanies this book in the Examples\Chap15\testing folder. If you're using CodeWarrior, just open the project file named testing.mcp. If you're using GCC, the Src sub-folder contains all the necessary files, along with a makefile. In either case, all the program code is in the testing.c file.

To create a data-driven dynamic form, you follow these steps:

1. **Design the data structures needed to generate a form dynamically.**

2. **Create the interface elements for the form, based on the data.**

3. **Initialize the contents of the dynamically created form.**

4. **Respond to events generated by the user when interacting with the form.**

5. **Extract the user-entered information from the dynamic form.**

6. **Remove the dynamically created elements from the form.**

Designing data for dynamic forms

The first step in our step-by-step process for dynamic forms is to design the data structures that describe what needs to be on the form. For our testing application, we need to create a structure that describes all the possible questions the application needs to display. The application displays:

✔ Multiple-choice questions with multiple answers

✔ Multiple-choice questions with a single answer

✔ Open-ended questions that require a written answer

The `questionType` structure defines the data structure represents a single question:

```
enum aType {
    mChoice,
    sChoice,
    freeForm
};

typedef enum aType answerType;

typedef struct {
    CharPtr prompt;
    answerType a;
    union qval {
        struct mChoice {
            CharPtr* answers;
            WordPtr selections;
        } mChoice;
        struct sChoice {
            CharPtr* answers;
            Word selection;
        } sChoice;
        struct freeForm {
            CharPtr answer;
        } freeForm;
    } qval;
} questionType;

typedef questionType* questionTypePtr;
```

The `aType` enum defines the three types of questions. The `questionType` structure holds a string in the `prompt` field, the type of answer expected in the `a` variable, and then a `union` named `qVal` that has the structures for the three question types.

For multiple-answer questions, we allocate an array of strings to hold the questions and store it in `answers`. We also allocate an array of `Words` to hold the user selections and store it in `selections`. For single-answer questions, we allocate an array of strings to hold the questions and store it in `answers`. There is a single `Word` to hold the user selections named `selection`. For the open-ended question, we will allocate a string and store it in the `answer` variable.

We need three global variables to keep track of the question data used by the program:

```
questionTypePtr fakeDatabase[3];
Int currentQuestion = -1;
Word firstIndex;
```

The `fakeDatabase` array holds three `questionType` structures. This represents our database. In a full implementation of this application, you'd store the data in a real Palm OS database. The `currentQuestion Int` holds the index (0-2) of the currently displayed question. We initialize it to -1 to indicate that there is no current question when the application first executes. The `firstIndex Word` holds the form element index of the first dynamically added element for the current question. We need to know this to know which elements to remove from the form when we display a different question.

In order to load the `fakeDatabase` array with some data, we create a function named `LoadData()`. This function just creates three `questionType` structures and puts them into the `fakeDatabase` array:

```
static void LoadData() {
   questionTypePtr newQ;
   Int i;

   newQ = (questionTypePtr)
      MemPtrNew(sizeof(questionType));
   newQ->a = mChoice;
   newQ->prompt = "What are the\rcharacteristics of fire?";
   newQ->qval.mChoice.answers =
      (CharPtr*)MemPtrNew(5 * sizeof(CharPtr));
   newQ->qval.mChoice.answers[0] = "Red";
   newQ->qval.mChoice.answers[1] = "Green";
   newQ->qval.mChoice.answers[2] = "Hot";
   newQ->qval.mChoice.answers[3] = "Cold";
   newQ->qval.mChoice.answers[4] = 0;
   newQ->qval.mChoice.selections =
      (WordPtr)MemPtrNew(4 * sizeof(Word));
   for (i =0; i < 4; i++)
      newQ->qval.mChoice.selections[i] = 0;
   fakeDatabase[0] = newQ;
   newQ = (questionTypePtr)
      MemPtrNew(sizeof(questionType));
   newQ->a = sChoice;
   newQ->prompt =
      "In which state is the city\rof Spokane?";
   newQ->qval.sChoice.answers =
      (CharPtr*)MemPtrNew(4 * sizeof(CharPtr));
   newQ->qval.sChoice.answers[0] = "Idaho";
   newQ->qval.sChoice.answers[1] = "Massachusetts";
   newQ->qval.sChoice.answers[2] = "Washingtion";
   newQ->qval.sChoice.answers[3] = 0;
   newQ->qval.sChoice.selection = 255;
   fakeDatabase[1] = newQ;
   newQ = (questionTypePtr)
      MemPtrNew(sizeof(questionType));
   newQ->a = freeForm;
   newQ->prompt = "Describe photosynthesis:";
   newQ->qval.freeForm.answer = NULL;
   fakeDatabase[2] = newQ;
}
```

Three questionType structures are allocated by using the MemPtrNew() Palm OS function. Refer to Chapter 9 for complete details on using MemPtrNew(). The first question is a multiple-choice question with four possible answers, the second question is a single answer question with three choices, and the last question is open-ended.

You can change this function and add additional choices to the multiple-choice questions, change the order of the questions, or even allocate additional questions to see how the dynamic Form is displayed, based on your changes.

Creating elements dynamically

Step 2 in the step-by-step process is to create elements on a form dynamically. We also need to create a form dynamically, so we use the same basic approach as we did with the Hello World example presented at the beginning of this chapter. First, we create a form with two buttons on it. This serves as the basic form for the application. We add and remove interface elements to this basic form as we display each question. The MakeMainForm() function creates the basic form:

```
static void MakeMainForm(void) {
    FormPtr newForm;
    EventType openEvent;

    newForm = FrmNewForm(Main_Form, "Tester", 0, 0,
        160, 160, false, 0, 0, Main_MenuBar);
    FrmSetActiveForm(newForm);
    FrmSetEventHandler(newForm, MainFormHandleEvent);
    CtlNewControl ((VoidPtr) &newForm, Main_Form+1,
        buttonCtl, "Next", 20, 145, 40, 14,
        stdFont, 0, true);
    CtlNewControl ((VoidPtr) &newForm, Main_Form+2,
        buttonCtl, "Previous", 100, 145, 40, 14,
        stdFont, 0, true);
    ShowQuestion(0);
    openEvent.eType = frmOpenEvent;
    openEvent.data.frmOpen.formID = Main_Form;
    EvtAddEventToQueue (&openEvent);
}
```

We create a new form and give it the ID of Main_Form. We defined this to be 1000. Then we make it the active form and associate an event handler function with it. Next, we create two buttons labeled Next and Previous. Their IDs are Main_Form+1 and Main_Form+2, which we need to know when it's time to write the code that handles the events they generate when tapped. We call our ShowQuestion() function to add the dynamic elements to display the first question, and then we insert a frmOpenEvent event into the event queue to display the first question.

Our ShowQuestion() function adds elements to the current form, based on the data of the selected question in the fakeDatabase array. It also loads the elements with the saved answer the user supplied, if they've already answered the question and are reviewing their answer. That's Step 3 in the step-by-step process. This is a long function, so we'll present it in four chunks:

```
static void ShowQuestion(int questionId) {
    Word id;
    Word choices;
    FormPtr frm;
    questionTypePtr theQ;
    ControlPtr newControl;
    FieldPtr newField;
    char choiceString[80];
    Handle h;
    CharPtr aVal;

    currentQuestion = questionId;
    theQ = fakeDatabase[questionId];
    frm = FrmGetActiveForm();
    firstIndex = FrmGetNumberOfObjects(frm);
    id = Main_Form+firstIndex+1;
    FrmNewLabel (&frm, id++, theQ->prompt, 20, 20,
        largeFont);
    switch (theQ->a) {
```

For all questions, we begin by saving the supplied questionId into the currentQuestion global variable. We need to do this so we know which question is displayed when it's time to save the user-entered information and remove the form elements.

We next retrieve the questionType data for the question. This is where you'd normally use a database. Then we set firstIndex to the number of objects currently on the form. We get that by calling the FrmGetNumberOfObjects() Palm OS function. We compute the first ID we will assign to the new elements by adding the number of current elements plus 1 to Main_Form. This ensures that we don't give new elements the same ID as either of the buttons on the basic form. Finally, we create a label at the top of the form that displays the prompt for the question.

When we're done with all that, we use a switch() statement on the answerType enum of the question, to determine what kind of question it is. The next three chunks are the three cases possible. Each adds the required elements for the specific question type:

```
case  mChoice:
    for (choices = 0;
            theQ->qval.mChoice.answers[choices] != 0;
            choices++) {
        newControl =  CtlNewControl ((VoidPtr) &frm, id++,
            checkboxCtl,
            theQ->qval.mChoice.answers[choices],
            20, 60+14*choices, 0, 0, boldFont, 0, true);
        CtlSetValue(newControl,
            theQ->qval.mChoice.selections[choices]);
    }
    break;
```

The multiple-choice question generates a form containing check boxes for each question. This allows the user to select more than one answer. We just loop until we find an answers string that is NULL. For each non-NULL string, we create a check box control. We compute the y position of each new check box such that they are spaced 14 pixels down from the previous one.

We use the CtlSetValue() Palm OS function to set the control value to the saved value in selections. Recall that this array is initialized to all 0s when we initially loaded the question data. We'll see a little later where this array is updated.

The next chunk of code generates the elements for a single-choice question:

```
case sChoice:
    FrmNewLabel (&frm, id++, "Select one:", 10, 125,
        stdFont);
    for (choices = 0;
            theQ->qval.sChoice.answers[choices] != 0;
            choices++) {
        StrPrintF(choiceString, "%d) %s", choices+1,
            theQ->qval.sChoice.answers[choices]);
        FrmNewLabel (&frm, id++, choiceString, 20,
            60+14*choices, boldFont);
        StrPrintF(choiceString, "%d", choices+1);
        CtlNewControl ((VoidPtr) &frm, id++,
            pushButtonCtl,
            choiceString, 60+12*choices, 125, 10, 11,
            boldFont, 1, true);
    }
    if (theQ->qval.sChoice.selection != 255) {
        FrmSetControlGroupSelection frm, 1,
            Main_Form+1+theQ->qval.sChoice.selection);
    }
    break;
```

For this type of question, we create a label for each possible answer, and then a set of push buttons in a group, one per possible answer. This lets the user tap any one of the push buttons to indicate their answer. We create a label at the bottom of the form to identify the push buttons, and then we loop much as we did for the last `case` creating both labels and push buttons. We create all the push buttons in group number 1.

If the user has a saved selection, then the selection variable will not be 255. If that's the case we just use its value to set the group selection by using the `FrmSetControlGroupSelection()` Palm OS function. Notice that we must calculate the element ID that corresponds to the saved selection.

The last case block generates the elements for the free-form question:

```
case freeForm:
    newField = FldNewField ((VoidPtr) &frm, id++, 20, 40,
        119, 95, stdFont, 255, true, true, false, false,
        leftAlign, true, false, false);
    if (theQ->qval.freeForm.answer != NULL) {
        h = MemHandleNew(StrLen(
            theQ->qval.freeForm.answer)+1);
        aVal = (CharPtr) MemHandleLock(h);
        StrCopy(aVal, theQ->qval.freeForm.answer);
        MemHandleUnlock(h);
        FldSetTextHandle(newField, h);
    }
    FrmSetFocus (frm, firstIndex+1);
    break;
    }
}
```

The free-form question just needs a field, so we create a field by calling the `FldNewField()` Palm OS function. If we have a saved answer from a previous viewing of this question, we allocate a new block of memory, copy the old answer into the block, and then set the field to use the allocated handle. We finish up by setting the form focus onto the new field by calling the `FrmSetFocus()` function.

Responding to events

Step 4 in the step-by-step process is to handle events generated by the form. The `MainFormHandleEvent()` event handling function does this job. The only interesting part of this function is the case block that processes the `ctlSelectEvent` event:

```
case ctlSelectEvent:
   switch(event->data.ctlSelect.controlID) {
      case Main_Form+1:
         SaveAnswer();
         EraseQuestion();
         if (currentQuestion == 2)
            ShowQuestion(0) ;
         else
            ShowQuestion(currentQuestion+1) ;
         FrmDrawForm(FrmGetActiveForm());
         break;
      case Main_Form+2:
         SaveAnswer();
         EraseQuestion();
         if (currentQuestion == 0)
            ShowQuestion(2) ;
         else
            ShowQuestion(currentQuestion-1) ;
         FrmDrawForm(FrmGetActiveForm());
         break;
   }
   handled = true;
   break;
```

We want to handle the events generated by the two buttons on the basic form (Next and Previous) while ignoring all other ctlSelectEvent events. This means we need to examine the controlID supplied with the event. Recall that we assigned the Next button the ID of Main_Form+1, and the Previous button the ID of Main_Form+2. We use those two values in a pair of case blocks, so we only process the event if it's from one of these two controls. The case blocks themselves just figure out the index of the Next or Previous question, wrapping around if the user goes past either end of the list. After the new question is displayed by calling our ShowQuestion() function, the Form is redrawn by calling the FrmDrawForm() Palm OS function.

Notice that in both cases, we call SaveAnswer() and then EraseQuestion() before we generate the new Form elements. Those two functions represent the last two steps in the process.

Extracting user-entered information

We need to save the user's answer when they move to the next or previous question. That's Step 5 in the step-by-step process, and it's done in the SaveAnswer() function:

```
static void SaveAnswer() {
   FormPtr frm;
   Word id, index;
   Word choices;
   questionTypePtr theQ;
   CharPtr ansStr;
   FieldPtr fld;
   Handle h;

   if (currentQuestion != -1) {
      frm = FrmGetActiveForm();
      theQ = fakeDatabase[currentQuestion];
      switch (theQ->a) {
      case  mChoice:
         index = firstIndex+1;
         for (choices = 0;
               theQ->qval.mChoice.answers[choices] != 0;
               choices++) {
            theQ->qval.mChoice.selections[choices] =
               FrmGetControlValue(frm, index++);
         }
         break;
      case sChoice:
         theQ->qval.sChoice.selection =
            FrmGetControlGroupSelection(frm, 1);
         break;
      case freeForm:
         id = Main_Form+firstIndex+2;
         fld = (FieldPtr)FrmGetObjectPtr(frm,
            firstIndex+1);
         ansStr = FldGetTextPtr(fld);
         if (ansStr != NULL) {
            if (theQ->qval.freeForm.answer != NULL)
               MemPtrFree(theQ->qval.freeForm.answer);
            theQ->qval.freeForm.answer =
               (CharPtr)MemPtrNew(StrLen(ansStr)+1);
            StrCopy(theQ->qval.freeForm.answer, ansStr);
            h = FldGetTextHandle(fld);
            FldSetTextHandle(fld, NULL);
            MemHandleFree(h);
         }
         break;
      }
   }
}
```

We get the data associated with the currently displayed question, and then use a switch() statement to correctly process the question, based on its type.

For multiple-choice questions, we calculate the index of the first check box and then loop for as many choices as there are in the question. For each question, we extract the setting of the check box by calling the FrmGetControlValue() Palm OS function, and we save the value into the corresponding slot of the selections array.

For single-choice questions, we simply get the selection of group 1 by calling the FrmGetControlGroupSelection() Palm OS function.

For free-form questions, we calculate the ID of the field and then get a pointer to the field text. If the text pointer isn't NULL, we need to save the text. If we had a previously saved answer, we free that memory first, and then we allocate a new chunk of memory large enough to hold the answer string and copy it in. The last thing we do is free the handle in the field, and set the field handle to NULL.

You must free any memory inside a dynamically created interface element before you remove it. This applies to fields and lists. If you don't free the memory, it will not be freed until your application exits.

Removing dynamic form elements

The last step in the step-by-step process is removing elements from a form. That's done by our EraseQuestions() function:

```
static void EraseQuestion() {
    FormPtr frm;
    Word index;

    if (currentQuestion != -1) {
        frm = FrmGetActiveForm();
        FrmSetFocus(frm, noFocus);
        for (index = FrmGetNumberOfObjects(frm) -1;
                index >= firstIndex;
                index-) {
            FrmHideObject(frm, index);
            FrmRemoveObject(&frm, index);
        }
    }
}
```

Notice that this function begins by setting the form focus to noFocus, by calling the FrmSetFocus() Palm OS function. You must do this or your form may retain an invalid focus on an element that no longer exists.

This function simply removes all form elements that were added by our ShowQuestion() function. It uses the value in the global firstIndex to know when to stop, and it uses the FrmGetNumberOfObjects() function to know where to start. For each element, first we hide the element by calling the FrmHideObject() Palm OS function, and then we remove it by calling the FrmRemoveObject() Palm OS function.

When removing form elements, you should remove them starting at the highest index number, and work your way down. That way, the memory is freed up more efficiently.

Using Multiple Menus

Menus are not nearly as flexible as forms. You cannot add or remove menus to the menu bar, nor can you add, delete, or even modify menu items in a menu. In other words, what you define in Constructor (or via pilrc if using the GNU tools) is what you get, as far a menus are concerned.

You've got just a few options:

- ✔ Don't use menus at all.
- ✔ Keep your menus somewhat basic, with general options that are always available.
- ✔ Put all the operations possible in your menus, and display an alert if the user chooses an invalid (at the given time) menu item.
- ✔ Create multiple versions of each menu, each corresponding to how the menu should look in a given state, and switch to the appropriate menu as needed.
- ✔ Use a combination of multiple menus and alerts.

The first option isn't very appealing. Menus are quite useful if your application has many operations. The second option isn't much better than the first. Crippling the menus too much makes them essentially useless.

The third option is actually what the built-in applications do, so you can follow the lead of the folks at Palm and do this in your own programs. If you do, be sure to use the correct icon in the alert. You should use the information or warning alert type for these kinds of alerts.

The fourth option can get unwieldy if you have many different states. If you have a menu bar with three menus, each with three items, there are 27 different combinations of menu items. Obviously, you don't want to create 27 menu bars!

We prefer the last option. For those key operations that are confusing (like a delete option when there is nothing to delete) consider making two versions of the menu bar, one with and one without the option. Another good example is if your application supports beaming, and the Palm device it's running on does not, a version of the menu bar without the Beam menu item is quite nice. We provide an example of this in Bonus Chapter 2 on the CD.

Chapter 16

Bugs on the Windshield

● ●

In This Chapter

▶ Understanding and avoiding bugs

▶ Using the CodeWarrior debugger

▶ Using the gdb debugger

▶ Debugging under emulation and the device

● ●

*A*mazing as it may seem, it's possible to create a program that doesn't work as expected. For reasons lost to prehistory, we call the errors that make a program misbehave *bugs*. When it's time to go on a bug hunt, you've got a wide array of tools you can use and a lot of helpful hints from this chapter.

A whole host of horrors can beset you when you're creating an application. Why, if we kept track of the *many* versions of the example programs that didn't work, we could have filled three or four CD-ROMS. Instead we only put the fully debugged (we hope) version of each example program in the book. That doesn't mean that we didn't have any bugs; it just means we spent plenty of hours resetting our Palm devices, staring at program code, and working with the debugger to get rid of the little beasties.

Knowing Your Bugs

What we learned from our debugging experience is that there are several different kinds of bugs and different ways of dealing with them:

- ✔ Source code errors are flagged at compile time. Your program won't run at all until you correct these.

- ✔ Linker errors can mean you've misspelled a function name, exceeded the 32KB program code limit, or forgot to add a source file to your project.

- ✔ Runtime errors that are resource related, such as running out of stack or dynamic memory, mean your program is either trying to use too much memory or is not freeing memory after it is done with it.

✔ Runtime errors that are related to data corruption, such as inconsistent or unexpected program behavior or result values, mean that your program has incorrectly modified a value via a pointer or has used more memory than allocated for some data. These errors are difficult to track down.

✔ Runtime errors that are related to what we lovingly call "programmer error," such as using a Palm OS function in a way it was never intended to be used, or passing the wrong value to a function, or miscoding an algorithm, mean that it's time to take a break and maybe walk the dog.

If there's one thing years of programming have taught us, it's that it's better to avoid a bug then to have to fix it. Another thing years of programming taught us is that caffeine is a reasonable substitute for sleep for several days at a time.

Programming defensively

You'd never know it from reading our code, but the best thing you can do to avoid bugs is to check the result of just about every Palm OS function call that you make. We left out this form of error checking from the examples because it tends to make the code very difficult to read and explain, but that doesn't mean that we don't believe in this approach.

The Palm folks believe in it, too, so they provide several macros you can use in your programs to test the results of function calls:

✔ To display an error alert when `ERROR_CHECK_LEVEL` is set to `ERROR_CHECK_PARTIAL` or `ERROR_CHECK_FULL`, call the `ErrDisplay()` Palm OS function and pass in the string to display.

✔ To display an error alert dialog if a specific condition is `true` and `ERROR_CHECK_LEVEL` is set to `ERROR_CHECK_PARTIAL` or `ERROR_CHECK_FULL`, call the `ErrFatalDisplayIf()` Palm OS function. The first parameter to this function is a Boolean expression that evaluates to `true` when the message needs to be displayed, and the second parameter is a message to display.

✔ To display an error alert dialog if a specific condition is `true` and `ERROR_CHECK_LEVEL` is set to `ERROR_CHECK_FULL`, call the `ErrNonFatalDisplayIf()` Palm OS function. The first parameter to this function is a Boolean expression that evaluates to `true` when the message needs to be displayed, and the second parameter is a message to display.

The great thing about these macros is that you can use them in your program while you develop it, and enable them by setting the `ERROR_CHECK_LEVEL` value to either `ERROR_CHECK_PARTIAL` or `ERROR_CHECK_FULL`. This turns on the appropriate error checking during development and debugging. After your program is debugged, simply set `ERROR_CHECK_LEVEL` to 0 to disable all these macros and recompile your application.

We wrote an example program for Bonus Chapter 3 (on the CD) that is a simple Web-page viewer. All it does is retrieve a file from a Web site by using the HTTP protocol and display it as text. It's not a Web browser; it doesn't do anything other than display the raw text of a file. As written, it does not use any of the debugging macros. See Bonus Chapter 3 for a complete description of the example code.

Our simple Web-page viewer example can make great use of these macros during development. Here's just one chunk of code from that example that has been rewritten using these macros:

```
if ((numRecords + 1) > indexBufSz) {
   indexBufSz += 5; // increase size of buffer
   error = MemHandleUnlock(DbIdsHandle);
   ErrFatalDisplayIf(error,
      "Could not unlock DbIdsHandle handle.");
   error = MemHandleResize(DbIdsHandle, indexBufSz *
         sizeof(UInt));
   ErrFatalDisplayIf(error, "Could not grow record Idx
         list.");
   recIds = MemHandleLock(DbIdsHandle);
   ErrFatalDisplayIf(recIds == NULL,
      "Could not lock DbIdsHandle.");
}
recIds[numRecords] = recordNum;
if (recordNum <= prefs.scrollPos)
   scrollPos = numRecords;
storedName  = (CharPtr) MemHandleLock (overviewRecHandle);
ErrFatalDisplayIf(storedName == NULL,
   "Could not lock overviewRecHandle.");
nameLen = StrLen(storedName)+1;
if ((choicesOffset+nameLen) > choicesBufSz) {
   choicesBufSz += (NAME_SIZE*5);
   error = MemHandleUnlock(ChoicesHandle);
   ErrFatalDisplayIf(error,
      "Could not unlock handle.");
   error = MemHandleResize(ChoicesHandle, choicesBufSz *
         sizeof(Char));
   ErrFatalDisplayIf(error,
      "Could not grow choices for list.");
   choices = MemHandleLock(ChoicesHandle);
   ErrFatalDisplayIf(choices == NULL,
      "Could not lock ChoicesHandle.");
}
StrCopy(choices+choicesOffset, storedName);
choicesOffset += nameLen;
error = MemHandleUnlock(overviewRecHandle);
ErrFatalDisplayIf(error,
   "Could not unlock overviewRecHandle handle.");

++recordNum;
overviewRecHandle = DmQueryNextInCategory (PinDB, &recordNum,
         prefs.categoryView);
```

This approach may seem a bit paranoid at first, but when you're hunting a bug, it's invaluable. What we do is use the ErrFatalDisplayIf() macro to test the return code of every MemHandleLock(), MemHandleUnlock(), and MemHandleResize() Palm OS function call. If any of these calls returns an error value (or null pointer in the case of the MemHandleLock() calls) we display a fatal error alert. After we've fully debugged the application, we disable all this error checking in one fell swoop by setting ERROR_CHECK_LEVEL to 0 and recompiling.

The Error manager has one more trick up its sleeve. If you've ever done Java or C++ programming, you've seen the very handy try/catch form of error handling. This mechanism lets you open a block of code with a try statement. Inside the block of code, you perform one or more operations that might fail. If any of them do, they raise an exception. Then at the end of the try block, you put one or more catch statements that detect the various errors that the block of code might throw. This is a lot simpler to write, because you don't need to check after every statement for an error and then try to handle the error. Rather, you can catch all errors of a specific class in one place and attempt to recover from the error there.

When you're coding a Palm OS application in C, you don't have this nice try/catch error handling. What you do have is a set of macros that (more or less) mimic this behavior:

- ✔ ErrTry: Begins a Try/Catch block.

- ✔ ErrThrow(): Throws an error from inside an ErrTry block. You supply a Long value that indicates the error. Execution passes to the ErrCatch() block.

- ✔ ErrCatch(err): Receives the error value when an ErrThrow() is executed.

- ✔ ErrEndCatch: Ends the Try/Catch block.

You can nest ErrTry/ErrCatch blocks. If you do, an ErrThrow() statement inside an ErrTry block transfers execution to the corresponding ErrCatch() block, but an ErrThrow() from within the ErrCatch() block transfers control to the next higher enclosing ErrCatch() block. Consider this example:

```
ErrTry {
    ErrTry {
        ErrThrow(1);
    }
    ErrCatch(err) {
        if (err == 1) {
            ErrDisplay("Caught inside try block 1");
            ErrThrow(2);
        }
```

```
      } ErrEndCatch
  }
ErrCatch(err) {
    if (err == 2) {
       ErrDisplay("Caught inside try block 2");
    }
} ErrEndCatch
```

This code example will display two error dialogs. The first `ErrThrow()` is caught inside the first `ErrCatch()` block, and then the `ErrThrow()` inside that block is caught in the outer `ErrCatch()` block.

A more realistic example of how this can be used is to catch and handle a number of different errors in one place. We wrote an example program for Bonus Chapter 1 that allows you to use a Palm device to communicate via the serial port. It does not use any of the debugging macros. Refer to that chapter for a complete description of the example code.

The Chat example of Bonus Chapter 1 initializes and opens the serial port in the `StartApplication()` function. That function, as coded in the chapter, does not use `ErrTry/ErrCatch`. If we did use it, it would look like this:

```
#define ERRSLIB 1
#define ERRSEROPEN 2
#define ERRSETSETTINGS 3
#define ERRMEMPTR 4
#define ERRSETRCVBUF 5

static Err StartApplication(void) {
    Err err = 0;
    DWord value = 0;
    SerSettingsType serSettings;

    ErrTry {
        err = SysLibFind ("Serial Library", &refNum);
        if (err) ErrThrow(ERRSLIB);
        err = SerOpen (refNum, 0, 19200);
        if (err) ErrThrow(ERRSEROPEN);
        serSettings.baudRate = 19200;
        serSettings.flags =
        serSettingsFlagBitsPerChar8 |
        serSettingsFlagStopBits1 |
        serSettingsFlagRTSAutoM | serSettingsFlagCTSAutoM;
        serSettings.ctsTimeout = (SysTicksPerSecond() / 2);
        err = SerSetSettings (refNum, &serSettings);
        if (err) ErrThrow(ERRSETSETTINGS);
        serLibOpened = true;
        newRcvBuffer = MemPtrNew(2048);
        if (newRcvBuffer == NULL) ErrThrow(ERRMEMPTR);
```

(continued)

(continued)

```
        err = SerSetReceiveBuffer(refNum,
            newRcvBuffer, 2048);
        if (err) ErrThrow(ERRSETRCVBUF);
    }
ErrCatch(tError) {
    switch (tError) {
    case ERRSLIB:
    case ERRSEROPEN:
        FrmAlert(Problem_Alert);
        if (err == serErrAlreadyOpen) SerClose (refNum);
        break;
    case ERRSETSETTINGS:
    case ERRMEMPTR:
    case ERRSETRCVBUF:
    }
    return err;
}
```

By coding the function this way, we can more clearly see the normal flow of the code within the ErrTry block, and place all the error handling within the ErrCatch block.

You can do one more thing to help avoid bugs: You can check to see if you've got the correct value before you pass it into a function. This is something we do use in our examples, and it's so simple that you might have missed it. For example, Chapter 13 includes an example that implements an Edit menu. That menu has a Select All function. Here's the case block that handles that function:

```
case Edit_SelectAll:
    frmP = FrmGetActiveForm();
    focusFldId = FrmGetFocus(frmP);
    if (focusFldId != noFocus) {
        fldPtr = (FieldPtr)FrmGetObjectPtr(frmP, focusFldId);
        FldSetSelection (fldPtr, 0,
            FldGetTextLength(fldPtr));
    }
```

Notice that we test the value of focusFldId to make sure that it is not noFocus before we pass it into FldSetSelection() Palm OS function. If we didn't make that test, and the user selected that menu option when no field had the focus, the program would crash in the FldSetSelection() call. If it did crash, we'd call that a bug.

Even if you code defensively, there are times you're just going to make mistakes. Although staring at the program code can be cathartic, it's not very helpful for most folks when they're trying to figure out why a program is misbehaving. What is helpful is being able to actually see the program source code while the program is running. The debugger's job is stopping program execution at specific source code lines, examining variable values and even changing them.

The combination of the CodeWarrior or gdb debugger, the Palm OS Emulator, the debug ROMs, and your program is the way to stomp out bugs in a hurry.

Debugging with CodeWarrior

We've done a lot of Palm OS programming using CodeWarrior, and we pretty much follow the same procedure when we're developing a program:

1. **Launch CodeWarrior, and from within CodeWarrior, launch the Palm OS Emulator (POSE).**

   See Chapter 2 for details on starting CodeWarrior and POSE.

2. **Write enough of the program so that we think we can run it. This means at a minimum, there is a** `PilotMain()` **function, an** `EventLoop()` **function, and a form event handler, along with a Form resource.**

3. **Compile the program. Correct any compile errors, and try again. Repeat until you successfully compile and link the program.**

4. **Download the program into POSE, and run it.**

   When the program blows up somewhere (and it usually does) you're presented with a dialog window from POSE, briefly explaining the error, offering options to Continue, Debug, or Reset. See Figure 16-1.

5. **Click Debug, and you'll see the source code line where the error occurred,**

6. **Figure out what went wrong!**

Figure 16-1:
Detecting
an error in
POSE.

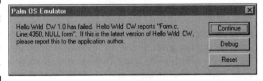

We've created a version of the Hello World example program from Chapter 8 with a simple bug in it. The full source code to the example is on the CD-ROM that accompanies this book in the Examples\Chap16\HelloWorld folder.

If you follow the steps outlined above with this example, your debugger window will look like Figure 16-2 after Step 5.

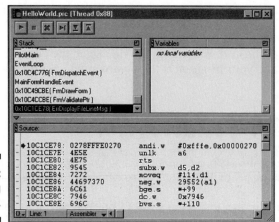

Figure 16-2:
Debugging
an error.

It seems that we've hit an error inside of a Palm OS function. You can tell this because the Debugger window isn't showing source code; it's showing assembly language code. To figure out what went wrong, we need to find out where in our program the error first occurred. Look at the Stack portion of the window. This shows the call stack (the nested function calls that lead up to the error). Looking backwards from the function where the error occurred, you can see that it came from within the ErrDisplayFileLineMsg() function, called from the FrmValidatePtr() function, called from the FrmDrawForm() function, called from the MainFormHandleEvent() function. That function is the first one without a leading hexadecimal number, so it's one of our functions. Click on this function name in the Stack window and the debugger shows the source code line in the program that started this whole mess off. Figure 16-3 shows the Debugger window after clicking on this function.

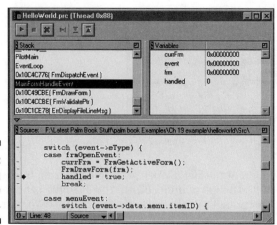

Figure 16-3:
Displaying
the source
line.

We see a small arrow pointing to the line:

```
handled = true;
```

This is the line after the one that caused the error.

Setting a breakpoint

We need to rerun the program and stop it just before the call to `FrmDrawForm()` to see what happens. The left edge of the Debugger window showing the source code has a dash (-) next to each executable line in the program. Click on the dash for the source code line that makes the function call:

```
FrmDrawForm(frm);
```

The dash changes to a red circle. This indicates that the program will stop executing before this source line, when run via the Debugger.

You can set as many breakpoints as you want in a program. When you save the source file, any breakpoints you've set are also saved. To remove a breakpoint, just click on the red circle again, and it changes back to a dash. To remove all breakpoints in a program, choose the Clear all breakpoints menu item from the Debug menu.

Click the Kill button in the Debugger (the large X), and POSE resets, and the debugger closes. Now run the debugger again by choosing the Debug menu item from the Project menu.

Sometimes, CodeWarrior loses its mind when you "kill" the running program. You might notice that the Debug menu item in the Project menu is grayed out, or if it isn't that choosing it yields an error window. When this happens, you must exit POSE, and then quit CodeWarrior. Then launch CodeWarrior with your project again, and re-launch POSE. The Debugger will work again, at least once. This is, as they say, a bug in CodeWarrior.

This time, the program will stop just before it executes the call to `FrmDrawForm()`, as shown in Figure 16-4.

Examining and changing variable values

You can now look at the variable values, and even change them. The Variables portion of the Debugger window shows the current variable values in the program. Notice that the `frm` variable's value is `0x00000000`. That's not a good value for a `FormPtr` variable. We put the pointer in a variable named `currFrm`, not the `frm` variable. We can set the `frm` variable to the same value as `currFrm`, and then continue execution to see if that fixes the program.

Figure 16-4:
Reaching a
Breakpoint.

Click the value of the `frm` variable, and enter the same value as is in the
`currFrm` variable. For us that's `0x00001A30`. Now you're ready to continue
executing the program.

Anytime you change a value this way, you can cause more problems than you
solve. For example, if you change the pointer value such that it points somewhere it shouldn't (for example, `0x0001A30`, which is missing a 0) then your
application will crash because that's not a valid address for a `FormPtr`.

Stepping in, stepping out

You can continue execution of the program in one of four ways:

- ✔ Click the Run/Debug button (the right pointing arrow) to run the program from the current source line.

- ✔ Click the Step Over button (the right pointing arrow followed by a vertical line) to run the next source statement and then re-enter the
  debugger. You use this to single step through your program a line at a
  time.

- ✔ Click the Step Into button (the downward pointing arrow with a horizontal line under it) to run the next source line. If that line calls a function,
  the program stops at the first source line in the called function.

- ✔ Click the Step Out button (the upward pointing arrow with a horizontal
  line over it) to run the program until it leaves the current function. It
  stops execution at the line after the one that called the current function.

Click the Run/Debug button, and then look at POSE. Now the Form displays correctly! We've figured out the bug, but we haven't corrected it yet. To do that, we need to stop the Debugger and edit the program source code.

Although you can edit the program source code while the program is running in the Debugger, your changes are not effective until you kill the program, recompile the program, and re-load it into the emulator.

Click the Kill button, and change the call to `FrmDrawForm()` to:

```
FrmDrawForm(currFrm);
```

Now compile the program and debug it. Notice that the program still stops just before the call to `FrmDrawForm()`. Click the Run/Debug button again and this time, the Form displays correctly without changing anything. It's a success!

Debugging with gdb

If you're using the GNU tools, there's a source code debugger named gdb that does pretty much what the CodeWarrior Debugger does. It's not quite as friendly to use, but it does work. Entire books have been written on using gdb, so we're not going to talk about it in great detail. This section will show you how to run your program from with gdb; the rest is up to you.

The gdb debugger works either directly from the Bash (or MS-DOS) command line, or it works from within the GNU Emacs editor. You can use it from the command line, but it's much nicer to use it from within Emacs. To use it with Emacs, you must first correct a small problem within Emacs.

To do this, copy the two files on the CD-ROM in the Examples\Chap16\Emacs folder into your GNU distribution. Copy both gud.el and gud.elc into your <GCC Directory>\emacs\lisp folder, overwriting the versions that are already there.

To use Emacs and POSE, make sure that you're using the Seed version of POSE, or any version 2.1 or greater. You can download the latest release and Seed POSE versions from www.palm.com/devzone/pose/pose.html. After you install this version, follow these steps to debug using gdb and Emacs:

1. **Build a debug version of your application, by using the** `-g` **flag to gcc.**

2. **Start POSE and install your application.**

3. **Open a bash shell window and use** `cd` **to get to your application source directory.**

4. **Enter** emacs& **from the bash prompt to launch Emacs.**

   Emacs opens, and the command prompt displays in the bash window. You can now use the bash window to make your application after saving changes in Emacs.

5. **Open your source (.c) file in Emacs.**

6. **Press the Escape key, then the x key.**

   The Emacs status line shows M-x.

7. **Enter** gdb **in the status line, and press Return.**

   The status line will show Run gdb (like this): m68k-palmos-coff-gdb.

8. **Enter the name of your application, without the** .prc **on the end, and press Return.**

   For example, if you're building the Chapter 8 GCC version, enter helloworld.

9. **The Debugger loads in one of the Emacs windows. At the (gdb) prompt, enter** target pilot localhost:2000.

   The Debugger will wait for you to run your application in POSE.

10. **Launch your application in POSE.**

    The Debugger shows a SIGTRAP and has stopped execution in PilotMain(). The source file containing PilotMain() is displayed in another Emacs window, with a pointer (=>) pointing at the next line that will execute.

11. **Set breakpoints by positioning the cursor on the desired source line and then selecting the temporary breakpoint menu item from the Guid menu in Emacs.**

12. **Enter normal gdb debugging commands at the** (gdb) **prompt in the Emacs window.**

You can only perform one debugging session per launch of POSE. If you need to load another version of the application, you need to use the kill gdb command to kill the program, exit POSE, re-launch POSE, load the new version of the application, and then perform Steps 6 through 11 again. If you can't seem to get a (gdb) debugger prompt, just re-launch the application in POSE.

If gdb seems to have a hard time showing you the correct source line while debugging, it's because you've saved your source file using DOS line breaks (both a carriage return and line feed character at the end of each line) instead of using UNIX line breaks (just a line feed). To correct this, you can use the free text converter located at www.tamasoft.co.jp/freesoft/cvret-e.html to change your program to use UNIX line endings.

Understanding Devices

You've actually got a number of choices when it comes to the device to debug against. You can use POSE, or you can use an actual Palm device. When you use POSE, you can use one of the debug ROMS (version 2.0, 3.0, and whatever other versions 3Com has released) or you can use a downloaded ROM image from an actual device. If you're using a Macintosh desktop computer, you can even use the Simulator to debug your programs. The following sections look at the tradeoffs of each option.

Using POSE and debug ROMS

As far as we're concerned, this is the best option for developing Palm OS applications. The debug ROMS contain a lot of extra error-checking built right in, and when they detect a problem (such as the NULL FormPtr in the FrmDrawForm() Palm OS function in our example) you get a lot of information as well as the option to enter the debugger.

You can download debug ROMs from 3Com, via the Internet. Surf on over to www.palm.com/devzone/pose/pose.html. You'll need to sign a license agreement to gain access to the ROMs, so scroll down on the POSE page to the section titled "Getting ROM image files" to see how to proceed. It's worth the effort, in our opinion.

Because the debug ROMs check for errors and display an alert when one is detected, many system functions will never return an error code. If you set a breakpoint on code that checks the result of a function call and the function fails when running against the debug ROMs, you will never get to the breakpoint. Instead, you'll see the alert in POSE. POSE itself allows you to select a ROM image file to use, so you can test how your application will behave when running on older and newer Palm devices. POSE also lets you select how much memory the emulated device has, so you can test your application in devices with small (128KB) and very large (4MB) memories. POSE also performs a lot of error-checking while it runs your program, so it may detect errors that would otherwise go uncaught.

POSE also includes the gremlins feature. Gremlins is a way to let POSE use your application just like a very persistent user. It will tap all the buttons, enter text, use menus, and even do Finds just like a real user. Unlike a real user, it never gets bored, so it will keep using your program as long as you let it, or until it uncovers a bug. One part of testing your applications is to let a Gremlin use it for at least a few hours straight. If it survives that, it's less likely to have hidden bugs in it. You can read more about Gremlins in the POSE documentation.

Using POSE with actual device ROM images

Before 3Com released the debug ROMs, this was the only choice you had for using POSE. Even now, you might need to use this method if you don't want to sign the license agreement required to get the debug ROMs. At any rate, POSE comes with documentation that describes how to upload the ROM image from a real Palm device into POSE.

You'll still get all the great features of POSE, including better error checking of your programs. You won't get detailed information about Palm OS functions when your program has a bug, however.

Using the real McCoy

There's nothing like the real thing when it comes to testing your application. However, for debugging, using a real Palm device is slow and cumbersome. It's possible, but it's so slow as to be unusable. We suggest you stick with POSE for debugging. Once you've got things to the point that you think all is well, it's time to take it to the device for a final test spin.

Using the Macintosh simulator

There's also little to recommend the Macintosh-based simulator these days. It also seems to be a throwback to pre-POSE days. About the best thing you can say about it is that it's fast. However, unless you've got a very old Macintosh, POSE will be quite acceptable in performance. POSE is also a much more accurate emulation of the device.

Part V
The Part of Tens

The 5th Wave   By Rich Tennant

IN A STROKE OF SELF RELIANCE, RAY EXTENDS THE POWER OF HIS PALM DEVICE ON HIS SLEEPING NEIGHBORS HEARING AID.

@RICHTENNANT

In this part . . .

Ah . . . The Part of Tens. This part is the place where we give you information in multiples of tens. Why? Because we don't have eleven fingers . . . that's why. First, we give some guidelines about using the inherent characteristics of the Palm devices to your application's advantage. Next, we broaden your world view of Palm OS programming by offering suggestions for ten development environments. Next, we give some pointers on things better left undone. Finally, we give plenty of great Web resources to all things involving Palm devices.

Chapter 17

Ten Things to Remember about Palm Devices

*T*his chapter covers the things to remember to keep you out of trouble when dealing with the Palm device's inherent characteristics, such as its screen size.

It's a Small World

Remember that your application's interface is only a 160 x 160 pixel screen. This makes things like 20-column spreadsheets unlikely candidates for Palm OS applications. The small screen size means that you'll have to pay particular attention to everything you display and when you display it. For example, menus are only shown when the user taps the Menu silk screen button, and forms fill the screen and don't display any borders. Keep repeating this mantra when designing forms: "Less is more."

My Memory Is All But Gone

Memory and storage space are hard to come buy in the Palm device. Doing simple things can usurp more memory than you expect. In light of this, you must be diligent in what you do and in what you store. Know your application's limits. For example, the local variable memory is limited to between 2KB and 4KB. This means that you cannot allocate large local variables nor can you use a lot of recursion. Also, because the dynamic memory your program can allocate, and the memory for global variables comes from the same place, you cannot declare very large globals or allocate very large amounts of dynamic memory. The best approach is to know how much memory you're allocating and where it's allocated, at all times.

Puny Palm Power

You should try to make your applications use as little power as possible. This makes sense on any mobile computing device. There is something a bit unique about Palm devices and their power — they never really turn themselves off. That's right. When the LCD is dark and the device seems to be "off," it's really in the sleep mode. It's actually in a very low-power state. It wakes from this state when the user presses a hardware button or an alarm goes off.

The doze mode is the preferred state. In doze mode, the unit is on, but in a reduced power state. The CPU is halted. The device wakes from dozing when a user or the system generates an event. Your goal is to write your programs such that the Palm device can get into this state as often as possible.

The last mode is the running mode. This is the mode in which the device actually executes program or operating system instructions. This mode uses the most power. Follow the general structure of a standard Palm OS application that we've given you in this book, and you'll be a long way toward conserving the batteries, because your application will be in doze mode whenever it is waiting for an event in the event loop.

Speed Is of the Essence

Palm Pilot users are usually on the go. They want information fast, and it's your job to get it to them. This means that your application's navigation should be fast, as we discussed in the preceding section. It also means that your application must be as fast as possible when retrieving and displaying information. Optimize your applications for speed. If a task seems to be taking too long for you, then it's certainly taking too long for your users.

Finding Your Way Around

Navigation should be easy. Palm Pilot users need to get to information without going through a lot of screens and commands. This means that your applications should never require more than a single tap to do something.

Also, you should provide a button to initiate or execute common commands and functions. Of course, your application should provide an overview form that displays a summary of the information that it holds and that allows selection of individual records or items of information. At the very least, applications should support the hardware navigation buttons (the up and down buttons in the center of the Palm device button array) and Graffiti next and previous field gestures.

Graffiti Is Not Vandalism

We don't agree with most legal statutes concerning graffiti on public walls and subways. We think graffiti is an art form not vandalism. In the same vein, we think Graffiti adds quite a bit toward helping users enter information into your applications. Your applications should include a Graffiti shift indicator in the lower-left corner of any form that has text entry fields. Also, an application should support Graffiti Help menu items and the Next/Previous Field Graffiti shortcuts.

Information Display Versus Information Entry

Palm devices were designed to be used as information-display tools, not information-entry tools. Sure, you can enter information into them, but that's not where their natural abilities lay. Use them to quickly retrieve and display information. Leave data-entry intensive tasks for desktops to contend with, and connect your applications via conduits and HotSync to transfer data to and fro. The folks at 3Com realized the display versus entry situation and have made data display evident in the built-in applications. Speaking of the built-in applications. . . .

Emulate the Built-In Applications

Be consistent with the built-in applications and do things their way. This is a simple rule to follow if you study the applications with the following in mind: the design of the forms, the ways in which menus are used and when they appear, how controls are used to prevent data entry errors, the feedback provided to users, the connectivity of the applications, the ways in which categories are employed. . . . We could go on and on. The gist of it all is to look and emulate. The answers are out there.

Simplicity Is the Mother of a Sane Application

Don't burden your applications with too many features. An application should do a small interrelated set of tasks well. Today it is easy to get trapped into thinking that "more is better." People want everything in one place and for one small price. Well, we won't give you advice about pricing, but we will tell you that trying to do everything you can think of in a single application doesn't work. Besides, with the limitations on-screen real estate, power, memory, and the requirement for speed, you need to be ever diligent in taking out extras, removing overhead, and streamlining functions.

The Desktop Is Your Friend

Palm applications are not meant to stand alone. That's why the device is called *The Connected Organizer.* Be sure to write conduits for your applications. It is imperative that your applications have the ability to exchange data with other computers. A standalone application is about as useful as a pair of glasses with one lens. Sure, you see some things, but to get the whole picture, you really need the other lens.

Chapter 18

Ten Other Development Environments

● ●

In This Chapter

▶ Developing directly on the Palm device

▶ Visual forms-based tools

▶ The rest of the story

● ●

Many more options are available for Palm OS Programming than just the two that we focus on throughout the book (CodeWarrior Lite and GCC.) Here are slightly more than ten other free, shareware, and commercial development environments you can use for Palm OS programming.

Before you dig into this chapter, you should know:

✔ We found all of these at www.developer.com/roadcoders.

✔ Within a category, we put the tools in alphabetical order so that no one's feelings would get hurt.

✔ Very brief descriptions were provided. These descriptions should be considered incomplete. Providing extensive descriptions was not our goal. Peaking your interest was.

Developing Directly on the Palm Device

PocketC

PocketC gives developers the ability to write C applets. PocketC is a C compiler for Windows CE devices and Palm devices. Some of the features of PocketC include a function library containing support for databases, serial I/O, and graphics. PocketC only works with Palm OS 2.0 and above. There is a shareware version of PocketC available for downloading that expires in 45 days. There is also a version available for purchase.

Quartus Forth

Quartus Forth is an ANSI standard Forth compiler and development environment. You develop applications directly on your Palm device. A free evaluation version is available as well as a registered version.

Visual Forms-Based Tools

CASLide

The Compact Application Solution Language (CASL) is a commercial for-sale language that can be used to create Palm OS applications. The CASL interactive Development Environment (CASLide) contains tools for editing source files, compiling programs, debugging, running CASL under Windows, and much more. To create an application, you point and click visual objects and place them into a simulated display. You then provide code for their behavior. There is a demo available for downloading.

PalmFactory

PalmFactory is a graphical Windows utility that allows developers to create Palm OS applications. PalmFactory takes you step by step through the creation of forms, menus, databases, and much more. PalmFactory can be downloaded.

Pendragon Forms

Pendragorn Forms is a custom forms software package for Windows. Pendragon Forms focuses on supporting the creation of data intensive applications. This is commercial for-sale software.

Satellite Forms

Satellite Forms is a visual rapid application development tool for Palm devices. With Satellite Forms, you lay out an application's interface by using drag and drop. Next, you add significant functionality via setting control properties and filters. You can also use the App Designer to add behavior and navigation. Satellite Forms also support scripting. A demonstration version is available as well as a for-sale version.

Visual Form Designer

Visual Form Designer is a visual application development environment for Palm devices. It provides a What You See Is What You Get resource editor, a code editor, and automatic resource file generation and compilation. There is a demonstration version as well as a registered version.

The Rest of the Story

ASDK

The Alternative Software Development Kit (ASDK) contains tools, files, and documentation for developing Palm OS applications for Windows 95 or NT. Features of ASDK include a compiler and previewer, an emulator, a debugger, and some support utilities. There is a version available for downloading.

cBasPad

cBasPad is a small interpreter for a subset of the BASIC programming language for Palm devices. cBasPad includes support for playing sounds, mathematical functions, serial port I/O, and simple graphics. You can download cBasPad.

Jump

Jump provides support for writing Palm OS programs in Java. It doesn't support writing Java applets. You can download Jump.

Pascal for the Pilot

Macintosh users can use Pascal for the Pilot to create applications. The development environment used is Think Pascal, although the author of Pascal for the Pilot states that other development environments can be used. To develop applications you create a set of resources with ResEdit. Next, you write and compile a code resource. The last step involves combining the two with the Swiss Army Resource Compiler (SARC). You can download both Pascal for the Pilot and SARC.

Pocket Smalltalk

Pocket Smalltalk allows developers to create applications for Palm devices by using the Smalltalk programming language. Pocket Smalltalk consists of a development environment for Windows 95 and NT. It also provides a compiler for generating .PRC files from Smalltalk code. A downloadable version is available.

Chapter 19

Ten Stupid Mistakes to Avoid

●●●

In This Chapter
▶ Building interfaces
▶ Communicating
▶ Programming tips

●●●

*H*ere are some things you are probably better off *not* doing in an application.

Building Interfaces

Alerts

When using custom alerts, your Alert message does not need to contain all three makers (^1 ^2 or ^3). However, the FrmCustomAlert() Palm function always requires three substitution strings. Always use empty strings when you call this function, for the unused markers.

Alerts and buttons

You must have at least one button on an alert. There is a practical limit of three buttons on an alert. If you need more than this, you have to use a dialog form. Dialog forms are explained in Chapter 9.

Button identification

The FrmDoDialog() Palm function returns the resource ID of the tapped button, not the index of the button. This is different from the Alert functions and also from the Palm documentation. The documentation is wrong.

Dynamically created elements

You must free any memory inside a dynamically created interface element before you remove it. This applies to Fields and Lists. If you don't free the memory, it will not be freed until your application exits.

The keyDownEvent

The Palm documentation for the keyDownEvent is incorrect. It says that when chr is 0, keyCode will be one of a set of virtual key codes. You'll find the definition of these codes in the Palm header file named Chars.h, but they include findChr (sent when the user taps the Find icon) and menuChr (sent when the user taps the Menu icon). For these and all other conmmand key codes, the value is provided in chr, keyCode is 0, and modifiers is commandKeyMask.

Label names

The FormCopyLable() function isn't very smart, so you can't pass in a string for the new Label that is longer than the original label text. If you do, very bad things happen. Also, the old label value isn't erased, so you have to do that yourself by calling the WinEraseRectangle() Palm OS function.

Communicating

Launch codes

Your application may not be running when it receives a launch code. This means you must:

- Use as little memory as possible when handling launch codes.
- Check to find out if your application was the currently running application, and if not avoid using any global variables when handling the launch code.
- If you're using the GCC compiler, you must use the CALLBACK_PROLOGUE and CALLBACK_EPILOGUE macros around the block of code that handles the launch code when the launch flags include the sysAppLaunchFlagSubCall flag.

Sockets

There is currently a limit of four open sockets with the Palm OS implementation of networking. This is a lot fewer than is available in other operating systems, so make sure that you close each socket when you're done with it.

Programming Tips

Alarms

An application can set only one alarm at a time. If it sets an alarm and it already has an alarm set, the old alarm is discarded.

Databases

You should always keep your databases in sorted order. This allows for quick access and sorted displays. However, the `DmFindSortPosition()` Palm function assumes that all deleted records are at the end of the database. If you delete or archive a record, rather than remove it, you must move it to the end of the database.

Hosts

The `GetHostByName()` Palm OS function has a little bug. Because of this bug, if the host you look up has four IP addresses, the first one returned isn't usable. That's why in our example programs we use a variable named `whichToUse`. We try to use the first IP address returned, but if it's zero, the bug has bit us, and we increment `whichToUse` so that we use the second IP address instead.

Pointers

Don't use memory pointers after you've unlocked the handle that you originally got the pointer from. In fact, try not to save pointers in global variables unless you are going to keep the handle locked for the duration of the program's execution.

Powering off

When you want to prevent the Palm device from powering off, the SysSetAutoOffTime() function is tempting. You might think that you can set the power off time so high that the unit will never power off. Resist the urge, and instead call the EvtResetAutoOffTimer() Palm OS function every so often. As its name implies, this function resets the auto off timer. Suppose that you're checking for some serial input every ⅙ of a second, as we do in the Chat example of Bonus Chapter 1. If you call EvtResetAutoOffTimer() every time you check for input, the device will never power off. When you stop checking for input (and resetting the auto off timer), the device will power off normally after the user-selected idle time has expired.

Chapter 20

Way More Than Ten Web Links

What would a Part of Tens chapter be without "Ten" in the title? We couldn't limit ourselves to just ten sites, though. You'll find links to the 3Com, to vendors on the CD-ROM, and to other Web sites that we thought were interesting or helpful. Surf's up dude!

The Mother Load

3Com

The www.pailm.com site is the place to start when you want to learn about 3Com and Palm computing. It also provides links to shareware and freeware sites, mailing lists and newsgroups.

Metrowerks

CodeWarrior Lite is used extensively throughout the book as the development environment for most of the example programs. The Metrowerks Corporation site is the place to find out everything you want to know about CodeWarrior. Go to www.metrowerks.com.

GNU

The `www.fsf.org` site gets you to the Free Software Foundation's GNU site. GNU is the other development environment that is extensively used throughout this book for the example programs.

RoadCoders

The `www.developer.com/roadcoders/` site is an invaluable site for mobile computing developers. It has links for developing applications for the Palm III and Windows CE devices. It also has a mailing list.

Groups and Lists

News Groups

- `comp.sys.handhelds`
- `comp.sys.palmtops`
- `comp.sys.palmtops.pilot`
- `comp.sys.pen`
- `pilot.programmer` — general Palm OS discussion group
- `pilot.programmer.codewarrior` — Codewarrior discussion group
- `pilot.programmer.pila` — Palm OS assembler discussion group
- `pilot.programmer.GCC` — Palm OS GCC discussion group

User Groups

The 3Com site has a great list of user groups so that you can communicate with people in your local area. Go to `www.palmpilot.com/resources/usergroups.html`.

Mailing Lists

The `www.roadcoders.com` site is mentioned previously in this Chapter. It is an invaluable source of information. Lucky for us it has a mailing list too.

The `palm3com.com/devzone/mailinglists.html` site provides links for 4 mailing lists. These can provide a wealth of information and an opportunity to interact with your Palm programming peers as well as many folks from Palm. You can ask questions, get help when you're stuck, and learn from other people's questions and answers.

Interesting Sites

GNU Pilot SDK

The `www.iosphere.net/~howlett/pilot/GNU_Pilot.html` site gives lots of links for GNU Palm OS programming.

IDG Books Worlwide

The `www.dummies.com` site is the source for this book and many more.

PalmPilotGear

This site gives you access to lots and lots of software for the Palm. Developers can get great ideas and learn what's out there. Go to `www.palmpilotgear.com`.

PalmZone

The `www.palmzone.com` site is a great site for information about the latest happenings in the Palm world.

WesCherry's PilRC

PilRC is a Win32 program for developing Palm OS applications. Go to `www.scumby.com/scumbysoft/pilot/pilrc`. You can even download the source code!

Appendix

About the CD

*H*ere's some of what you can find on the *Palm OS Programming For Dummies* CD-ROM:

- ✔ CodeWarrior Lite from Metrowerks and 3Com
- ✔ Pilot-GCC Win32, a GNU C development environment
- ✔ The Java™ 2 SDK, Standard Edition, v1.2.1

System Requirements

Make sure that your computer meets the minimum system requirements in the following list. If your computer doesn't match up to most of these requirements, you may have problems using the contents of the CD.

- ✔ A PC with a 486 or faster processor, or a Mac OS computer with a 68040 or faster processor.
- ✔ Microsoft Windows 95/98/NT or later, or Mac OS system software 7.5.3 or later.
- ✔ At least 24MB of total RAM installed on your computer.
- ✔ At least 120MB of hard drive space available to install all the software from this CD. (You'll need less space if you don't install every program.)
- ✔ A CD-ROM drive — double-speed (2x) or faster.
- ✔ A monitor capable of displaying at least 256 colors or grayscale.

If you need more information on the basics, check out *PCs For Dummies,* 6th Edition, by Dan Gookin; *Macs For Dummies,* 6th Edition, by David Pogue; *Windows 98 For Dummies, Windows 95 For Dummies,* or *Windows 3.11 For Dummies,* 4th Edition, all by Andy Rathbone and all published by IDG Books Worldwide, Inc.

How to Use the CD Using Microsoft Windows

1. **Insert the CD into your computer's CD-ROM drive.**

   Give your computer a moment to take a look at the CD.

2. **When the light on your CD-ROM drive goes out, double-click on the My Computer icon (It's probably in the top left corner of your desktop.)**

   This action opens the My Computer window, which shows you all the drives attached to your computer, the Control Panel, and a couple other handy things.

3. **Double-click on the icon for your CD-ROM drive.**

   Another window opens, showing you all the folders and files on the CD.

4. **Double-click the file called License.txt.**

   This file contains the end-user license that you agree to by using the CD. When you are done reading the license, close the program, most likely NotePad, that displayed the file.

5. **Double-click the file called Readme.txt.**

   This file contains instructions about installing the software from this CD. It might be helpful to leave this text file open while you are using the CD.

6. **Double-click the folder for the software you are interested in.**

   Be sure to read the descriptions of the programs in the next section of this appendix (much of this information also shows up in the Readme file). These descriptions will give you more precise information about the programs' folder names, and about finding and running the installer program.

7. **To install programs to you computer, find the file called Setup.exe, or Install.exe, or something similar, and double-click on that file.**

   The program's installer will walk you through the process of setting up your new software.

8. **To install programs to your Palm, use the PalmInstall Tool to find and install the .prc or .pdb files from the CD.**

How to Use the CD Using the Mac OS

To install the items from the CD to your hard drive, follow these steps:

1. **Insert the CD into your computer's CD-ROM drive.**

   In a moment, an icon representing the CD you just inserted appears on your Mac desktop. Chances are, the icon looks like a CD-ROM.

2. **Double click the CD icon to show the CD's contents.**

3. **Double-click the Read Me First icon.**

   This text file contains information about the CD's programs and any last-minute instructions you need to know about installing the programs on the CD that we don't cover in this appendix.

4. **To install programs to your computer, simply open the folder on the CD and double-click the icon with the words *Install* or *Installer*.**

5. **To install applications to your Palm, use the Install menu option in HotSync Manager to find and select the .prc and .pdb files from the CD.**

   After you install the programs that you want, you can eject the CD. Carefully place it back in the plastic jacket of the book for safekeeping.

What You'll Find

There are lots of useful tools and example files on the *Palm OS Programming For Dummies* CD-ROM.

Sample files

All of the demonstration files you need to follow this book's tutorials are organized by chapter number in the Examples folder. I've included a self-extractor, Examples.exe, to make it easy for you to copy all the files to your hard drive. Please note: If you happen to have a 16-bit CD-ROM driver in your computer, long filenames may appear truncated, or folders containing files with long filenames may appear empty. If this happens, just run Examples.exe to place all the files with the correct long filenames on your hard drive.

Adobe Acrobat Reader

Required tool for reading documentation in Acrobat format. I've included two versions — 4.0 is the latest version, but it doesn't offer any search capability. If you want to be able to search documents, you can install Version 3.

CASL for the Pilot demo by John Feras

The Compact Application Solution Language (CASL) is a commercial development environment that can be used to create Palm OS applications. To create an application, you point and click visual objects and place them into a simulated display. You then provide code for their behavior. This demo lets you try CASL out.

CodeWarrior Lite

CodeWarrior Lite is a demo version of CodeWarrior by Metrowerks and 3Com. You can compile the example programs using this version. And the extensive legalese goes like this: Selected programs Copyright (c) Metrowerks Inc. and its Licensors. All rights reserved.

Technical support from Metrowerks is available by acquiring any of Metrowerks' commercial products. For more information on upgrading from this limited version of CodeWarrior to a commercial product, contact Metrowerks at 1-800-377-5416, or via email at sales@metrowerks.com.

And oh yeah, the CodeWarrior end-user license is on the CD. Check it out.

Return Character Converter by Tama Software Ltd

This is a great little Freeware utility that converts files from DOS to UNIX format. This is handy when using GCC. Look for the program in the Tools/Conv folder. Copy the executable to your hard drive and it's ready to roll.

Microsoft Internet Explorer 5.0

It's where you want to go today. It's also needed to read documentation in HTML format, so if you don't have it, this saves you about 45 minutes of download time!

Pilot-GCC Win32

This is the finest free C development environment for the Palm OS you'll ever find. You'll find it in the GNU folder. It includes the GCC compiler, a linker, the GDB debugger, an emacs editor, the bash shell, and many other things. Since this is a GNU product, we have to say this: The use of this program is subject to the terms of the GNU General Public License contained on the CD.

PilRC Version 2.3 by Wes Cherry

This tool lets you define and view the user interface for your applications, when you use GCC. It's in the Tools/PILRC folder on your CD. The PilRC Web page is at `www.scumby.com/scumbysoft/pilot/pilrc`.

The Java™ 2 SDK, Standard Edition, V 1.2.1

The latest and greatest version of the Java Developer's Kit. Look for it in the Tools folder. We also have to tell you the following: Use of this software is subject to Binary Code License terms and conditions at the end of this book. Read the license carefully. By opening this package, you are agreeing to be bound by the terms and conditions of this license from Sun Microsystems, Inc. Copyright 1998 Sun Microsystems, Inc., 901 San Antonio Road, Palo Alto, CA 94303-4900 USA, All rights reserved. Java, JavaBeans, JDK and other Java related marks are trademarks or registered trademarks of Sun Microsystems, Inc. in the U.S. and other countries. Use of the software contained on this CD is subject to the license agreement(s) contained therein.

Shareware and Freeware

These are various Palm development tools and sample programs. Many come with their source code. You'll find these in the Share_fr folder. Browse them over!

ErrorFinder, Shareware from Shuji Fukumoto

Flash! v2.0.6, Shareware from Jaime Quinn

5 Graphics-Effects-ASM-Source v1.1, Freeware from Thomas Jawer

TUserData Class for Delphi v1.1, Freeware from Art Dahm

Astro Info v1.10, Freeware from Michael Heinz

HackMaster example sources, Shareware from Wes Cherry

Chess Timer v1.2, Freeware from Ethan Shayne

Doodle sources and binaries v0.6, Freeware from Roger E. Critchlow Jr

If You've Got Problems (Of the CD Kind)

We tried our best to compile programs that work on most computers with the minimum system requirements. Alas, your computer may differ, and some programs may not work properly for some reason.

The two likeliest problems are that you don't have enough memory (RAM) for the programs you want to use, or you have other programs running that are affecting installation or running of a program. If you get error messages like `Not enough memory` or `Setup cannot continue`, try one or more of these methods and then try using the software again:

- ✔ Turn off any anti-virus software that you have on your computer. Installers sometimes mimic virus activity and may make your computer incorrectly believe that it is being infected by a virus.

- ✔ Close all running programs. The more programs you're running, the less memory is available to other programs. Installers also typically update files and programs. So if you keep other programs running, installation may not work properly.

- ✔ Have your local computer store add more RAM to your computer. This is, admittedly, a drastic and somewhat expensive step. However, if you have a Windows 95 PC or a Mac OS computer with a PowerPC chip, adding more memory can really help the speed of your computer and allow more programs to run at the same time. This may include closing the CD interface and running a product's installation program from Windows Explorer.

If you still have trouble with installing the items from the CD, please call the IDG Books Worldwide Customer Service phone number: 800-762-2974 (outside the U.S.: 317-596-5430).

Index

● *G* ●

IDG Books Worldwide, Inc., End-User License Agreement

READ THIS. You should carefully read these terms and conditions before opening the software packet(s) included with this book ("Book"). This is a license agreement ("Agreement") between you and IDG Books Worldwide, Inc. ("IDGB"). By opening the accompanying software packet(s), you acknowledge that you have read and accept the following terms and conditions. If you do not agree and do not want to be bound by such terms and conditions, promptly return the Book and the unopened software packet(s) to the place you obtained them for a full refund.

1. **License Grant.** IDGB grants to you (either an individual or entity) a nonexclusive license to use one copy of the enclosed software program(s) (collectively, the "Software") solely for your own personal or business purposes on a single computer (whether a standard computer or a workstation component of a multiuser network). The Software is in use on a computer when it is loaded into temporary memory (RAM) or installed into permanent memory (hard disk, CD-ROM, or other storage device). IDGB reserves all rights not expressly granted herein.

2. **Ownership.** IDGB is the owner of all right, title, and interest, including copyright, in and to the compilation of the Software recorded on the disk(s) or CD-ROM ("Software Media"). Copyright to the individual programs recorded on the Software Media is owned by the author or other authorized copyright owner of each program. Ownership of the Software and all proprietary rights relating thereto remain with IDGB and its licensers.

3. **Restrictions on Use and Transfer.**

   (a) You may only (i) make one copy of the Software for backup or archival purposes, or (ii) transfer the Software to a single hard disk, provided that you keep the original for backup or archival purposes. You may not (i) rent or lease the Software, (ii) copy or reproduce the Software through a LAN or other network system or through any computer subscriber system or bulletin-board system, or (iii) modify, adapt, or create derivative works based on the Software.

   (b) You may not reverse engineer, decompile, or disassemble the Software. You may transfer the Software and user documentation on a permanent basis, provided that the transferee agrees to accept the terms and conditions of this Agreement and you retain no copies. If the Software is an update or has been updated, any transfer must include the most recent update and all prior versions.

4. **Restrictions on Use of Individual Programs.** You must follow the individual requirements and restrictions detailed for each individual program in the "About the CD" appendix of this Book. These limitations are also contained in the individual license agreements recorded on the Software Media. These limitations may include a requirement that after using the program for a specified period of time, the user must pay a registration fee or discontinue use. By opening the Software packet(s), you will be agreeing to abide by the licenses and restrictions for these individual programs that are detailed in the "About the CD" appendix and on the Software Media. None of the material on this Software Media or listed in this Book may ever be redistributed, in original or modified form, for commercial purposes.

Installation Instructions

The *Palm OS Programming For Dummies* CD offers valuable information that you won't want to miss. To install the items from the CD to your hard drive, follow these steps:

1. **Insert the CD into your computer's CD-ROM drive.**

   Give your computer a moment to take a look at the CD.

2. **Windows users: When the light on your CD-ROM drive goes out, double-click on the My Computer icon. (It's probably in the top-left corner of your desktop.)**

   This action opens the My Computer window, which shows you all the drives attached to your computer, the Control Panel, and a couple other handy things.

3. **Windows users: Double-click on the icon for your CD-ROM drive.**

   Macintosh users: Double-click the CD icon to show the CD's contents.

   Another window opens, showing you all the folders and files on the CD.

4. **Double-click the folder for the software you are interested in.**

   Be sure to read the descriptions of the programs in the appendix (much of this information also shows up in the Readme file). These descriptions will give you more precise information about the programs' folder names, and about finding and running the installer program.

5. **Windows users: Find the file called Setup.exe, or Install.exe, or something similar, and double-click on that file.**

   The program's installer will walk you through the process of setting up your new software.

   Macintosh users: To install most programs, just drag the program's folder from the CD window and drop it on your hard drive icon.

   Some programs come with installer programs — with those you simply open the program's folder on the CD, and double-click the icon with the words Install or Installer.

For more information, see the "About the CD" appendix.

IDG BOOKS WORLDWIDE
BOOK REGISTRATION

Register
This Book
and Win!

We want to hear from you!

Visit **http://my2cents.dummies.com** to register this book and tell us how you liked it!

- Get entered in our monthly prize giveaway.
- Give us feedback about this book — tell us what you like best, what you like least, or maybe what you'd like to ask the author and us to change!
- Let us know any other ...*For Dummies*® topics that interest you.

Your feedback helps us determine what books to publish, tells us what coverage to add as we revise our books, and lets us know whether we're meeting your needs as a ...*For Dummies* reader. You're our most valuable resource, and what you have to say is important to us!

Not on the Web yet? It's easy to get started with *Dummies 101*®: *The Internet For Windows*® *98* or *The Internet For Dummies*®, 6th Edition, at local retailers everywhere.

Or let us know what you think by sending us a letter at the following address:

...*For Dummies* Book Registration
Dummies Press
7260 Shadeland Station, Suite 100
Indianapolis, IN 46256-3945
Fax 317-596-5498

™

**BESTSELLING
BOOK SERIES**